Matt Zabitka

Sports

---

60 Years
of Headlines and Deadlines

---

by Ed Okonowicz and Jerry Rhodes

Myst and Lace Publishers, Inc.

Matt Zabitak: Sports
60 Years of Headlines and Deadlines
First Edition

ISBN   1-890690-09-0

Published by
Myst and Lace Publishers, Inc.
1386 Fair Hill Lane
Elkton, Maryland 21921

www.mystandlace.com

Printed in the U.S.A.
by Thomson-Shore Inc.
Dexter, Michigan

The Historian

"Every city of any size needs a Matt Zabitka, who I respectfully call a chronicler, someone who has a history and picture of the past. You need someone with deep roots in the community. Wilmington is fortunate to have that in Matt."

—**Pat Williams,** senior vice president
Orlando Magic basketball team

The Man

"When I first met him, he immediately struck me as the classic sportswriter. If they were going to do a movie about Matt's life, it's a shame that Walter Matthau died, because he could play Matt—with a cigar hanging halfway out of his mouth, banging on a typewriter, talking on the phone and working late into the night."

—**Kevin Tresolini,** sportswriter
The News Journal

ALSO AVAILABLE FROM MYST AND LACE PUBLISHERS, INC.

Spirits Between the Bays Series

Volume I
Pulling Back the Curtain

Volume VI
Crying in the Kitchen

Volume II
Opening the Door

Volume VII
Up the Back Stairway

Volume III
Welcome Inn

Volume VIII
Horror in the Hallway

Volume IV
In the Vestibule

Volume IX
Phantom in the Bedchamber

Volume V
Presence in the Parlor

DelMarVa Murder Mystery Series

FIRED!
Halloween House

Stairway over the Brandywine
A Love Story

Possessed Possessions
Haunted Antiques, Furniture and Collectibles

Possessed Possessions 2
More Haunted Antiques, Furniture and Collectibles

Disappearing Delmarva
Portraits of the Peninsula People

Terrifying Tales of the Beaches and Bays

Ghosts

Matt Zabitka: Sports
60 Years of Headlines and Deadlines

Dedications

To

My grandson, Bobby; my daughter, Shirley Ann;
and my beloved wife, Helen Vera
Matt Zabitka

To

Catherine, Mary Ann and Michael
Jerry Rhodes

To

Theresa Radulski Okonowicz, my Mom and hero
Ed Okonowicz

Acknowledgments

The authors and designer appreciate the assistance of those
who have played an important role in this project, including

Anne Haslam, for her research assistance;

John Brennan, Barbara Burgoon, Marianna Dyal
Sue Moncure and Ted Stegura
for their fine proofreading and excellent suggestions;
and
The News Journal, for granting permission
to reprint Matt Zabitka's columns.

Table of Contents

Introduction

This project originated with a message left on my home answering machine in the fall of 2000 from a guy named Robert "Bob" McCreary. He said he was Matt Zabitka's grandson, and that he wanted to talk to me about writing a book on the life and achievements of his grandfather, one of Delaware's best known sportswriters.

Having grown up in the city of Wilmington and gone to high school at Salesianum in the early 1960s, I—along with anyone else who ever read *The News Journal* sports section—was familiar with the name Matt Zabitka. He was better known than most state politicians and had been at his desk a heck of a lot longer. I had first come in contact with Matt when he interviewed me and my friend, Andy Ercole, after we had written a book on boxing champion Dave Tiberi in 1992. We were delighted to include one of Matt's columns about Philadelphia's Blue Horizon boxing club in *Tiberi: The Uncrowned Champion*. In fact, we got the idea for the book title from one of Matt's columns following Dave's nationally televised match in Atlantic City.

In 1997, I put Matt on the other end of the tape recorder and lens, interviewing him and taking his picture for my book *Disappearing Delmarva*. So I knew about Matt's colorful past and—with his raspy voice and often-present cigar—I thought he might have been the model for the Oscar Madison character in Neil Simon's *The Odd Couple*.

But as interesting as Matt and his career were, I was committed to a full-time job and an equally hefty schedule of books waiting to be completed. There was not enough time. I told Bob that I was flattered at being considered for the job, but that I really couldn't add another project, no matter how interesting. Then I tried to get off the hook and end the conversation by adding, "And I know next to nothing about sports."

"How about if I call you back in October?" Bob suggested, but it didn't sound like a question. It was more of an announcement to expect to hear from him again. Apparently, my earlier comments hadn't been understood.

"Make it November," I replied, hoping Bob wouldn't call back, and I hung up feeling good that I had survived the Grandson of Matt's first assault.

Just after Thanksgiving 2000, I answered the phone. It was Bob.

Probably because the spirit of the Christmas season had softened my resolve, I agreed to meet with Bob and his parents—Matt's daughter, Shirley, and her husband, Jim—one evening after work.

I told them that Kathleen—my wife, business partner, graphic designer, artist and boss of our two-person publishing company—would come with me to discuss "the book."

On the drive over, I told Kathleen, "No matter what they say, no matter what happens, we cannot agree to do this book. We don't have the time to get it done. Understand?"

She listened and nodded.

After five minutes of conversation with Bob and his mother, my responses during the conversation had changed from "we can't" to "we could," and from "if I were you, I would," to "if we can get this started by this date, we can."

It was a short meeting. We left with an appointment to meet with Matt and his wife, Helen, in their north Wilmington home.

As we walked to our car, Kathleen said in a teasing tone, "I thought we weren't going to do this project."

I shook my head and smiled, then began trying to figure out how to get Matt's book done.

After meeting the Zabitka family it was impossible to decline their request to work on a project that would recognize one of the state's premier writers and share some of the thousands of stories about Matt's experiences and the wonderful columns he had written during his decades of work.

In order to move this project along, we decided to enlist the help of my friend, co-author Jerry Rhodes, a fellow Delaware native, Newark High School graduate, University of Delaware journalism major and former reporter for the *Oxford Tribune*. Also, for almost a year, Jerry had worked with Matt during the evening shift at *The News Journal*, so he was familiar with both sports and our subject. All that, plus his being an excellent reporter would be an immense help in the project.

For months Jerry and I double-teamed Matt, each of us interviewing him separately and sometimes together. We also tracked down some of Matt's friends, admirers and colleagues, to add their comments to the book. There was no way to interview or include everyone. Matt's contacts and the lives he has touched through thousands of columns is incalculable.

After our first meeting, when Matt spent the initial minutes trying to talk us out of writing this book, he played an active role—making himself available for interviews, securing copies of some of his favorite columns, sharing his wonderful stories, providing names of leads and, most importantly, checking over what Jerry and I had written.

During the interview and research process, we've learned so much from Matt—about writing and interviewing, his work and the times when he played sports and the places where he had worked. Through his columns, articles and memories, readers don't just read the results of a game. Instead, they meet the people—the ever-important focus of Matt's columns. They also learn about the changing role of sports and its personalities in society during much of the last century.

In these pages we've tried to capture the essence of one of Delaware's major sports personalities, who is both a professional writer and a fascinating and colorful character.

In contrast to today's college-educated writers, Matt learned his craft in the newsroom instead of the classroom. Where modern journalism students sign up for college credit internships to learn from experts in the field, Matt signed on as a Navy seaman and taught himself, by trial and error, how to write. He sent columns back home that were published in his local paper while he was serving in the Pacific during World War II.

Today, his readership stretches beyond the state's boundaries, and his headlines and bylines have hung on refrigerator doors, been mailed to relatives around the world, been displayed on locker room bulletin boards and been framed by former jocks—some now playing corporate games in executive offices and others existing alone in nursing homes.

In the limited space available in these pages, we will share only a few of Matt's thousands of stories and meet only a handful of the people he has known and featured over the years. From major sports personalities to regular Joes and Janes, from has-beens to wannabes, from coaches to fellow sportswriters, from overlooked Negro National Baseball League players to top-earning Hall of Famers who hire assistants to keep their schedules, Matt has captured them all in print.

Lou Romagnoli, a former University of Delaware baseball player during the early 1950s, referred to Matt as "prolific, like a snowball going down a hill. Matt has a fantastic memory. He has written so many words about so many people, it's nice to have somebody write some words about him."

Matt's work demands more than some words. His experiences could easily fill several additional volumes about topics other than sports. As Matt said during one of our final interviews, "This isn't just a book on sports, it's a history of how things were, how the athletes lived."

It was as if, while selecting material and rereading some of his work, he realized that his contributions to his readers go far beyond a sterile record of box scores and statistics associated with wins and losses.

Matt Zabitka: Sports

During thoughtful moments, famous politicians and front porch philosophers tell us that we must learn from our past in order to appreciate the present and prepare for the future.

They say knowing what has happened will give us a sense of who we are, and, if we are smart enough to take advantage of that knowledge, we will benefit from the successes and mistakes of others.

Their advice applies to every sport and, more importantly, the game of life. For sports is really a version of the challenges of the real world compressed into nine innings, four quarters or two halves.

In that finite amount of time there are joy and sadness, luck and skill, things within our grasp and factors beyond our control. Every decision is not the best and every penalty or judgment is not fair. More players quit than continue. More lose than win. More disappear into the crowd than make headlines.

Matt has given us thousands of columns containing tens of thousands of stories and anecdotes. Within his well-crafted, cleverly worded and entertaining presentations is a generous quantity of lessons waiting to be discovered.

If we read beyond Matt's humorous and touching descriptions of the great and the forgotten, we might realize we have more opportunities than we think. We might understand that sports stars are not super-heroes, just talented people who worked hard. Quite often, they stumbled into Lady Luck and took advantage of the opportunities she offered. And we might learn that being successful doesn't mean getting one's face on a Wheaties box. Achieving a personal goal or winning a hometown championship is just as important and much more realistic.

Matt Zabitka's story is not about writing, it's about surviving, persevering and caring about others. By example, he's showed what can be achieved if we work a little harder, hang on a little longer and share our knowledge and talents.

He is a living connection with many of the greatest athletes of the 20th century. He sat with them, touched them, listened to their stories and selected their best messages and recollections to pass onto us. Now it's time to take a look at the writer often referred to as "Zee," and find out what it's been like working behind the sports desk for more than half a century.

Ed Okonowicz
December 2001

4

At the Banquet

It was Sunday evening, June 3, 2001, in Essington, Pennsylvania. Nearly 350 guests had arrived six hours earlier, at 3:30 in the afternoon, at the Radisson Hotel ballroom located within sight of the Philadelphia Airport. There was excitement in Philly and throughout the entire Delaware Valley, because the come-from-behind, Cinderella 76ers were playing the Los Angeles Lakers in the second game of the NBA championships. In city row houses and suburban two-story colonials, in neighborhood corner bars and in members-only country club lounges, longtime basketball fans and playoff converts were anticipating the tip off.

Jerry Rhodes

Matt Zabitka entertains the audience at the Pennsylvania Sports Hall of Fame, Delaware County Chapter, induction ceremony.

The effects of Game 2, being played 3,000 miles away in L.A., had extended across the continent and could be measured by the number of vacated tables in the half empty banquet hall. Apparently, many of the guests who had filled the room during the 5 o'clock dinner had slipped out during the extended awards program to see if their Philly hometown team could run its slim series lead to two games in a row.

They had arrived at the Radisson hotel in mid-afternoon and sat through 11 acceptance speeches given by members of the Class of 2001, who were being inducted into the Pennsylvania Sports Hall of Fame, Delaware County Chapter.

5

Matt Zabitka: Sports

As is the rule with seating assignments in kindergarten, attendance checks in college classrooms and listings in telephone books—if your name starts with "Z" it's safe to bet your paycheck that you will be introduced, called on, recognized or mentioned dead last.

This day was no exception.

Matt Zabitka, the 80-year-old sportswriter who had been born in Chester, Delaware County, Pa., in 1920, and worked for a number of newspapers—including the *Chester, Pa., Times* and Wilmington, Del., *News Journal*—and contributed articles to national sports magazines, was asked to come forward and accept his award.

After thanking the club's president, master of ceremonies John Furlow, president of the Pennsylvania Hall of Fame, Delaware County Chapter, Matt approached the microphone. Working full time and approaching his eighth decade as a writer (he started at 13, but that's a story for later in the book), the 6-foot-2 awardee, with a raspy voice and accent betraying his East Coast, inner city roots, looked over the crowd.

It was obvious the audience was exhausted from the lengthy awards affair and was ready to head for their cars if Matt paused to take a long breath.

But from the opening comment of "To all you survivors out there," Matt demonstrated his ability to read the crowd. He quickly tossed out a litany of major-name sports figures about whom he had written—Jimmy Karas, Gorilla Monsoon, Jessie Owens, A.J. Foyt, Ted Williams, Joe DiMaggio, Stan Musial, Ralph Kiner, Mike Schmidt, Duke Snider, Judy Johnson, Mickey Vernon, Mike Ditka, Joe Montana, Wilt Chamberlain, Red Auerbach, Bob Cousy, Arnold Palmer, Rocky Graziano.

In his few moments at the microphone, Matt recalled a meeting in Imburgia's Bar, a Marcus Hook waterfront gin mill, with boxer Graziano, and how he, Matt, was mistaken by a fan for the champ.

The crowd's applause and laughter, indicated its enthusiastic response—not because Matt Zee was the last speaker of the evening, but because of his style and material. Perhaps, too, there was the realization that Matt is a real, live link with many of the sports legends that most people only read about or see in documentaries and old newsreels.

In ending his brief time at the podium, Matt recalled a lesson he said he had learned while in prison in California for driving without a seatbelt.

"I was sentenced to jail for five months," Matt said, ignoring scattered chuckles rising up from the audience. "I didn't want to waste my time, so I enrolled in a public speaking course. My teacher said, 'If you want to be well known and get a good response from the people, there are three rules you have to follow. If you follow these three rules, you will always be popular.' "

Raising his finger for emphasis, Matt smiled at the audience and said, "Be brief, be appreciative and be seated. Thank you." The experienced toastmaster knew those in the audience were ready to head for the parking lot, and he gave them what they wanted—an early out.

Unfortunately, the limited time kept the guests from hearing some of Matt's wonderful stories, learned across banquet tables, in motel rooms, in the booths of diners, over telephone lines and at nursing home bedsides. Many of his stories cause listeners to laugh; some even make them cry. But they all offer insight into the professionals and the amateurs who have played the game—whatever game it was that Matt happened to be covering at the time.

Fortunately, in this 220-page forum we have a bit more space to share the steppingstones and milestones of Matt's lengthy and fascinating career.

As he welcomed Zee to the microphone, master of ceremonies Furlow said Matt had "covered every sport and has probably written more articles than anyone." By the time Zee had finished his remarks, Furlow returned to the podium and had elevated Matt to "one of the greatest sports journalists in the world! He really is!"

Ed Okonowicz

The Zabitka clan poses for a family photo at the Pennsylvania Sports Hall of Fame, Delaware County Chapter, banquet. From left (standing) are Steve Kalatucka (brother-in-law), Matt and Robert McCreary (grandson); (seated) Jim McCreary (son-in-law), Kelly McCreary (granddaughter), Shirley Ann McCreary (daughter) and Helen Zabitka (Matt's wife). Also present were Brian McCreary (grandson) and his guest Jen Bowman.

Matt Zabitka: Sports

Colleagues and friends have described Matt as a mentor, survivor, organizer, friend and a real guy. He has been called persistent, dependable, honest and top notch. *Sports Illustrated's* Gary Smith used the words "zest for life" and "gloriously silly," and several of those interviewed have provided what is perhaps the best description of all: "classic."

When asked to offer his opinion, Pat Williams, senior vice president of the Orlando Magic basketball team, said: "Matt loves what he does. He's got enormous passion and a relentless work ethic. He cares for the people he writes about. They're not just names and numbers."

Williams added that Joe Falls, a Detroit sports columnist, once said there were two keys to satisfaction and success: Enjoy your life and be good to people.

"That," Williams said, "captures Matt."

CHAPTER I

It All Started in School

'They wanted you to write an essay.... I made it different. It was a letter from a great Notre Dame football player at the time. It was like he sent me a letter about why I shouldn't drink. It had more emphasis, 'cause somebody was talking to me. But he didn't do it. I made it up. It won second prize in the state of Pennsylvania.'

—*Matt Zabitka*

Matt Zabitka was born Oct. 25, 1920, in the first quarter of the last century in a narrow, semi-detached, row house in Chester, Pennsylvania. It was a booming, industrious blue-collar, immigrant town with factories, shipyards, alleys, street vendors, ethnic neighborhoods, corner stores, clubs, saloons and people sporting nicknames based on how they looked or what they did for a living.

Matt's parents were immigrants from the Galacia section of Austria. His father, John, worked in the salt mines near Detroit and in coal mines in upstate Pennsylvania. Matt recalled a small coal miner's cap that used to hang in the family's Chester home.

"He was a hard working man," Matt said. "At one time, he gathered tomatoes in New Jersey. He worked all his life, but he always looked old. He used to say, 'Here comes my engineer,' because I worked for the paper.

"He used to go through the coal ashes, after they cooled," Matt said, "and would pull out the larger pieces to burn again. That will give you an idea of how rough it was in those days."

Matt described his mother, Anastasia, as a "busy housewife."

But 21st century Chester is no longer a hustling hub of humanity. Its population has shrunk to half what it had been in 1950. Once tidy, stable neighborhoods have been consumed by urban blight. Crime, poverty, boarded up homes and vacant storefronts depress oldtimers and scare off newcomers. But in its prime the city along the Delaware was a hot place to live, work and play. To some it might seem like Chester's heyday was ages ago, but to others, like Matt, the changes took place during the course of a single lifetime.

Matt grew up when television was only an idea, party line telephones were common, money for children's toys was rare and computers and space travel were fantasies of science fiction writers and comic book artists.

For adults, recreation after a day at the railroad, factory or shipyard was listening to the radio, playing sports and sharing some cold ones at the club.

Young Matt—and his friends from Chester and nearby Marcus Hook, usually referred to as, "the Hook"—was always eager for a pick-up game.

Their playing fields were empty lots and paved streets on which Matt loved to play sports—baseball, football, basketball. There were no fancy playgrounds or parks like today. Balls were hard to come by, so they taped and patched up many a hardball that had to be recycled more than once.

As kids, Matt recalled, they got excited when they knew they were going to play a game. In addition to informal pick-up contests, Matt and his friends took advantage of any opportunity to play organized sports, often playing for several neighborhood club teams at the same time.

Matt (seated at far left), representing the Rosemont Athletic Club, in this All-Star team photo taken in the late 1930s

One of their regular pick-up game sites was located beside the Pennsylvania Railroad tracks, in an industrial area only a few blocks from their row house neighborhood.

"So what we would do," he said, "was get a wagon and go from the 'cinders field' down towards the riverfront, the Delaware River, which is quite a few blocks away. We hauled reddish dirt back up to the field that was near the railroad tracks and that was all black and filled with cinders.

"You know how, on a baseball field, you put white lines on the field, from home plate to first base. We would take the red dirt and spread it out for a line, to make the markers."

There was no grass, Matt said, and in left field, just past the short-stop position, there were railroad tracks.

"They used to haul a lot of coal there," he said, smiling. "We'd play baseball, and while the guys were batting, the trains were coming through. So the left fielder, he could either stay in back of the train, where nobody could see him, or in front of it. We didn't know whether it was a home run or not. Sometimes it landed in a train. If it landed in a boxcar—mostly they hauled coal and were open on the top—so if you valued the ball, the left fielder would climb on the train and try to retrieve that ball.

"Trains were slow, too," Matt added, explaining how the team would be able to catch up with the moving cars and retrieve the ball. "In right field there was a little rubbish plot, with cinders on top of the rubbish plot. But," he added, waving a hand, "if you loved baseball, you played where you played."

Matt said that when he was young, kids knew their way around the rail yards, but not just because they played there.

"In those days," he said, "everybody was poor in the neighborhood. A lot of the people who lived in the area, they would get two or three of their boys, and they would climb on

Ed Okonowicz

Matt returned to Front and Ward streets, the site of Cinders Field in Chester. Notice the railroad tracks in the background that run through the outfield.

the train and throw coal down to the guy on the ground with a bag. Then he would put the coal in the bag and take it home, and that's how they kept warm through the winter."

One of Matt's first encounters with a real major leaguer was on the streets of his South Chester neighborhood. The guy's name was Ernie Vinson, and he lived in different places around Third and Highland Avenue and Third and Wilson Streets.

"He swept up in front of Bomberger's Drug Store," Matt said. "He always needed a shave, with a two to three weeks old beard. He chewed tobacco always. He had all decrepit clothes, just hanging on him. But this guy had a reputation that he played in the major leagues.

"There was a little place where I lived on Third Street, and right next to me was a small garage. Two brothers ran it. They fixed cars. In the back it was all open. Sometimes I would go over there and would have a catch with the guys.

"I'd come out there with a glove, looking for a guy to catch with. He [Ernie] lived in a cellar in a house across from me at that time. He saw me. He used to see me around there all the time. I never talked to him at all. One day, he said, 'I'll have a catch with you.' I said, 'All right!' I gave him my glove. I didn't want to throw fast, because I didn't think he could see the ball. I was standing too far away from him. I lobbed the ball to him, and he said, 'Don't throw the ball that fast, I can't see.' "

Later, Matt looked up the older man in the baseball record book and discovered that his pitching partner was Ernie Augustus Vinson,

Murderer's Row of the Rosemont Athletic Club pose for a formal photo in their finest on Easter Sunday, April 13, 1941. The sluggers include (from left) Matt Zabitka, Sonny Brown, Edward "Doc" Biely and Russ Rosenberg.

who had played with the Cleveland Indians and Chicago White Sox in the early 1900s.

Matt's next door neighbors used to make moonshine. But that was no surprise. Families throughout America brewed illegal whiskey to make ends meet during Prohibition. "We knew he was making moonshine," Matt said. "He would go to the A & P with a wagon and get 100 pounds of sugar, to use in making moonshine, which he sold for 25 cents a pint. He was always drunk with his own creations. It was exciting in those days."

When Matt was growing up, characters seemed to hang out on every corner. Most of them were born in the area and never left the neighborhood, and you knew them by name—and what names they had.

"One guy, his name was English. They called him 'English,' " Matt said. "He had a bulbous nose and a red face. These guys would sit on the steps and sit there and drink. They had brown bags with booze or wine in them.

"They didn't bother anybody. You knew where they were from. One guy was always drunk. He lived a block away. He would stagger up there in the evening and sit on that stoop with the other guys. The guys would say, 'This guy is Jack, he's always drunk.' Nobody ever saw him sober.

"Somebody told me he was in World War I, and he was gassed, and that's why. And then they had another guy down on the West End. He was a short guy. He had parts of Army clothes. I don't know where he got them.

"He was maybe 5-1, and he lived in abandoned cars, and that's where he slept. The people in the neighborhood, they would maybe give him some food, and that's how he survived. I think there was something wrong mentally with him. It was something maybe from the war. He would go up the street screaming his head off. They would call him Spoch. The kids would taunt him, and he would run after them.

"He was not the kind of guy you would fraternize with. He was of foreign descent, too. You could tell by the accent. Where he got money for the booze, I don't know, but he always had booze, too. When I would see this guy on the corner walking by, the guy would say, 'Could you spare a quarter?' You would say, 'What's the quarter for?' and he would say, 'That's to buy booze. I want to buy booze.'

"This is a joke. The other guy would say, 'Yeah. How do I know you are going to spend it for booze? How do I know you're not going to spend it for soup?'

"We had a funeral director in the neighborhood," Matt said, "and he kept his coffins in a big old building. And all the drunks would be found sleeping in the coffins."

In the West End of Chester, everyone knew everyone. Even into the mid-1950s different blocks in the area resembled small European villages.

Neighbors knew the names of every kid on the block, and each section had its own special ethnic group with their distinctive names, accents, customs, clubs and foods.

"St. Hedwig's Church, which is still there," said Matt, "is a huge church, which will stand for thousands of years. It's all stone. They had a school, also a St. Hedwig's Club. They had everything there in this one section. Also, the Ukrainians, they had a church, and then there were the Russians.

"Now and then, interspersed, you would find a Jewish merchant—a tailor, maybe a candy shop or something like that. Not many Italians in this section of town."

And even after more than 70 years have passed, Matt said, he still can recall their names and what they did. Majeski the shoemaker, Wojiehowski the court interpreter.

But when they were on the team, a player's nationality was never an issue. "Nobody looked on a guy like, he's Russian, or he's Polish or Ukrainian. They were just part of the gang, part of the team, that's it. That's the kind of environment I grew up in."

Ed Okonowicz

Matt in front of his elementary school on Grace Street in Chester

Writing Award

In addition to playing sports, Matt also loved to read and write. He realized he was good at writing and spelling, and he used the skills to follow the progress of his favorite ballplayers in the newspaper.

While a sixth grader at Chester's Dewey-Mann School, he entered a contest sponsored by the Women's Christian Temperance Union (WCTU) on why people should not drink.

"They wanted you to write an essay," Matt recalled. "Hell, I never had a drink in my life at that time. I went to some magazines and cut out pictures of a football player and some other different things. And I wrote an essay and pasted the pictures into a little booklet.

"I made it different. It was a letter from a great Notre Dame football player at the time. I forget his name now, and it was like he sent me a letter about why I shouldn't drink. It had more emphasis, 'cause somebody was talking to me. But he didn't do it. I made it up. It won second prize in the state of Pennsylvania."

The award presentation was held during the commencement ceremony at Smedley School Auditorium, and all the graduating eighth graders were in the room, with guests seated on bleachers.

"I was a sixth grader. A woman on the stage called me up," Matt said, "and I got a suit on, which I don't wear too much. All dressed up. And I'm nervous in front of all these people. She was praising me and I start walking away, and she says, 'Come back here!' So I go back, and I'm standing real stiff, and that's when she gave me an inscribed, leather bound dictionary and a five dollar gold piece.

"I'll never forget it. My mother and father were there. They couldn't read or write English. But they went there for me, and they were all dressed up, too.

"On the way home, I gave the five-dollar gold piece to my mother and said, 'Give me a nickel.' I wanted an ice cream cone. I never had an ice cream cone in my life. We always had penny yum-yums, which was ice and flavored water. So I got my ice cream, but I wish I had kept that gold piece today. Imagine what it would be worth."

It was three years later—in 1934 when Matt was 13 and in the ninth grade at Chester High School—when he got his first newspaper job. How the job developed demonstrates how at an early age Matt began to use initiative and creativity, two attributes that would serve him well throughout his writing and public speaking careers.

"I was walking to Chester High School," Matt recalled, "and every Thursday they put out a paper. It was called the *Progressive Weekly*. It was a good paper, about 32 pages. I used to love to read it, because it was all local.

"I noticed that they didn't have any sports. Nobody asked me, but I sat down one day and wrote a column, 'Sports of All Sorts,' by hand. I didn't have a typewriter. I just printed it. I had good penmanship."

Matt said he put in a lot of local stuff, including plenty of names and information on who starred in the high school scene. He sent the unsolicited manuscript to the paper and waited for the following week's edition to hit the streets.

"When I opened the paper," he said, still excited with the memory from long ago, "on page three, there were two full columns all the way down. It was all my stuff. Not only that, they had 'Sports of All Sorts' and my name, in half-inch letters, 'by Matt Zabitka.' I was shocked. To me it was like a million dollars, my name in print."

Matt sent another column in the following week, and it was printed, as was a third column in the subsequent issue.

"Now, I didn't ask for any compensation," Matt said. "I was just thrilled to see my name there. I didn't want money. A lot of people were calling me up, a lot of older guys, giving me information for new stories.

"The paper called and asked me to continue doing it for five dollars a week. Man, I was in Seventh Heaven. With that five dollars, I went and bought a used typewriter. I never owned one, didn't know anything about them. Later, I learned it was a left-handed one. It didn't make any difference to me. I started typing the stories after that and taught myself to type. My pay increased to $10, $15 and then to $20 a week.

"I can't type with all 10 fingers to this day. But I can put out 60 to 70 words a minute, using three fingers. With all the copy I put out now, I have to move fast."

Matt bought that first typewriter for $30, and paid $5 a month until it was paid it off. He kept it until about 15 years ago, when he had a flood in his home, and he threw it out along with mountains of sports memorabilia.

"With that typewriter," he said, "I sold stories to a lot of publications, including *Sporting News*. That was one of the top baseball papers in the country in those days. I sent a story in unsolicited, and they called me at my home and asked me if I had any more story ideas. I said, 'Yeah!' and I was writing for them for 13 weeks. That was big time. I remember interviewing Whitey Witt. His real name was Witkowski, and he played center field with Babe Ruth on the New York Yankees. I went over to his house in New Jersey to interview him. He showed me all his scrapbooks.

"He told me how happy Babe Ruth was that he was playing center field. He said that Babe Ruth liked to carouse all night. The next day, they played in the afternoon then, when the ball would come to the outfield to Babe Ruth, he was too lazy or too drunk to go after it. Whitey Witt would go over and catch the ball."

While in high school, Matt received a call from the *Chester News* and started providing another weekly column to that paper.

"Everybody saw my stuff. I got a good response. I was getting a lot of leads," Matt said. "People were calling me with ideas and I was playing a lot of sports, knew a lot of people."

Matt's reputation as the neighborhood sportswriter would continue to grow through his high school years. He would polish his skills, and add more stories to his portfolio during his service in the Navy during World War II.

CHAPTER 2

Working for Uncle Sam

'There were a lot of big-time writers aboard,
but I was the only guy who got a byline for a story.'
—Matt Zabitka

On the morning of Dec. 7, 1941, at approximately 7:53 a.m. Hawaii Standard Time, the forces of Imperial Japan launched a sneak attack on American military bases at Pearl Harbor and Hickam Field. Described by President Franklin Delano Roosevelt as "a day that will live in infamy," the attack took the lives of 2,403 Americans and left 1,178 wounded. The attack at Pearl Harbor got the United States into World War II, and it also got a lot of guys like 21-year-old Matt Zabitka into the Armed Forces. They would leave cities, farms and small towns and end up fighting for their country in places with names like Guadalcanal, Salerno, Midway, Coral Sea, Iwo Jima and Normandy.

On the other side of the world it was early afternoon when Matt— who had just gotten off work at the Sun Shipyard and Drydock Co. in Chester, Pa.—first heard the bad news.

"A bunch of us guys were on our way home from work, and we stopped at a gas station in the west end of Chester, because a guy wanted to get something at the store there," Matt recalled. "All of a sudden, this guy came running back out to the car and told us the Japanese had bombed Pearl Harbor. We didn't even know where Pearl Harbor was."

But they would soon learn.

Although the U.S.A. was going to need all of the soldiers, airmen, sailors, marines, coastguardsmen and merchant marines it could muster, it also was going to need a lot of ships to fight a two-ocean war. This meant that guys like Matt would be encouraged to take a deferment to keep working at Sun Shipyard and Drydock, which was one of the country's major shipbuilding centers throughout the war.

But Matt had his own plans.

When he graduated from Chester High School in 1939, Matt's brother-in-law, Pete Schneider, got him an application to Sun Shipyard. He recalled wearing steel-plated shoes and three or four sweaters to keep off the chill. But nothing would keep out the noise that was constant at the yard that was running full tilt 24 hours a day, seven days a week.

"When I arrived there," Matt said, "they lined us all up, about a dozen of us. There was noise so loud you couldn't hear yourself talk. Steel plates flying all around, over your head, with pounding that never stopped. This big bull of the woods came out; he was head of the '47 Department,' where they hammered steel plates for ship keels. He was chewing tobacco and had snow white hair."

Matt said the man walked down the line, looking the fresh meat over, like it was a slave auction.

"He stopped and looked at me," Matt said. "I towered over him. He wasn't big, but had a lot of meat on him. 'Are you from the coal mines?' he said. I told him, 'No. I'm from Chester.' He spit tobacco on my shoes and said, 'I'll take you.' I didn't know what that meant or what I was going to do."

Matt found out that he would be on a crew swinging mauls—large heavy, long-handled hammers—that were used to shape mostly keel plates, which protected the bottoms of ships.

"It was hard to handle in the beginning, but I got the rhythm and eventually liked the work," he recalled. But a serious accident occurred when a piece of steel plate sliced open Matt's leg, sending him to the hospital.

"Almost every day," Matt recalled, "it seemed like somebody was killed or hurt in there [shipyard]. It was rough work. I was working seven days a week for $35. The shipyard was geared to work on 50 ships at a time."

As expected, his "personal invitation" from Uncle Sam arrived in the mail.

"Sun Ship told me to come to the main office when I got my draft notice, and they could keep me out," Matt said. "But it was rough work, and I wanted a change. I got my physical exam and got hell from Sun Ship for not reporting to them about my draft notice immediately."

Matt went to the Navy recruiting office to take his tests. He recalled spending several hours walking around "bare assed" and reading inkblots.

After a couple of hours he went into a room to learn the results of his tests.

"A guy said, 'You got a choice.' I stood there and asked if I went in the Army, when would I report. They said, 'One and a half months.' Then I said, 'How about the Marines?' And they said, 'On Christmas Eve.' And I said, 'How about the Navy?' And they said, 'You report right now.' I said, 'I'll take the Navy.' I left a week before Christmas."

Like all young men heading toward an uncertain future, Matt remembered leaving his Chester home and reporting for duty. "We said goodbye and headed for Philadelphia, where we found out where we were being assigned," Matt said. "I found out I was headed to Sampson, New York, and that I had a couple of hours before we shipped out."

Although he could have gone back to Chester for an hour or two, Matt felt that it would just be too hard saying goodbye to his family all over again, so he and a couple of buddies decided to do some window shopping before stopping in at the Earle Theater in downtown Philadelphia.

It was here that Matt had his first encounter with the crooner who would later become known as the "Chairman of the Board," the legendary Frank Sinatra.

"We just walked into the theatre, and it was real dark inside, and Sinatra was up on stage practicing," Matt said. "Some guys in the audience didn't like Frank's singing, and they kept throwing pennies up on the stage, which bothered the hell out of Sinatra."

Never known for being mild-mannered, Sinatra told the guys if they kept it up, they would step out into the alley behind the theatre after the rehearsal to settle things.

"The guys throwing the pennies told Frank they weren't worried, because they thought they could beat him up," Matt said. "Sinatra told them that if he couldn't beat them up, he had a couple of big guards who could."

The guys got the message. There were no more pennies on the stage after that.

Matt in uniform during World War II

But Matt wouldn't be enjoying Sinatra up close and personal for quite some time. Instead, he would hear the sounds of "Reveille" and "Taps" at boot camp in Sampson, which could only be reached by train or plane. Matt said most of that railroad journey was done standing along with hundreds of other scared recruits, and breakfast was an apple and orange. But, at least, he wasn't enduring the new experiences alone.

Matt recalled the sad atmosphere during his first evenings at boot camp. "It was cold up there, and we were in a big room with 50 guys in double bunks, about 25 sleeping on a side. At night you could hear sobbing coming from underneath pillows that some of the guys put over the heads. It was rough being that far away from home, and a lot of us for the first time."

Even while undergoing training, Matt found time to write for the base newspaper, *The Sampson News*, sending copies of his articles to *Chester Times* sports editor Bill Burk, who noted Matt's efforts in his "Sports Shorts," column.

Matt Z: Medical Corpsman

After boot camp, the Navy gave sailors a test, and Matt said he was to be assigned to the signal corps.

"I qualified and was put on supernumerary. Then, somebody failed the test for the medical corps, and they put me in his place," Matt said. "The daily classes were hard, and there was a test every night."

Matt graduated in three months and was shipped to the Jackson Naval Station in Florida, where he awaited further assignments.

For a time, Matt said, it didn't look like he was going to put his medical corps training into practice. Instead of working in sickbay or the base hospital, he found himself sweating it out in the ship laundry.

"It was awful hot, and when the officer in charge came in I told him I wanted to know where my grades from Portsmouth where," Matt recalled. "Well, we got into a heated argument, and the whole laundry stopped what they were doing to listen."

His grades finally arrived and Matt was assigned a special mission that was like something out of Joseph Heller's WW II novel, *Catch-22*.

"There was this patient, a pilot, and he was in a special room," Matt said. "I was just supposed to stay outside of the man's room all night and keep an eye on things."

Because his barracks buddy had told him this was good duty and that the patient never made so much as a whisper, Matt took some magazines to help pass the time during his boring shift.

Settling down for what he thought would be a nice evening of reading and relaxation, Matt was startled to hear a moaning sound coming from the patient's room.

It was dark inside the room, so Matt fumbled around for the light switch, and when he finally got the lights turned on, he was surprised to see a creature from *The Mummy* sitting up in bed.

Matt figured the patient must have been a burn victim, because the only parts of his body that were unbandaged were two slits over his eyes and a third thin opening over the mouth.

"He was trying to tell me something, and he got madder when I couldn't understand him," Matt said. "The nurses came running in and found out that all the poor guy wanted was a straw and a glass of water."

That pretty much unhinged Matt, who thought, "If this is what the medical corps is like, I don't want any part of it."

"Right away, I asked to see the captain, and I told him what had happened," Matt recalled. "I told him I was used to rough work, and that I might kill somebody working as a medical corpsman. I told him I had worked in a shipyard, swinging a maul."

The captain laughed, but he agreed with Matt and decided that the duties of a shore patrolman (SP) might be more suited to his talents and temperament.

"I got a club and a badge," Matt said. "It was a huge base, so I ended up walking patrols and settling fights through the night and early morning hours."

The Shore Patrol walked a beat inside as well as outside of the medical wards, and it was while on duty that Matt was placed into the unlikely position of translator. A Russian patient in one of the wards had developed a difficult attitude because nobody understood what he was saying. He spoke only Russian and was a young pilot injured in battle. At that time Russia was a U.S. ally.

Matt, who could speak some Russian, approached the wounded foreign serviceman."I went up to him and asked him if he understood Russian," Zabitka said. "He was insulted—of course he could speak Russian. Then, he asked me the same question in Russian."

That broke the ice. Matt said he and the Russian managed to have a nice talk between them.

Shore Patrol duty turned out to be temporary, and Matt returned to medical corps duties and more training in Newport, Rhode Island, while the ship to which he would eventually be assigned, the *U.S.S. Randolph*, was being built in Virginia.

On the way from Rhode Island to the *Randolph* in Virginia, Matt suffered a bad case of homesickness as the train he was on passed through his native Chester, on tracks where he had played ball, only about a block away from his home.

"I wanted to stop the train and go say hello to my family," Matt said. "I felt a real heart pang as we went by the old neighborhood."

After a shakedown cruise off Cape Hatteras, where many of his ship-mates got their first taste of seasickness en route to the British West Indies, the *Randolph*, a new aircraft carrier, was ready for sea duty. But the ship was so huge it couldn't make it through the Panama Canal with its guns mounted. So the long gun tubes and turrets that protruded on either side of the ship were shipped by train to California.

Following passage through the Panama Canal, the *Randolph* sailed up the Pacific coast to Hunter's Point Naval Yard in San Diego, where the big guns were mounted.

While the technicians and engineers got the ship ready for combat duty, Zabitka and his shipmates were given a week of liberty.

"A shipmate of ours named Richard Swift, whose father was a stock-broker, invited us to his home in Hollywood, while on leave on the West Coast," Matt said. "He had a nice car, so we set out to take a look at some of the mansions in Beverly Hills."

They also took in famous of Hollywood landmarks, including Grauman's Chinese Theater, the Brown Derby, plus UCLA and facilities where famous radio shows were staged. It was shortly after this that the guys had another encounter with Old Blue Eyes.

There were a lot of radio studios in Los Angeles during the war, and famous entertainers like Bob Hope and Frank Sinatra would do live shows there.

One afternoon, when Matt and his friends were looking for some-thing to do, they decided to check out a theater where they heard Sinatra was scheduled to sing that evening.

"We went up the back alley, and the door was open, so we just walked in," Matt said. "The Alex Stordahl Orchestra was rehearsing, and Sinatra was on stage singing 'Night and Day.' "

The guys were listening to him sing when a guard appeared and got upset at the sight of the uninvited audience, standing in the wings while Sinatra was on the stage rehearsing.

Running up to Matt and his buddies, the guard demanded to know how they got in. Matt and the guard got into such an argument that Sinatra stopped singing and asked what the matter was.

"I broke away from the guard," Matt said, "and told Frank we were only in town for a week, and that we were going to Pearl Harbor after that. Frank told the guard, 'These guys are heroes,' and he told us where to go and get tickets for the show that night."

When the sailors came back that night, the lines were already stretched around the block, and many people couldn't get in.

"He put on quite a show," Matt said. "The people went crazy."

While Frank was wooing the bobbysoxers in Tinsel Town, there was still a war going on in the Pacific, and with her new guns now in place, the *Randolph* steamed off to Hawaii to pick up those two essentials—food and ammunition.

When the *Randolph* reached Hawaii, there was another wait for the ship's complement of planes that were being flown in from the mainland, so Matt and his shipmates took advantage of another leave to tour the big island of Oahu.

"We were tired and wanted a place to sleep, so we went to a YMCA and found the auditorium was dark," Zabitka said. "Down in the front there were some couches, so we laid down and went to sleep."

Soon the sleeping sailors were awakened by the noise of a large group of servicemen being marched in to watch that most traditional of Hawaiian entertainments, a hula show. Somehow Matt was volunteered to go up on stage, and one of the dancers gave him a crash course in hula dancing. "She told me to put my hands on my hips, then she taught me how to hula," Matt said. "After that, she thought I was going to leave, but I just stood there."

Matt was waiting for a Hawaiian kiss from the island sweetheart, but despite all his pleadings, all he got was a lei of flowers placed around his neck.

The fun and games were short-lived, and the *Randolph's* crew departed the safety of Hawaii for its first tour of combat duty.

The entertainment that particular night was not Matt's friend Sinatra, but instead the sounds of big band music being played on a radio show hosted by the infamous Tokyo Rose.

Although the crew appreciated the music by Tommy Dorsey and Benny Goodman, they were in anything but a swinging mood when Rose interrupted the broadcast to tell her audience that the Japanese pilots knew the *Randolph* was leaving Hawaii and promised that her countrymen were going to bomb the ship that night.

"There were a lot of spies in Hawaii, and that's how they knew about us," Matt said. "We never saw any planes, but I remember our guns going off a lot that night."

Matt (standing, at left) with his teammates of the H Division basketball team on the deck of the aircraft carrier Randolph

The *Randolph* went out to sea, and stayed there for a while, joining a large group of battleships massed for a major attack, and it was here that Matt witnessed the grim reality of war for the first time.

Kamikaze attack

"On March 11, 1945, at 8:07 p.m., a twin-engine Japanese 24 Yokosuka Pyl 1 (nicknamed Frances), loaded with bombs flew into our ship and went through the wooden flight deck, with the plane's engine crashing down to the steel hangar deck," Matt recalled. "The entire rear part of the ship was afire, flames were shooting sky high."

The Japanese pilot was a member of the Kamikaze Corps, a special air corps organized by Rear Admiral Arima in 1944, whose sole mission was crashing into U.S. ships and setting them on fire before exploding their bombs.

The Kamikaze pilots were expendable, and Matt recalled the sight of the charred body of the Japanese airman as it was being placed into a burlap bag onboard the *Randolph*.

When the Kamikaze hit the *Randolph*, Matt was in the front of the ship, and he recalled how he joined his shipmates running towards the rear of the carrier trying to get to one of the two hatches to escape from shrapnel that was flying everywhere, just inches above the hangar deck.

"When the plane hit the flight deck, sailors were laying flat on the deck," Matt said. "You prayed, wishing you were back home."

A burial was held at sea for the 25 sailors killed in the Kamikaze attack. As the crew searched for three missing sailors, Matt and the other medical corpsmen were busy tending to the 106 sailors who had been wounded.

Thinking back to the incident that occurred more than 50 years ago, Matt said he has mixed feelings. "I was sad that it happened, but I was glad that I had survived," he said. "We were also glad because we thought our ship would not be in the next action because of the damage we had sustained."

The respite was short-lived because a whole team of welders and carpenters arrived immediately with a floating shipyard to repair the *Randolph's* damaged flight deck. But they couldn't repair the big guns that were twisted like pretzels from the flames and heat generated by the Kamikaze plane.

While the ship was being put back into fighting condition, another vessel took its place and suffered even more tragic consequences.

"In one of the supreme ironies of the war, another ship, the *Franklin*, took our place in the action," Matt said. "While they were unloading bombs below decks, a Kamikaze hit the ship and dropped its bombs down the elevator, detonating the bombs stored below decks on the *Franklin.*"

Commanded by Captain Leslie H. Gehres, the *Franklin* was part of a three-carrier group that also included the *Wasp* and the *Yorktown*, charged with launching a series of air attacks on Japanese cities.

The attack on the *Franklin* claimed the lives of 832 sailors, the most casualties on any U.S. ship, and left 265 men wounded. The *Wasp* also suffered heavy casualties, with 101 sailors killed and 269 wounded.

Despite suffering such a huge loss of life and damage to the ship, the *Franklin* did not sink, and was towed clear by the heavy cruiser *Pittsburgh*, under Captain John E. Gingrich.

As the ship limped back on its eventual 12,000-mile journey to New York City, it pulled alongside the *Randolph*, which took survivors on board. "The guys that came on board were afraid to go down below decks because of what had happened on the *Franklin*," Matt said. "You can't blame them for that."

The *Franklin's* survivors at first thought they would be returning to less hazardous duty, but many were reassigned to the *Randolph* which, after being repaired at Ulithi, joined the Okinawa Task Force on April 7, 1945.

The *Randolph* was under daily air attack, but continued to send her aircraft on support missions throughout April, and in May the carrier became the flagship for Task Force 58, as part of the American occupation of Okinawa. Matt remembered what it was like being under constant threat of Kamikaze attack, and the efforts of her skipper, Captain Felix Baker, to keep the *Randolph* out of harm's way.

"When we went back into battle, there was a moonlit night, and it lit up our ship and made us a sitting target," Matt said. "The captain comes on the speaker system and says he is going to take us on a zigzag course and throw up a lot of smoke. It worked, because we didn't get hit that night."

During her next assignment, the *Randolph* became part of Admiral Halsey's 3rd fleet, carrying out attacks up and down the Japanese home islands. In a 15-day period during July 1945, pilots from the *Randolph* estimated they had destroyed 25 to 30 ships, from small barges to a 60,000-ton freighter. Strikes from the *Randolph* were being carried out at the Kisarazu Airfield when the Japanese surrender finally came on Aug. 15.

"We were about 100 miles from Japan, when the news of the first atomic bomb came," Zabitka said. "Our ship was getting away from Japan as fast as we could."

Although they had been told that atomic bombs had been dropped on Hiroshima and Nagasaki, the sailors on the *Randolph*, like the rest of the world, really had no idea what an atomic bomb was. But they did know that it ended World War II

The *Randolph* was part of the huge armada that had gathered on Sept. 2, 1945, for the official Japanese surrender onboard the battleship *Missouri* in Tokyo Bay.

General Douglas McArthur accepted the surrender on the behalf of all the Allies, while Admiral Nimitz signed for the United States and Admiral Fraser accepted the surrender on the behalf of Britain.

While the ceremonies were going on, the *Randolph* narrowly missed being the last great casualty of the war.

"A Japanese submarine shot a torpedo that just barely missed the *Randolph*," Matt said. "They probably did not know the war was over."

Following the surrender, the *Randolph* and her crew headed for Hawaii and eventually back to the eastern United States, where they were given a big welcome-home parade in Baltimore.

Now that peace had returned, America faced another formidable task, getting its servicemen, scattered around the globe, back to the homes many of them had not seen for several years.

To accomplish this mission, ships like the *Randolph* were rigged to become part of the "Magic Carpet" service that would transport large numbers of servicemen back to America and a return to civilian life.

After a week of liberty in December, Matt was sent to the Brooklyn Shipyard, where the *Randolph* was picking up new sailors for the ship's latest mission, transporting occupation troops overseas to Naples, Italy.

The planes were gone, and in their place were

Matt Zabitka (left) and Carl Folk walk the streets of Honolulu, Hawaii, on Sept. 12, 1945, soon after the end of the war.

stacks of bunks four tiers high on the hangar deck, where the planes were usually kept. It was around this area that some of the younger sailors would gather to discuss the *Randolph's* wartime exploits.

"The young guys going to Italy for occupation duty thought I was new, too, so they were telling me what had happened during the war," Matt said. "When I told them I was part of the crew that had been through all of the action, well, that really impressed them."

After a rough passage across a stormy Atlantic Ocean, the *Randolph* arrived in Naples, and it was here that Matt, who had seen his share of wartime causalities, saw that civilians had not been spared the effects wrought by the war.

"When we landed, a cyclone fence was put up between us and the civilians, and our guys were taking the garbage off our ship," Matt said. "The poor civilians saw the food and other stuff in the garbage and broke through the fence to get it. They were pretty ragged looking."

Matt also said that the disruption caused by the war in Europe had taken its toll on the younger members of the Italian population.

"It was cold, and I was walking through Naples, with my pea coat on," Matt said. "A little girl about four or five years old, wearing tattered clothes, came up to me and took my hand. You just felt so sorry for those people."

While the *Randolph* was getting ready for the return leg of the first of two trips made to Italy to retrieve American servicemen, Matt and his buddies had a private mission to complete.

It seems one of the sailors was an Italian fellow from Brooklyn, and his relatives had given him a package to deliver to some folks in Naples. Matt said the guys hired a taxi, which turned out to be a one-horse, open buggy, and found themselves being driven down cobblestone streets by a driver whose main concern was getting his hands on American cigarettes.

Having travelled 3,000 miles to deliver the package, the sailors found the place they were looking for, but nobody answered their knocks on the door.

"We kept knocking, and somebody inside said there was nobody home," Matt said. "Then, the *Randolph* crewmate said he had a package from America, and they let us in. They were glad to see us. They offered us hard candy and nuts in their apartment, wearing coats and scarves to keep warm."

Like most homes in Naples that winter, the building had no heat, and after a short visit the sailors from the *Randolph* set about getting a ride back to their ship.

"We found our horse and buggy driver, who was running around the buggy, trying to keep himself warm," Matt said. "He took us around

Naples and we ended up at this big hotel occupied by high ranking American officers. When me and my two buddies went inside, we were met by a young lieutenant who was very impressed with the battle ribbons we were wearing. He offered us a trip to a local officers' club in the hills outside the city."

The people running the club did not want a bunch of enlisted men on the premises, but the young officer reminded his colleagues that the sailors from the *Randolph* were war heroes, so a special table was set so the guys could enjoy themselves for a little rest and relaxation.

"But," Matt said, "they put us in a secluded wing off the stage where we couldn't be seen, because it was an officers' club and we were not officers."

Matt said that while there were some grim times, he also had good memories. He said he would never trade the experiences and knowledge that he learned during the war and, in particular, on the *Randolph*.

Writing during the war

Through it all, Matt created opportunities to keep busy writing.

On one occasion, he developed a small newspaper while on the *Randolph* and gave a copy of a two-pager to a yeoman in charge. He told Matt that his content was "damn good," just what the ship needed, and said he'd show it to the commander to get the necessary approval.

Unfortunately, when the yeoman reached the officer's cabin, he was asleep.

No one had told Matt, and his newspaper was circulated throughout the ship the next morning.

"There were bombing missions the next day," Matt recalled, "and everyone was locked in areas (condition Zebra) around the ship. And I'm in the hole at the bottom of the ship and a call comes down telling me to report to the bridge. They had to open all the sealed doors and compartments to let me pass up through each level, and I'm wondering what is so important.

"As I pass by, everybody is waiting for me. When I get up to the bridge, up high, looking down on the planes taking off, the yeoman was standing there pissing his pants. He was shaking all over.

"The officer is shouting at him, asking, 'Are you running this Navy?' and holding a copy of my paper in his hands. And I said, 'He had nothing to do with it. I wrote it!' Then he tells me, 'You go back to the engine department and after this mission you report to me in my cabin.' He wanted to see me after the early morning attack on Japan.

"At this point, I'm so upset that I don't give a damn if the ship sinks. I don't even care if I die."

Eventually, Matt went in the wardroom, prepared for his dressing down from the highly annoyed officer, anticipating a possible court martial.

"What the hell," Matt said. "I'm thinking, I don't give a crap. I'm in the middle of a war. So what could be worse? Then the officer says he had a conversation with the captain, and tells me the captain liked my paper. Then he asks could I do the paper every day. And I said, 'I don't think so.' I went through humiliation and a lot of emotional feelings. But what I did do was something else. I would type up pieces of paper and put them on a large sheet of paper to make it look like a newspaper. I even had cartoons."

Each morning, he would post the paper on the back of a door in the muster area, where other sailors would gather to take a look at the goings-on aboard their ship. The officer in charge of that area noticed that all the commotion about what was in the latest edition of Matt's newspaper caused the sailors to report for muster in a less than orderly manner, so he took what he thought was appropriate action.

"He told me I could put the paper up, but not until after muster," Matt said. "Then, he asked me if he could keep a copy of the paper as a souvenir."

Perhaps Matt's most enduring writing project during his years in the Navy was working on a history of the *Randolph* and her crew.

"Some of the people on board had mentioned something about putting out such a book," Matt said. "I was the only non-com sitting in the ward room to discuss the book. The others were all gold braid, writers and editors from major newspapers and magazines."

With hostilities over in the fall of 1945, work began on the book while at sea, financed from the ship's recreation fund. Final copies were available for $5, and they were to be sent to the homes of the soon-to-be discharged sailors.

The result was *Gangway*, described as "A Pictorial History of the *U.S.S. Randolph's* first year at sea, October 9, 1944, to October 9, 1945."

"I wrote about the medical division and there were pictures of the sick bay and the sailors getting dental treatment, and so forth," Matt said, adding that when he met for the first time with the group of writers—most of them officers and experienced journalists—assigned to the project, he stood out like a sore thumb. "There were a lot of big-time writers aboard, but I was the only guy who got a byline for a story."

The article that earned Matt this singular honor was "Randy is a Lady." This animated account of the exploits of the ship's only female crew member during World War II is early evidence of Matt's creative talent and his ability to know his audience and develop and deliver an interesting story that other writers overlooked.

Randy is a Lady

BY MATT ZABITKA

The only female amongst thousands of sea-going sailors aboard an aircraft carrier is the dire predicament which confronts Randy, a young, zestful, blossoming, buxom brunette from San Francisco, California, who was shanghaied from her place of employment in early January of 1945, to go out to sea with the greatest navy on this globe.

Handsome Jack Salling, MA1c, of Cleveland, Ohio, who was a travelling salesman in civilian life, selling tobaccos and smoking pipes, was the brains behind the shanghai movement.

Salling, from the very first moment that he laid his sky-blue eyes on Randy in the Frisco store, knew it was love at first sight. Randy's sparkling, big brown eyes . . . her well-lined thin lips . . . her long, dainty fingernails . . . and the way she carried her body appealed to Salling so much that right then and there, on the spot, he decided he would never leave the States minus Randy.

Then he thought, "What if the Navy doesn't allow it! So what! This may be my last trip and I want to get as much fun and enjoyment out of life as possible while I am still alive. I'll try anything once!"

And with that self-consolation, Salling cunningly devised a plan.

Due to military regulations concerning the movement of troops, ships, cargoes, etc. . . . we can't reveal at this writing just what the plan was, or when and how it occurred.

Anyway, Randy was soon smuggled aboard.

As soon as Salling had led her past the O.O.D. [officer of the day], on the quarterdeck, under the veil of darkness, he quickly hustled her to Sick Bay Country where he works, on the 3rd deck, aft part of the ship. He didn't know where to hide his precious cargo. He tried several places . . . behind the sofa in the doctor's office . . . in the pharmacy . . . in the pea coat locker . . . But none of these places offered too much security for the only female aboard this man-loaded ship. Finally, Salling decided to share his own personal sack with Randy. Randy objected at first, but finally gave in.

The following day, the news broke out in Sick Bay Country that a female had been smuggled aboard by Salling the nite before. The Corpsmen made a mad rush for Salling, who was nonchalantly brushing his teeth in the head. They demanded a peek at the femme.

Salling, realizing it was quite impossible to keep it a secret much longer, went to the medical storeroom and cautiously emerged with his valuable and precious souvenir from the States.

After a few seconds of minute observation, they all made a sudden dash for the beautiful creature. Randy became so frightened that she let out a terrifying, spine-tingling yelp and made a head-on dash for security underneath a table.

Then tall, blond-headed Richard Mickelberg, PhM3c, of Aurora, Illinois, blurted out, "Suppose the Captain finds out about her . . . then what?"

All the Corpsmen chimed in, "Yeah, how about it?"

A few days later, practically everybody aboard ship knew of Randy's presence, including the captain . . . who wanted to know . . . "HOW COME?"

Explaining Randy's presence aboard, Salling stuttered out something which ran like this, "Well, uh, you see, sir, she just came aboard to visit me while we were still in port. Then I escorted her off of the ship after a couple of hours of sight-seeing. . . and a funny thing happened . . . just as our ship was pulling out, she must have climbed back on via one of the extended lines . . . or somehow . . . for I discovered her near my sack after we had already left port and were underway. And you wouldn't want me to throw her over the side now . . . would you? That would be murder."

So now Randy is doing sea duty in the South Pacific aboard a hospitable carrier.

On the first leg of her journey towards the battle zone, Randy really got seasick. She ate hardly anything. She could barely walk. Her legs wobbled, and after taking a few steps she would flop down flat on the deck. But she never griped. She seemed determined to acquire sea legs if it was the last thing she would ever do.

After a couple of weeks of sea duty, Randy gained her sea legs, plus all the zip and vitality she had lost the previous two weeks. She now walks around the decks in true sailor fashion, no matter how rough the sea.

Randy has been selected by the Hospital Corps Division aboard the ship as "The girl we'd most like to take home with us." . . , and she has been made an HA2c, with promises of advancement if she shows the ability to do what is asked of her.

She does duty in the dispensary, and the sick-call line-up is twice as great now than it was before she came aboard.

Her G.Q. station is on the 3rd deck, forward part of the ship, with the No. 2 Damage Control Party. She keeps cool and relaxed thorough every GQ alarm.

In trying to delve into Randy's past history, not much could be dug up . . . except for a few facts.

Randy has lived all her life in San Francisco, Cal., up 'til the time she was shanghaied . . . she doesn't know her mother or father from Adam and Eve . . . and she's a cross between a bulldog and fox terrier.

Yep . . . Randy is a dog . . . . But . . . Randy is a lady!

She has been made an honorary member of the crew of the "USS Randolph" (CV-1S), an Essex-class carrier.

She had a health record on file, a dog tag around her collar and a sick call card in the Sick Bay files.

The following information is contained in Randy's personal U.S. Navy Health Record, which is in the files of the clerical office aboard the "Randolph," along with the records of the rest of the crew. . . .

Full name: Randy Flattop . . . birthplace: San Francisco, Cal. . . . service number: 100,000,000 . . . Rating: Pharmacist Mascot . . . Date of shanghai: Jan. 1, 1945 . . . next of kin: Jack Neal Salling, HA1c, Cleveland, Ohio . . . nationality: Dog . . . complexion: dark . . . hair: brown . . . general appearance: good . . . head and face: normal . . . ears: large . . . eyes: brown . . . color perception: good . . . vision: 20/20 . . . weight: 6 lbs., 8 oz.. . . . pulse before exercise: 60 . . . after exercise: 70 . . . after rest: 65 . . . blood pressure: systolic-110 . . . diastolic-70 . . . urinalysis: albumen-neg . . . sugar-neg. . . . nervous system: normal, except occasionally urinates on the deck. . . .

The aforementioned exam results were the findings of the Senior Medical Officer aboard the ship.

Randy, the ship's "Lady" and the subject of Matt's article, is shown with members of the Randolph *crew. Matt was the only writer to receive a byline for his story about the mysterious female smuggled aboard ship.*

The record of Randy's first dental examination, made by a Lieutenant of the Dental Corps, states she has deciduous dentition present, and is dentally qualified for aviation and submarine duty.

Randy's blood type has been classified as "Type k-9." Her Kahn test proved negative, and she has already been inoculated for rabies.

The following note is carried in Randy's Health Record of the page devoted to her medical history:

"USS Randolph" (CV-5) . . . 14 Feb., 1945 . . . Examined this date and found physically qualified and aeronautically adapted for duty involving riding as a passenger but not for duty involving the actual control of aircraft . . . signed by the Flight Surgeon.

Randy herself had to attend sick call twice thus far, and both times for seasickness. The first time, the doctor advised complete rest and liquid diet. . . and the second time, the treatment prescribed was to eat crackers and cheese, take a good shower and forget the thing.

Reprinted from Gangway, *a pictorial history of the* U.S.S. Randolph.

Although the *Randolph* would continue to proudly serve her county until 1969, and would welcome famous visitors such as Sir Winston Churchill, with the close of World War II it was time for Randy, Handsome Jack, and guys like Matt to face the challenge of returning to civilian life.

CHAPTER 3

Writing for Real

'I had a lot of guts.... So I told him what I wanted to do. I said, "You sign a contract. We run it in the Chester paper, top paper in Delaware County. We run it on the sports page—one full column. I would have my picture on the top of it." He looked at it and started reading. I thought he was going to throw it in the wastebasket. But he looked up and said, "I like it! I like the idea! We'll take a 13-week contract." And he agreed to pay me for writing the weekly sports column!'

—*Matt Zabitka*

Matt married Helen Kalatucka on April 8, 1944, while he was in Navy medical school in Portsmouth, Va. The better half of the couple that has been together for more than 50 years has a number of memories of her own regarding her relationship with Delaware's longest-writing sports reporter.

"We met through Matt's sister, Marie," Helen said. Since Helen grew up in Sun Village, on the east end of Chester, she and Matt had a number of friends in common. "She wanted me to date Matt. He stood me up several times. I said, 'If he didn't want to date me, that's all right by me.' I couldn't care less.

"I thought Matt was beautiful. But I also thought he'll never date me. And he didn't, for about three or four weeks. He would call me up and say, 'I'm coming over Wednesday night, I'll be over around seven,' or something like that. Then, he wouldn't come. His sister and I were in the same class, and he would send a message with her, saying, 'I'm sorry I didn't get a chance to come see you.' "

Helen remembered that Matt didn't have a car at the time, but he told her he had a Cadillac convertible, in his garage.

"He used to tell me it was a brand new yellow coupe. I went down to his house one time, and he'd say, 'My car's in the garage and I've got a flat tire.' I said the heck with that guy. I'm not paying any attention to what he says. But, after that, we finally got along together real well. I fell in love with him, really deep.

"The first date was near Christmas. They needed Matt at the shipyard because he had brawn and brains. He used the maul to hammer steel plates."

Soon afterwards, Matt joined the Navy. Helen kept in touch with him through letters and later visits when Matt was stationed in Virginia. Eventually, he told her to come down and see him, before he left port.

"His ship is supposed to sail, so he said to get my clothes ready," Helen recalled. "I went to Portsmouth, Virginia, and we were married there in a little chapel. Matt got one of his buddies to be his best man. Once they sail, they don't tell you where they are going. That's it."

While Matt was overseas, their son, Donnie, was born. Five years later, the couple had a daughter named Shirley.

"I lived with my mom and dad while Matt was in the war," Helen said. "You always worry when your husband or brother is in the service. When he came back, we lived with my mom for a couple of weeks, but we knew we had to find another place, because my brothers were coming home from the service. So when he came back, he was working at the shipyard for a few months. We got this apartment, and it was loaded with cockroaches."

Matt described his first residence.

"When I got out of the Navy, we lived in an apartment house for $5 a week. It was roach infested," he said. "There was a small kitchen and stove. Once, we pulled the old wallpaper back off the wall, and 50,000 cockroaches were behind there. When I hit the typewriter keys, 10,000 cockroaches came out of my typewriter."

Matt and his bride, Helen, pose for their wedding portrait in Virginia in April 1944.

"We saw this house for sale on Morton Avenue in Chester," Helen said. "Sun Ship had built it. Matt said to call the next day and see how much they want for it. We borrowed money for a down payment and bought it right on the spot. Later we moved to Ashbourne Hills and now we're here in Afton. We're still together after more than 50 years and three houses and one cockroach apartment."

After returning from the service, Matt went back to his old job at Sun Shipyard.

"After you got out of the service," he said, "the place where you worked before had to hire you back. I went back to the shipyard in 1946. I was making $35 a week. I stayed there about six months before being laid off."

But Matt was always trying to figure out a way to land a job doing what he liked best—writing.

His first stop along the way was working as a probation officer for Delaware County government.

"I had an office with gold lettering on the door, 'Matt Zabitka Probation Officer,' in the Media Courthouse. But that was only a title," he explained. "I was really the head of a Recreation Department for the county. I organized athletic leagues—basketball, track, boxing. I did that for a while, but I still wanted to write. I tried to get a job at the *Chester Times*, but they had no openings."

But he continued to work at finding a full-time writing position. During one evening interview session, Matt described himself as a "survivor," making it through three life-threatening incidents—one while in the Navy and two others that occurred years later in Delaware.

He said he was thankful that he had lived through a Kamikaze attack on his aircraft carrier on March 1, 1945, off Ulithi, an atoll in the Pacific.

Then, in the summer of 1978, he would survive an accident in Brandywine Springs Park when a metal bar attached to the top of a backstop fell, inflicting a serious head injury that sent Matt to the hospital for nearly a month.

Finally, in the late 1990s, he survived a serious traffic accident when tire remnants from a passing truck smashed into his windshield while he was driving to work on Interstate 95. He was hospitalized and said he still feels physical pain associated with the auto accident.

But perhaps his most significant attribute is ingenuity.

Realizing that creativity helped him capture second place in a state writing contest while in grade school, Matt applied this same skill—plus a healthy dose of a young veteran's bravado—to the business world in an effort to land the position he wanted. Thinking back more than 50 years, Matt said he came up with a great idea.

He recalled that he eventually had gotten hired as editor of a weekly Delaware County, Pennsylvania, paper, the *Marcus Hook Herald*, where he did everything—sports, editorial and delivery.

"I used to take bundles with me on the bus to deliver," Matt said. "If you love what you do, it was a lot of fun. It was in your blood. You looked forward to doing it."

But Matt wanted to get on the staff of a daily.

"I thought of this idea, right off the top of my head," he said. "Nobody solicited it or anything. I would write a column and suggest they put it in the *Chester Times*. It would be filled with names, lots of names of local people in it. But it also would be associated with a product—such as Ortlieb's Beer.

"There were a lot of clubs and bars in the area at the time," Matt said, "and I would put something in there about sports and then mention the different clubs serving Ortlieb's Beer. It's subliminal advertising, actually. My plan was to sell the column idea to some company. For no special reason I picked Ortlieb's Beer."

Matt called the brewing company in Philadelphia, got the name of the advertising company handling the account and tried to explain what he had in mind over the telephone—but got the brush off.

"The Ortlieb's advertising representative said they were busy and that I 'had to come in person' to discuss my idea. Make an appointment. Then he threw the phone down. If he hadn't done that, I would have said, 'That's okay.' But that brush-off angered me. I called back, made an appointment and went to Philadelphia. I found his agency. I don't know how I found it, but I did.

"I had a lot of guts. I went in there. I was outside in the office cooling my heels, waiting and waiting. I had a feeling I wasn't going to sell anything to these people. Then I walked into the office and I knew things were going to be bad right off the bat. He was sitting behind the desk with a scowl on his face, taking pills and drinking a glass of water.

"So I told him what I wanted to do. I explained everything. I had a dummy column of what I had in mind. I said, 'You sign a contract. We run it in the Chester paper, top paper in Delaware County. We run it on the sports page—one full column. I would have my picture on the top of it. You pay me and pay the paper for the space.'

"He looked at it and started reading. I thought he was going to throw it in the wastebasket. But he looked up and said, 'I like it! I like the idea! We'll take a 13-week contract.' And he agreed to pay me for writing the weekly column!"

Matt's "column" that was really an advertisement, ended up capturing a very good readership.

"I figured if it could work for one product," Matt said, "it would work for another."

He added J. D. Jewelers, which ran his column in the society/gossip page section. Matt also used the same approach for Collins Clothes and the Surplus Store. (See an example of these columns in "Spot Light on Sports" printed below.)

"Collins Clothes would pay me in clothes," he said. "After 13 weeks, Ortlieb's wanted to renew the contract, but in the meantime the *Chester Times* hired me as a reporter. Bob Finucane was the sports editor at the time. There was an opening on the sports staff and he especially sought me. He wanted me because of my familiarity with sports in Delaware County, and I was someone who could step in immediately and take over when he was off or going on vacation.

Finucane arranged an interview for Matt with the publisher, Alfred G. Hill.

"I arrived 20 minutes late," Matt recalled, "but at Bob Finucane's insistence, the publisher hired me. Bob was a hellava fine writer. He told me that one of the reasons he wanted me was because the sports column I was writing for Ortlieb's Beer, which appeared in the *Chester Times*, was attracting a lot of readers.

"I also had the experience to take over for him when he was off or on vacation, plus the fact that I had a lot of sports contacts."

Surplus Store Presents

Spot Light On Sports

Every Thursday

BY MATT ZABITKA

CONTEST WINNER

JOAN DU HADAWAY, 417 W. Baltimore Ave., Clifton, a ninth grade student at Clifton Heights High School, won the SURPLUS STORE'S "Mystery Phillies" contest and with it the reward of two box seat tickets for each of the Phillies' home games during the entire month of August.

THE 15-YEAR-OLD lassie correctly identified the "Mystery Phils" as being (1) Seminick, (2) Ennis, (3) Ashburn, (4) Church, (5) Silvestri and (6) Meyer. She was thrilled to pieces when she learned that she was the winner.

JOAN WAS one of 86 persons who correctly identified the six Phillies players. Her entry, along with the other correct 85 entries, was placed in a receptacle and a drawing held to determine the ultimate winner. The winning entry was picked by PAT SMITH, of 140 W. 21st St., Chester.

MORE THAN 400 entries disqualified when they named the No. 5 Mystery Phi (Silvestri) as Sawyer, Nicholson and even Bengough. Others mistook No. 4 (Church) for Sisler, Hamner and Waitkus.

TO EACH AND every person who took the time and effort to enter the contest, genial OTTO ROSENBLATT, proprietor of the mammoth SURPLUS STORE extends a cordial "THANK YOU."

OBSERVATION PLATFORM

BOBBY DENT, Essington third sacker, is currently experiencing one of this greatest seasons on the diamond. His hitting and fielding has been terrific all year. . . . Handsome LOU MUTZEL, one of the betting boxing refs in this area, chews gun like mad when officiating in the squared circle, but that doesn't stop him from turning in an excellent job at all times . . . LAYTON McGAW, pitcher for the Media Boys' Club nine, bears watching, he's equipped with some goods.

ALSO EQUIPPED with the goods is the gigantic SUR-PLUS STORE on Sproul Street, where you find something new every day. Man, you should get a gander at the wide and varied array of merchandise on sale at the big store with the small front. Sporting goods, work clothes, sports clothes, tools, camping equipment—YOU NAME IT, THE SURPLUS STORE HAS IT! Stop in tonight and browse around.

ODDS 'N ENDS

HANK MASON, former N. Providence High School grid ace, is slated to start at Lincoln U. this fall . . . Local photog JOHN BARON is an official picture-taker for the Pimlico and Laurel race tracks which open in the fall. He also takes pics of Delaware Park. . . The Norway team of the Chester Pike Little League has a couple of very promising players in catcher PAUL TERHAS and first sacker "LEFTY" HEISNER. "LEFTY" is the "SHY" HEISNER, who, while a member of the old Crowther Bros. team, was one of the greatest hoopmen in the area.

PLANS ARE afoot to start a Little League in Upland next year.. .. BILLY BURK, JR., son of the former *Times* sports ed, has received over 15 college athletic scholarships because of his outstanding athletic feats at Phoenix, Arizona, High School. Incidentally, BILLY, a former St. James High student, made the Arizona All-State football team and will play in the big All-Star game out West on the 24th of this month.

ACCORDING to several leading Delco sportsmen, the SURPLUS STORE TROPHY put into competition this year in the annual Valley-Delco all-star series, "is one of the finest trophies ever presented hereabouts by anyone for any sport." Which certainly speaks highly of the top quality trophies available at the SURPLUS STORE. If you're in the market for any type of trophies, at any time, make it a point to visit the SURPLUS STORE where you always get the best for less.

Paid advertisement that appeared in the Chester Times *in 1952*

Matt began working at the *Chester Times* (later renamed the *Delaware County Daily Times*) in March 1952. During his years at the Delaware County daily, Matt covered the lives and achievements of local athletes in Chester and throughout Delaware County, Pennsylvania. His columns featured such celebrities as football great Billy "White Shoes" Johnson, two-time American League Batting Champion Mickey Vernon and Pittsburgh Pirates World Series manager Danny Murtaugh, voted National League manager of the year three times.

He also got to meet major celebrities as they passed through the area. In a 1955 issue of the *Chester Times*, a photo caption (which Matt wrote) entitled "The Beauty and the Beast" described an odd couple. "Lee Ann

Matt chats with former Chester Times *sportswriting colleague Ed Gebhart at a roast held in Delaware County, Pa., in March 2001.*

Meriwether (Miss America 1955) The Beauty," and "Matt Zabitka (Mr. Nobody 1955) The Beast."

Chubby Imburgia grew up in Marcus Hook, Pa., and now lives in northern Delaware. In athletics all his life, he has been officiating high school football for more than 35 years.

"I remember Matt when he worked for the *Chester Times*," Imburgia said. "I moved to Claymont in 1957. Matt sees me very often. He has written numerous articles about me. We hold a lot of events [sports banquets] in the community. Whenever we need a write up, to get the word out, Matt is always there for us. This is important to us, because a lot of people who grew up in Marcus Hook now live in Delaware . . . . Matt has been 2000 percent for sports. He likes people and he likes writing stories about them."

Sportswriter Ed Gebhart worked with Matt at the *Chester Times* in the 1950s and early 1960s. The longtime friend and colleague, who still writes a column twice a week for the *Delaware County Daily Times*, said, "Matt was a horse. He must have worn out 15 typewriters. He was a delight to work with. If you had a bad day, Matt would step in and carry the load for you."

Gebhart recalled filling in for Matt as host of his *Sports Page of the Air* radio show when Zee went on vacation to Miami in the summer.

"My buddy Al Cartwright lured Matt away to *The News Journal*, and I think it was a real loss to Delaware County sports. One of Matt's big secrets is that he was always local. He was very likable and he always wrote about the local guy. His favorite lead would be, 'Former outstanding local athlete so-and-so is now . . . .' "

Boxing

One of Matt's favorite sports is boxing.

"I had breakfast, lunch and dinner with three of the most famous boxers of all time," he said. "One was Rocky Graziano, middleweight. I had breakfast with him. He stopped at Imburgia's Bar in Marcus Hook, because he knew the guy who owned the place. Not far from the waterfront—rough town."

Matt said he got word that Rocky was going to be there, and someone suggested Matt try to get an interview.

"I said, 'Yeah. I'll do that!' So I went down there. They don't serve any kind of breakfast or anything. Only dinners. In the lower level they have a U-shaped bar there. Then you go up three steps into the dining room.

"There was nobody in the dimly-lit dining room. They had a guard outside. They didn't want to let anybody in. They didn't spread the word that Graziano was there, because all of the Hook would be there. It was an Italian community with strong family roots, and Rocky Graziano was their hero.

"So Rocky was there with his manager and trainer. I was there—I was seated at one end of the table. Rocky was seated at the other end. The other guys were on either side—Rocky was wearing a beat-up sweater.

"I'm sitting there, pasta in front of us with a jug of wine. And here comes this elderly gentleman into the dining room. He knew the owner of the bar, and they let him in.

"He looked like he hadn't shaved for about four weeks, old clothes on. He comes up to me, takes his hat off and bows to me. He thought I was Rocky. Rocky and the guys on the other side were amused and broke out laughing.

"I said, 'I'M NOT ROCKY!' I was the biggest guy at the table. Rocky is a little guy. He wouldn't believe me. He thought I was putting him on. I think Rocky finally acknowledged himself later on. All the elderly gentleman wanted, he said, was Rocky's autograph for his grandson. And he thought I was Rocky.

"Then, I had dinner with Tony Zale. Another world-famous middleweight boxer. He fought three really bloody bouts with Graziano, on TV, all title bouts. I ate with him in a Wilmington restaurant. I remember Zale was a short guy, bald and shy.

"I heard he was coming into Delaware for a banquet. I think it was the St. Anthony's banquet. I went to the restaurant. There was a guy there who was an agent for Tony Zale. Tony said to me, 'Who the hell would remember me? I'm in my 50s.'

"Then the agent told me, 'I had Zale come to visit me in New York, and we're walking down the Times Square area there. Tony was there with me. There were big trucks going by. This guy in a truck yelled out, 'HEY TONY! TONY!' You think they don't remember you—they remember boxers forever.'

"At the restaurant, Zale was seated at our table," Matt said. "The other guys who were with me were smoking—and Tony, he can't stand smoking—asked the people at the table to put out their cigarettes. Most boxers are real nice guys and humble. But they're animals in the ring."

The News Journal

May 3, 1968   Wilmington, Del.

Zale Still Can Fight,
He Says, for 3 Rounds
BY MATT ZABITKA

"Boxing is at its lowest ebb mainly because there's too much spoilage among the white people," reflected Anthony Florian Zaleski. "The whites shun boxing because they have too easy a life."

Better known as Tony Zale, the Man of Steel from Gary, Ind., who held the middleweight title longer (5 years, 7 1/2 months) than any boxer in history, was here last night for a St. Anthony's Catholic Club Sports function.

"When I fought times were tough. The whites were eager to get into the sport to make a couple of bucks," noted Zale, a veteran of 95 fights as an amateur and 88 as a pro before retiring in 1948 at 35. "This is not the situation today."

Zale, who reaped $280,000 as his share for three memorable middleweight title fights with Rocky Graziano, said boxing was good to him and for him. But he admitted he has little to show for it, "outside of a new car, some nice clothes and a few dollars in the bank."

"Bad investments," he explained. "There was this restaurant I had in Chicago that folded because I wouldn't go with the syndicate. Then there was a separation from my wife that cost me, plus a number of other bad deals."

But Zale, now in a field training program with Metropolitan Insurance Co., weighs 170, 12 pounds over his best fighting weight, but he has no paunch. His nose isn't flattened and his face is fairly smooth. His hair is thinning and he uses a hearing aid.

"I'm 55, but I feel I could go three rounds against the best fighter my weight in the country today and not disgrace myself," he said. "I still keep in shape. For 20 years I was the boxing coach at the Chicago CYO before I hooked up with Metropolitan last January."

Zale said he probably would have continued fighting long after his career-ending bout with Marcel Cerdan in 1948, but he was afraid of losing his right arm.

"When I was attending high school in Gary, Ind., I hurt my elbow pitching for a sandlot team. The injury would flare up in later years.

"I remember just before my third title fight with Graziano my arm started paining something terrible. I fought anyway, knocking out Rocky in the third round.

"In my next fight, which turned out to be my last, I was knocked out by Cerdan in the 12th round, losing my title. I went the entire way using only one arm. After the fight, my doctor warned me that if I continued to fight I could possibly lose my arm. I never fought after that."

He said the toughest fighter and hardest puncher he ever faced was Al Hostak. "I beat him on a decision the first time I met him; it was a very big upset and shot me into prominence. I later knocked him out twice. But I never met a harder puncher."

Zale scoffed at stories about his "grudge" match with Graziano.

"That was newspaper publicity," he said. "I was never mad at Graziano or anyone else I fought. When I was in the ring, I held nothing back in trying to win. But once the fight was over, I was friends with the other guy."

Zale also offered these observations:

On Cassius Clay, "Speed rather than punching has been his greatest asset. In his present predicament I sort of sympathize with him. I don't know if he's more afraid of the United States government or the Black Muslims."

On Joe Frazier: "He looks rough, tough, he's always in there scrapping. He has endurance. Reminds me of Rocky Marciano."

On Jerry Quarry: "He doesn't go forward enough. If he had moved in he would have done much better against Jimmy Ellis."

On advice to aspiring boxers: "They shouldn't take up the sport unless they have natural ability and are willing to sacrifice."

Reprinted with the permission of The News Journal

"Then," Matt said, "I had dinner with Jersey Joe Walcott, who was world heavyweight champion. He had lost to Rocky Marciano. That fight I remember, because I read all about the background on that fight. The 9th or 10th round, Wolcott, who towered over Marciano, who wasn't very big, got a lot of cuts. Rocky was bloodied up in the late rounds. They wanted to stop the fight. Rocky pleaded with his corner, 'No, no, no! You can't stop the fight.'

"It was a title fight. The doctor said, 'It will be my ass here, if anything happens.' But Marciano said, 'Give me just one more round.' So they did. They don't know where in the hell he got the stamina from. Marciano beat him and became the heavyweight champ, and he never lost a fight after that. He retired undefeated."

Other boxers

Matt regularly featured boxers with a local connection, including:
- Wesley Watson, who once trained with world heavyweight Lennox Lewis and was a sparring partner for Gerry Cooney;
- Former world heavyweight champion Michael Spinks;
- Former International Boxing Federation (IBF) world light featherweight and middleweight champion Bernard Hopkins;
- Heavyweight Vaughn Bean;
- Fight promoter and manager Nick Tiberi;
- Middleweight boxer "Pinching Postman" Tony Thornton;
- Dave "The Uncrowned Champion" Tiberi; and
- Light heavyweight Henry Milligan, among others.

"I used to cover boxing a lot," Matt said, speaking at length on the careers of local boxers Henry Milligan and Dave Tiberi, who he described as, "two of the brightest fighters since I have been here."

Matt remembered receiving a phone call from Milligan, asking Matt for advice on finding a trainer early in the Delaware boxer's career.

Tiberi, Matt said, was the local boy who got the biggest shot in his Atlantic City bout against James Toney, who Matt described as "pound for pound the greatest boxer in the world."

"Before the fight," Matt said, "they thought if Tiberi lasted two rounds it would be a moral victory. Tiberi lasted the entire fight, all 12 rounds. Nationally televised. There was a lot of controversy. A lot of Tiberi fans were at ringside, loudly protesting the split decision."

Is Matt at ringside covering fights?

"Always," he said, almost seeming hurt by the thought he might be anywhere else. "I covered Dave Tiberi at Cheyney University. He was fighting a guy from Pittsburgh. I was seated right at the corner of a ring post. I had my notebook. There was blood splattering all over it. I kept ripping pages off and tossing them under the ring. It was a title fight, held under the auspices of a neophyte boxing rating organization. Tiberi won on a knockout."

Matt explained his fascination with and respect for those brave enough to enter the ring.

"I like boxing. There's a lot of excitement and thrills, especially when the fans are rooting for the home guy. No matter what bout it is, there's usually a favorite. I get more excited when someone's pulling off an upset. I'm always for the underdog when two boxers are fighting with whom I have no connection.

"In boxing, the guy doesn't have a teammate to depend on. He is there, one-on-one. His whole life is at stake. It's not that somebody is going to foul up and make a mistake, or lose the fight for you, like a pitcher in baseball or a quarterback in football. In boxing, you're by yourself, facing an opponent. Everything rests on you. You lose by what you do, what you don't do.

"I think it's probably the easiest sport to cover, because you only have to remember two names. The only thing is, you have to be fast, and a lot of what you write comes from memory after each round. What kind of punches are thrown—because they are going so fast—you record in your memory. Then you write it down at the end of the round, because you have a minute to do it then."

Matt recalled a Henry Milligan fight he was covering in Atlantic City. The opponent was a head taller than Milligan and looked like an ex-Marine.

"He was a big, tough guy," Matt recalled. "He hit Milligan on the side of his cheek. His whole face went red. Milligan was moving around, trying to shake the cobwebs out of his head. That blow would have knocked anybody else out.

"He took a few more blows. I'm at ringside with the other reporters. This one guy with the Atlantic City paper, he knows me, he said, 'There goes your man. That's it!' Then, just as the first round is going to end, Milligan had him on the ropes, right in the corner, just where I was sitting, below the ring post. He gave this guy an uppercut. The other guy went down. Like a piece of string. They counted him out in one round."

After a fight, Matt said he goes to the locker room of each fighter.

"Usually," he said, "everybody rushes to the to the victor's dressing room. But many times you get a better story from the loser."

After the Milligan victory, Matt said he was initially barred from entering the room by the loser's manager and trainer. But, he said, the beaten boxer told them to let Matt stay.

"The boxer," Matt said, "had a guy on each side of him, asking him questions, trying to get his senses back. He said to me, 'I'm a little discombobulated right now. But when I come around, I'll talk to you.'

"Also, when you are covering boxing, you don't have to remember a lot of names, like in football and basketball. In football, as soon as one team loses the ball on offense, there are 11 defensive players that come in to replace the offensive team.

"Basketball is fast paced, but many times the result boils down to the last few minutes."

Baseball

"Because baseball goes at a slower pace than boxing, you have more time to organize your story," Matt said. "You got the players there. Stationary. You could carry on a conversation while a game is going on, or you could eat or go to the bathroom, read a book. You don't loose track of the game completely."

Baseball also, said Matt, has the ability to attract hard-core fans throughout the year and also pulls in larger audiences as pennant fever adds more excitement going into the late stages of the season.

"During the World Series," he said, smiling, "everybody's a baseball fan. Almost everyone turns out in droves when a team is going for the pennant or competing in the World Series. They want to tell everybody, 'I was there in 1948 when this or that happened.'

"I covered the World Series in Yankee Stadium when the Pittsburgh Pirates played the Yankees in the 1960. I got a field pass and was there in 'the house that Ruth built.' It was an enormous place. Danny Murtaugh, the manager of the Pittsburgh team, he was from Chester. He was a small guy when he played baseball as a kid. But he had guts, was a daredevil type. Used to steal bases diving head first into the bag.

"I went into the Yankee dugout before the game. There were all New York reporters—seven or eight of them. I was the only one from out of town. Yankee manager Casey Stengel had a bit of a reputation for being a flake. He came out scowling, plants one foot on the bench of the Yankee dugout. He knows the reporters, and he was answering their questions. But he kept looking at me, like, 'Who's he?' I see Danny come out of the Yankee bullpen in left field. We met at shortstop, talking about Chester and the pinochle league. He moves his head back several times, looking up, surveying the mammoth stadium, and says, 'Gawd almighty. This is one hellava big place.' "

Matt explained that although Murtaugh had played and managed in the majors for years, he had never set foot in Yankee Stadium because his big league career was entirely in the National League and the Yankees were in the American League.

During that year, Matt wrote an article for the *Chester Times* about hometown friend Danny Murtaugh and his baseball career--from the minors to the majors and on to become the Pittsburgh Pirates' manager.

After getting permission from his paper, Matt sent a copy of his six-part series on Murtaugh to the *Pittsburgh Post Gazette*, which used Matt's work in a special supplement it ran during that team's participation in the World Series.

In 1976, upon Murtaugh's death, Matt wrote a column about his longtime friend.

The News Journal

Dec. 4, 1976   Wilmington, Del.

Murtaugh: A man to remember

BY MATT ZABITKA

It's October, 1960. World Series time, Pittsburgh Pirates vs. the New York Yankees.

Danny Murtaugh, who guided the Bucs to their first National League pennant in 33 years, was an instant hero in his bailiwick of Delaware County, Pa., not to mention Pittsburgh.

I was then writing for the Delaware County Daily Times and was assigned to cover Danny and his Pirates in Yankee Stadium.

Maybe fifteen minutes before any of the players put in an appearance on the field, I spotted Murtaugh coming out of the left field bullpen area. I ran out on the field. Met him at the spot where the shortstop usually plays.

We shook hands and exchanged pleasantries. He flooded me with questions, wanting to know everything that was happening back in his hometown of Chester, Pa.—how was the St. James High football team doing (his son was an athlete there), who was leading the Delco Pinochle League (in which he played during the off-season), how was his old buddy Mickey Vernon (two-time American League batting champion with the Washington Senators) making out . . . on and on the questions came.

Danny talked about everything but the Series coming up.

Then he tugged the visor of his cap, stuffed his hands in the back pockets of his uniform and glanced upward at the huge stadium, slowing doing a 180-degree turn with his head. He spit out a stream of tobacco juice that caught the toe of his shoes and shook his head.

"Gawd almighty," he sighed, "this is one helluva big place."

It was then I learned that Danny, in organized baseball since 1937 when he broke in as a fuzz-faced, 19-year-old infielder with Cambridge, Md., of the old Eastern Shore League, had never previously set foot inside Yankee Stadium. This was his first trip ever inside the House That Ruth Built and it was as a manager of a team involved in the World Series.

He told me that he saw only three major league games in his life before he ever played in the bigs himself.

"First big league game I ever saw was in 1927, when I was 9. Never forget that one. I wanted so much to see Ty Cobb, then with the Philadelphia Athletics. Went up to Shibe Park and sat in the grandstands with my uncle (Tim McCarey).

"Cobb didn't play that day and I was disappointed. There was a situation that came up in the last inning when all the fans thought Connie Mack (A's manager) would send Cobb in to pinch-hit. But he didn't.

"Second big league game I saw was at the old Baker Bowl (then the Phillies' home park). Went up specifically to see local boy (from Delaware County, Pa.) Stouts (Hack) Wilson, who was a big star with the Chicago Cubs. I sat in the bleachers and marveled at the play of Cub shortstop Wood[y] English.

"Third and last big league I saw before I first played in the majors was one in which Detroit's Schoolboy Rowe was trying for his 17th win against the A's in Philly."

These and many, many other memories surfaced when I learned that the lovable Irishman died Thursday night at age 59, after suffering a stroke Tuesday.

Gawd, I must have written a half-million words chronicling Danny's activities and accomplishments—for the *Delaware County Times, The Sporting News, The Pittsburgh Post Gazette*, as well as *The News Journal*.

I couldn't even venture to guess how many banquets I attended, gracing the dais, seated next to Murtaugh.

Danny, a product of Chester High, was a jewel of a speaker. In great demand, he never accepted a cent for his services, not even gas money, when addressing organizations in his hometown. I heard Danny on numerous occasions save sagging banquets with his main addresses. He was a frequent guest at the Wilmington Sportswriters and Broadcasters Association fetes.

I recall at several banquets, after the meal, he'd light up a huge stogie, lean over and comment, "Matt, this looks like a one-cigar banquet."

I recall a specific Delaware County Old Timers Sports banquet at Chester's YMCA. One segment of the program was reserved for intro-duction of former outstanding sports personalities in the audience. Manning the "mike" and doing the introductions was a late 70-ish man with failing eyesight [Dick McDonald].

After about a dozen-or-so introductions, the gentleman manning the "mike" cried out, "and there's old Baron Dougherty. C'mon Baron, stand up and take a bow."

Now Baron Dougherty had been dead maybe 10 years. He had been a celebrated figure in Delaware County, a close friend of Jack Dempsey, Maxie Rosenbloom, Tony Galento, Damon Runyon. He also had been a boxing referee, worked one of Dempsey's big fights.

Murtaugh, seated next to me, almost swallowed his cigar when he heard Baron Dougherty being asked to "stand and take a bow."

"If Baron Dougherty gets up," Murtaugh quipped, "I'm getting the hell out of here fast."

One banquet that gave Murtaugh goose pimples was a testimonial in his honor, tendered the winter of 1960 by the fine people of Delaware County who wanted to pay their hometown hero a tribute in recognition of his leading the Pirates to the World Series championship.

One of the worst blizzards in many years struck Chester the day of the banquet. I was then living in Claymont's Ashbourne Hills section. En route to the banquet that night, at Chester's Columbus Center, twice I got stuck in the heavy snow. I thought for certain the banquet would be post-poned. Who in their right mind would venture out on a night like that.

But I was wrong. Man, but was I wrong!

The banquet hall was packed to capacity. Even Bob Prince, then the Voice of the Pirates, showed up to perform his role as toastmaster. It was a night to remember and Danny was ever so humble in his appreciation of the mass turnout.

I'll never forget how close Murtaugh came to never managing in the majors.

He went to Charlestown, W. Va., in the American Association as manager in 1955, but was released when the club ran into financial difficulties and had to trim its payroll.

He was slated to manage the Williamsport club in the Eastern League in 1956. In early '56, he paid me a visit in the sports department of the Delaware County Daily Times. Asked if I knew of any place where he could find a job. Said he was through with baseball and was going to stick at home. Said he had an ulcer that was bothering him. He did get a job as a playground instructor for the Chester Recreation Department.

But it wasn't long before he was back in baseball. He was selected by manager Bobby Bragan, who had played with him with the Phillies, as a coach for the Pirates, when Tom Tatum dropped out to enter business.

I asked Danny later why he was returning to baseball, after telling me he was through with the game because of an ulcer.

"I figure it this way," he explained. "A guy could get an ulcer being a janitor. Why not do something you like and get paid much, much more than a janitor gets paid."

Danny succeeded Bragan as Bucs' manager on Aug. 3, 1957, and went on to create some of the greatest chapters in Pirates' baseball history.

Three times voted manager of the year, Danny's success never spoiled him. The hat size never swelled for this product of the Depression, Franklin Fire Co. volunteer, Sun Shipyard worker, and World War II foot soldier, who trudged across Europe with the infantry and was ambushed by German snipers.

He was a deeply religious, quiet, conscientious and a patient man. A baseball manager who knew how to get the best out of his players without all the raucous of a Billy Martin or the abuses of a Woody Hayes.

That's how I remember Daniel Edward Murtaugh Jr.

When Danny stepped down as manager of the Bucs after the 1976 season in October, after managing 15 years during four different terms, he explained, "I think I've been around long enough. I'm approaching the age of 60 and I've also reached a point where I would like to spend some time with my grandchildren."

He admitted he neglected his own children a bit while in the process of playing and managing during his younger years. "So I'm going to try to make up for it by spending a little more time now with my grandchildren," he said.

It's three weeks before Christmas and Danny never lived to watch his grandchildren greet Christmas Day.

Published with permission of The News Journal

Letter from Ty Cobb

In the late 1950s, Matt received what he described as "the most memorable letter I ever got from the greatest baseball player in history, Ty Cobb—even though I never met him, never saw him play."

Matt had written a six-part series for the *Delaware County Daily Times* on Hack Wilson, a local baseball player who had an outstanding career that included appearances in the World Series, and unloaded 191 RBIs and 58 home runs in one season. To get the story, Matt conducted interviews with more than 50 of Wilson's contemporaries, who were living in Delaware County, Pennsylvania, where Wilson was raised.

Matt's series asked the question: Why was Hack Wilson not in Baseball's Hall of Fame? After the series ran, he sent copies to all of the voting members of the hall of fame veterans division selection committee, who voted on ex-players for induction into the Baseball Valhalla in Cooperstown, New York.

Thinking that Ty Cobb, who had played with Wilson, might enjoy the series, Matt sent the Georgia ballplayer a copy of his series. Since he did not know the baseball great's correct address, or even if he was still alive, Matt addressed the envelope simply: "Ty Cobb, Atlanta, Georgia."

Cobb got the letter.

Matt received a three-page, hand-written response from Cobb, who mentioned that Hack Wilson would never get into the Hall of Fame as long as some of the old time voters were still alive.

"I was surprised to get the personal letter," Matt said. "It was hand written. He started the letter, 'Dear Matt.' It was like we were friends."

Matt eventually got in touch with a person who specialized in collecting signatures of famous individuals, wondering what the Ty Cobb letter might be worth. He agreed to sell the letter for $150 to a fellow in New York City, a stockbroker named Lyons.

After the deal was made, the buyer told Matt the $150 check was in the mail, and he requested that Matt send Ty Cobb's letter to New York, but first instructed Matt to go to the post office and insure it for $10,000.

Matt said he kept a photocopy of Ty Cobb's personal letter in his basement office. It was destroyed, along with hundreds of other files and letters and pictures, in the early 1990s, when four feet of water flooded Matt's home and destroyed many of his possessions—including the left-handed typewriter he had bought to write his first columns for the *Progressive Weekly* when he was 13 years old.

CHAPTER 4

'Sports Page of the Air'

'It was not a scripted show, where you know what everything is—and it's going to be flat. My show was ad libbed—I would take cold calls. The people didn't know what was going to be going on. I didn't know sometimes. You had to make things up as you went along. That's what made it really interesting.'

—*Matt Zabitka*

Sports talk radio—it's all the rage these days. It's also a big, corporate-run business, with not a whole lot of room for the little guy to get a foot in the door and a hand on the mike.

It wasn't quite so tough to break into the broadcasting business in the mid-1950s, when Matt Zabitka had a hit radio show that seemed to generate as much controversy as it did ratings.

The radio station, WDRF (Delaware River Ferry Station), was located on Edgmont Avenue in Brookhaven, Pa., just on the outskirts of Chester, and was owned by local businessman Lou Kapelski. Described by Matt as a "big money man," Kapelski had a charitable side, often donating large sums of money to institutions such as Widener University, where the Lou Kapelski Education Building honors the businessman's generosity.

At the time that Matt started in the radio business, the station had a guy doing an afternoon program. He concentrated mainly on national news, giving the results of major league games. What Kapelski wanted was somebody to cover local sporting events and the people who participated in them. He asked Cy Swingle, his radio station manager, to see if Matt was ready to bring his passion for local sports coverage to the airways.

"Cy came to me and asked me to do this local program for the station," Matt said. "I was flattered. I had no experience, but I told him I would take it."

What flattered Matt even more was the fact that they were going to pay him for the show, which would be on the air weekdays from 4:30 to 6 p.m., a time slot that fit nicely with Matt's other job at the *Chester Times.*

"They told me they would pay me $25 a week. Hell," he said, laughing, "I would have done it for free. It was great."

Now that he had his own show, all Matt needed to do was to learn how to operate the dizzying array of knobs, buttons and switches that made the whole thing work. Cy promised he would give Matt a crash course in radio broadcasting, and all he had to do was show up at the WDRF studios about an hour before airtime. Matt arrived on time for his first show, but Swingle was nowhere to be found.

As the 4:30 deadline crept closer, a very nervous Matt asked the station engineer for some help, but it wasn't until they started playing the show's theme song that Swingle came running into the studio to give Matt an abbreviated lesson in the fundamentals of broadcast journalism.

"He was in a meeting," Matt said, "and I guess he forgot about me. It's getting down to airtime and he's not there. Now they're playing the theme song," Matt recalled, singing, " 'You've got to be a football hero . . . .' and he runs in and starts pressing buttons and shouting directions, like, 'press this and that.' "

Matt said Cy tried to explain the complex process and procedures the new host would need in about a minute and a half.

"I said to myself, 'What the hell am I going to do?' I was tense, sitting there. The palms of my hands were wet. I was sweating profusely."

Tense and jittery, Matt remembered sweating bullets as he got through the program, and afterwards he wondered just how awful he sounded on the air.

"After I left the station that first day, heading for home, I was so ashamed that my speech was all stilted and slanted, that I took the back streets coming home," Matt said. "I was lousy, and I didn't want anybody to even see me in the car."

He told his wife, Helen, that he would probably quit after a few days—maybe by the end of the week—if he lasted that long.

Matt need not have worried, because once he got the knack of it, he found radio work was something he really loved to do. Instead of getting the axe, Matt thought that after a couple of months he ought to be getting a raise.

The show was spontaneous—for there was no delayed-time button at that time. The program soon turned out to be something special, and the people in Delaware County made it a point to listen to Matt and his guests after school or on their way home from work.

"What made the show popular was the fact that it wasn't scripted," Matt said. "I interviewed the guests and took calls over the phone, and some of the calls were wild."

In the beginning, Matt said he didn't know what to expect from callers. Anyone with any comment could get on the air.

"One guy called in and he told me, 'You reprimanded somebody for playing for two teams. I remember when you were playing baseball, you were playing for a lot of teams at the same time. You have a lot of nerve.'

"There wasn't much I could say, so I said, 'Why don't you go back in the woodwork?' or something like that. But most of the calls were more pleasant."

Matt explained that while hosting the show he would attempt to switch roles and put himself on the other side of the microphone. He also tried to think like his listeners and would ask his guests questions that people in the audience would pose if they were in his place.

Sometimes the inquiries were humorous, sometimes they focused on the guest's sport or their life and sometimes the questions were a bit controversial or blunt. But, he said, that's why the audience was tuning in.

The Zee connects with The King (almost)

It was during his time behind the mike, that Matt became connected—although distantly and indirectly—with the hot-at-the-time, swivel-hipped guy they called the King of Rock 'n' Roll.

Back in the mid- to late-'50s, not only was Elvis Presley very much alive he also was the most sought after entertainer in America. Record stores, as they were called then, couldn't get enough of his music, and fans couldn't get enough of the guy with the sideburns and Southern swagger from Memphis.

Now while it's true that the King never personally called the station asking to talk to Matt Zabitka, a lady named Margie Glover did.

Glover and her family in Thorofare, New Jersey, were in the habit of listening to the radio during their evening meals. One night, just by chance, they happened to tune into the new show that was somehow different from anything they had heard before.

"They turned on the radio and turned the dial, and there I was," Matt said. "They were so enamored that, even though they didn't know the people I talked about, they turned my show on every night after that."

Although the Glover family, living across the Delaware River in New Jersey had no idea what was going on in the sports community of Chester, Pa., they did like the controversy Matt always seemed to generate on the airwaves.

Margie never met Matt, but she did send him letters and a picture of herself on a horse and another on a motorcycle.

At that time, Betty Hardesty, a public relations director for the Philadelphia Arena was trying to generate ticket sales for the boxing matches, ice hockey games, rodeo shows and circuses that took place there. She sought Matt's help in getting a plug on his radio show that Elvis Presley was scheduled to perform in the Arena.

On his end, Matt was trying to raise some money for a local charity called Camp Sunshine, a vacation haven of a week or two for underprivileged children. He worked out a plan with the Philadelphia Arena public relations person that would benefit both parties.

Matt would receive a piece of Elvis Presley's wardrobe, preferably a dress jacket that could be auctioned off over the air, with the proceeds going to Camp Sunshine. The accompanying radio publicity would plug Presley's performance at the arena.

Two weeks later, a package arrived from Memphis containing a stunning dress jacket from Presley's personal collection.

"At least it said Tennessee on the mail label," Matt said, recalling the incident.

Matt said he tried on the King's coat, but never really got a chance to break it in, since it was auctioned off during his radio show. Of course, Margie Glover, Matt's number one fan, made the top bid. The promotion was such a big hit that Matt requested a Presley sports shirt, which he carved up with scissors into 4-inch squares and sold the pieces for $1 each.

Matt also was involved in a sports promotion for the March of Dimes.

At Easter break, when Delaware County athletes returned home from college, Matt arranged a basketball all-star game. The charity contest involved college players from the south end of Delaware County playing their peers from the northern end. To increase interest in the event, Matt turned it into a doubleheader, with a second game matching high school all stars from opposite ends of the county as well.

"The problem," Matt said, "was getting someone to help finance the project with a donation to buy uniforms for the four competing clubs."

Matt was a personal friend of Lord Jim Ferguson, manager of Bill Haley and the Comets, still known for their groundbreaking rock 'n' roll hit "Rock Around the Clock." Ferguson arranged a meeting with Matt and Haley at the singer's Delaware County home.

"He lived in Booth's Corner," Matt said. "I went to Bill Haley's home with *Chester Times* photographer Walt Chernokal, who took a photo of Haley presenting me a check in the kitchen. He didn't hesitate to donate $1,000 for the uniforms." Matt said. "We had a long talk over a couple cups of coffee. I kept a copy of the 8-1/2 by 11 photo for years, until it was lost in a flood in my basement."

While the show was a lot of fun and offered opportunities to meet even more interesting people in the area, broadcasting's demands called for long workdays, with Matt starting at the *Chester Daily Times* at 6 a.m., working until about 4 in the afternoon, then rushing over to WDRF to do his Monday-through-Friday, 4:30-to-6 p.m., radio gig. It meant that he wouldn't get finished until early evening. If there was a banquet or some other affair where he was needed that evening, he would arrive home even later.

"The show would usually start off with a theme song," Matt said. "I might be in another part of the studio, but when I heard my theme song coming on, I'd rush right back and sit at the mike."

Matt even had a bunch of photos put together in a sort of album, to give fans an idea what the show was really like, and what went on behind the scenes.

"I had all the ashtrays in the station filled to the brim and brought them into my studio," Matt said. "I had them piled up in front of me as the show continued and the caption said "This is what goes on when I'm doing the show,' with photos of me stripping to my bare chest as air time elapsed."

The photo album was put up for sale, and the first customer was, you might have guessed, none other than Matt's biggest fan from the Garden State, Margie Glover.

While the show was popular with a lot of people, it was even more popular with the sponsors, who were lined up waiting to buy a commercial spot from 4:30 to 6 p.m. every weeknight. "Sometimes," Matt said, "I would get 25 sponsors for an hour-and-one-half show. Some of the sponsors were 15 seconds, maybe 30 seconds, but they wanted the time."

One of these advertisers was the old Claymont Diner, and Matt told listeners the food wasn't that good, but the waitresses were something else.

"I got a call the next day," Matt recalled. "The guy said the waitresses were ugly—the food was better."

Another time Matt was supposed to air an advertisement for a loan company in downtown Chester. They had a taped commercial by a big name announcer named Del Parks, who did the commercial for the hit television show *The Life of Riley*, starring William Bendix.

The commercial was supposed to air at exactly 4:30, when the show began, but nobody at the station could find the tape. The engineer told Matt he would have to ad lib the commercial.

Fortunately, Matt knew where the loan company was, so he told his audience "This afternoon, I'm all dressed up in my new white suit, and during my lunchtime, I went down to the ICC Loan Company, to see a friend of mine there.

"Well, just as I got there, I see this big 18-wheeler backed up to the front door of the place, and they were shovelling money into the place.

The money was newly minted. It was so fresh that the green ink was still wet."

As Matt was working his way through the commercial, his engineer was having fits. He couldn't believe what Matt was saying, and he was sure they would both be fired when the sponsor called up to complain.

He couldn't have been more wrong. The ICC loan company loved it. They got more attention from Matt's commercial than they ever did from Del Parks' tape.

Once Matt got a call from the manager of a local kids' baseball team, who had received a lot of criticism from a parent whose son was not used during an all-star game. Matt got them both on the show and told them it was a shame they were at such odds, because they had been friends for years. He wanted them to make up and settle their differences on the air. The audience also thought it would be a good idea to bury the hatchet, and they were glued to their radios to hear what would happen. But the show ran out of time.

"The station was flooded with calls," Matt said. "The sad thing is they never shook hands. They nearly came to blows."

Creative prediction

One prediction that really rattled a listener had to do with a state of Pennsylvania high school championship basketball contest, slated to take place one evening at the Palestra, a legendary Philadelphia sports arena.

The game, which pitted Chester High School against Farrel High School, was the talk of the local sports world, and Matt wanted to go in the worst way, but he couldn't figure out how to finish his radio show at 6 p.m. and still get to Philly on time.

"I figured it out in my mind before I went to the radio station," Matt said. "I brought a whistle with me, and I mentioned on the air that the Palestra was sold out. No tickets left."

The solution was that Matt would broadcast a *War of the Worlds*-style, simulated version of the hottest game in town that night, and how it was going to end. The tape was to be played between 4:30 and 6 p.m.

Before going on the air, Matt made a stop at the station's library, and got some phonograph records of past sporting events—like boxing matches and championship games—complete with fans cheering their heads off.

"I told the engineer, when I make a signal with my finger, you play the records with the people cheering," Matt recalled, still smiling at his ingenuity. "Then, I arranged another signal, which meant that the engineer was to keep turning up the volume. I wanted it loud, real loud, as the game was reaching the final seconds."

The more Matt got into it, blowing his whistle and calling the play by play, the more it seemed like a real game was actually being broadcast on the air.

As the time came for Matt to give his final prediction, he screamed into the microphone that is was the last seconds of play, and that the game, a real thriller, was going right down to the wire.

He remembers describing how a player from Chester High put the ball up in the air just as the simulated buzzer went off.

This was against the background noise of fans cheering at a fever pitch (at least on the records that the engineer was spinning).

"He shoots the ball. It's going to sink IT'S GOING IN! CHESTER WINS BY A POINT! CHESTER WINS BY A POINT!!!!"

All this was recorded on a WDRF tape, and was being played while Matt was on his way to the Palestra to cover the real basketball game.

"I told the audience what I was doing and why I was doing it," Matt said. "I went to the game and didn't think any more of it. It was just a creative way of predicting the outcome of the game."

Matt learned of the far-reaching results of the whole affair about three months later, when he was sitting in a booth at Kelly's Restaurant in Marcus Hook, having dinner with Nick Sciochetti, a friend who has since died.

"It was about 8 or 9 at night, and there was this guy, John Gattone, sitting in a booth across from us, and I thought I knew him from somewhere," Matt said. "He recognized me and came over to our booth and introduced himself."

Not only did the guy know Matt but he had been looking for him ever since the night Matt ran his "creative" version of how the high school basketball championship was going to turn out.

"He told me that three months ago he was ready to kill me," Matt said. "I asked him why, and he told me his story."

Gattone had been on his way home from work at Sun Oil on the night of the championship game, hoping to get a quick change of clothes and head for the Palestra. Like all true sports fans in Chester and Marcus Hook at that time, he had his car radio tuned to WDRF, and that's when he heard Matt's voice screaming over the crowd, telling anyone within range that Chester High had won the game by a basket at the buzzer.

Unlike most of Matt's listeners that afternoon, Gattone had not heard the disclaimer at the beginning of the broadcast. He had only caught the last minutes of the tape. He couldn't believe his ears. He thought they must have moved the game up a couple of hours for some reason.

Still, he headed home, got a change of clothes and dropped by Sid Stesis' newsstand in Marcus Hook, where his buddies were congregating. They were supposed to meet there and go up to the game together.

When his friends tried to tell Gattone that they are just about leave for Philly, the confused fan tried to explain to them there was no use going—that Chester High won the game by a point. He said he had heard it on the radio!

This was the first that his buddies heard of this, and they told him he was crazy—that no game had been played—it was still on for that night.

Now, the man's dander was up, and he told his friends he would bet them $100 that Chester High had already won. He was sure, because, after all, he had heard it on the radio.

He made a $100 bet with Sam Moschella. To prove his point, Gattone went into the newsstand and picked up a copy of the *Chester Times*. To his dismay, he saw that the game was on for 8 o'clock that night. That's why his pals were waiting—they were ready to leave.

As Matt remembered, "He was so shocked—he had lost $100—he was going to kill me. He only heard a little bit of the tape. He didn't hear the beginning, because he was in a hurry to get home and get dressed. He was pretty much calmed down by the time he found me three months later. Time helped to heal that loss. But that was a lot of money—big money. I guess it sounded realistic. I had the whistles blowing in the background and everything else, fans cheering to make it sound realistic—and it did."

Guests and callers

"I remember one time I was on the air," Matt said, "they gave me a wire story that somebody brought in. It was a big, wide yellow sheet—somebody thought I should read it. It just came over the wire.

"So here I am in the studio, I'm reading it. And these guys are playing a prank on the studio. I'm reading the paper, and somebody gets a match and lights it. While I'm reading, it's going up in flames. I said, 'I'm reading some hot news here.' I put that out in a hurry."

One of Matt's more unusual interviews was with an old-time Phillies catcher Andy Seminick, who had been with the team during its days at Connie Mack Stadium. Matt had arranged to conduct an on-air interview, over the phone, from the stadium dressing room before the game.

"They gave me a number to call him in the training room," Matt said. "I introduced him, and I said, 'Hi, Andy. What are you doing right now?' He said, over the air, 'I'm in the nude, and I'm laying on the table right here, getting a rubdown.' So I interviewed him while he was getting a rubdown."

Thinking back more than 40 years, Matt said his radio show was popular because "it was local and spontaneous." Nobody, particularly Matt, knew for sure what any given show would be like. "I would give opinions about things that were going on," Matt said. "I made predictions, with scores. That really rattled some people."

When talking about *Sports Page of the Air*, Matt seems to be proud that his show featured the little guy. It got the club football player, the bowler and high school baseball player and college football star from Chester or the county's suburbs on the air and in the spotlight during a time when being interviewed "on the radio" was a big thing.

"That's how people got to know about them and got to know about me," Matt said. "Then they would call me with more leads and information. And that's why people got to know you. The other thing was, it was not a scripted show, where you know what everything is—and it's going to be flat. My show was ad libbed—I would take cold calls. The people didn't know what was going to be going on. I didn't know sometimes. You had to make things up as you went along. That's what made it really interesting."

While Matt received a fair share of positive comments, he also found out that you can never please everyone all of the time.

"I was at a bowling banquet, during the time when I was on the air," Matt recalled, "and after the banquet, a number of people cornered me and talked about the radio show. This guy was standing there, and I knew he wanted to get into the conversation. He looked me in the face. I knew him—not real well—and he said, 'I listen to your show every day. It stinks.' I said, 'Why do you tune in every day?' "

In the news

But Matt's show was such a hit that he began to make the news. In addition to his role as a news reporter, Matt also was becoming a newsmaker.

Versions of the following column, a WDRF radio promotional story distributed throughout the area, appeared in several local newspapers. This press release presents a good summary of both Matt's show and his special creative broadcasting style. While the article presented several favorable opinions of *Sports Page of the Air*, not everyone thought Matt's broadcasting talents deserved airtime, especially the teenage boy who offered a rather strong complaint about Zee's daily radio broadcast.

WDRF's 'Sport Page of the Air'

For 69 consecutive weeks, people of the Delaware Valley area (Southeastern Pennsylvania and parts of Delaware and New Jersey) have been eating their suppers and riding to and from work tuned in to a garrulous-voiced announcer named Matt Zabitka, who conducts what he calls the "longest radio sports show in the entire world today."

The program, heard daily, Monday through Friday, 4:30 p.m., to 6 p.m., emanates over Chester, Pa., station WDRF, 1590 on the dial.

Zabitka has emerged as one of the most controversial radio announcers in radio in this neck of the woods as a result of his "on the spot" type questioning of local and nationally-famous athletes.

Of professional prizefighter Fred "Rocky" Jones, who pulled one of the biggest upsets in the past 20 years when he defeated heavily favored Roland LaStarza, Zabitka asked, "Did you ever accept a bribe?" and "Were you told to lay down to LaStarza in the return match?"

Of Phillies' coach Andy Seminick (an ex-catcher) Zabitka asked whether he would be interested in taking over May Smith's job as manager of the Phils?

These are the type of questions Zabitka has been asking and getting straight answers from hundreds of local athletes, as well as such well-known national sports figures as Don Cardwell, Jack Meyer and Richie Ashburn of the Phillies; Villanova University's head football coach Frank Reagan; Yale University's backfield coach Art Raimo; National League umpire Shag Crawford; American League umpire Johnny Stevens; Boston Red Sox first baseman Mickey Vernon; Pittsburgh Pirates coach Danny Murtaugh; Indianapolis Speedway 550-mile race winner Pat Flaherty; former Philadelphia Eagles grid stars Bill Mackrides, Jack Ferrante and Jay MacDowell; Philadelphia Warriors' basketball star Neil Johnston; professional tennis promoter Jack Karmer; NBA referee Lou Bonder; former Minneapolis Lakers standout Jim Pollard, and many others.

Zabitka has interviewed more than 700 guests in the 68 weeks he has been on the air.

You either like his program or you hate it vehemently . . . but you listen to it.

As one listener put it—"I'm afraid to turn him off for fear that he may be attacking me."

Zabitka averages 200 letters and phone calls per week, mostly from women, many of them invitations to free suppers.

He has changed the eating habits of thousands of listeners. As one 13-year-old lad from Woodlyn, Pa., wrote in: "I don't see what in the world my old man sees in your lousy show, but he tunes you in every day, and it's disrupting our entire family life. Because of your stinking show our family has to eat very early every day so that no one will bother my old man while he's listening to your show. I hope you croak."

On his show, titled "Sports Page of the Air," Zabitka takes on all comers. He has interviewed people representing 31 different sports, everything from hunting and fishing to skin diving and cock fighting.

One listener wrote in, "I like your program because I don't know what to expect next." And that's a fact. One time, Zabitka tried to serve as a peacemaker between two quarrelling local sportsmen and almost touched off a riot within the studio while both men were on the air. Cooler heads jumped in to save the day and possibly the station.

One of Chester's leading contractors, Dan Clendening, has a special aerial installed on his 37-foot boat to make sure he pulled in Zabitka's sports show every day while deep sea fishing, more than 150 miles from Chester.

And that's the way things have been going ever since Zabitka, a sports staff member of the *Chester* (Pa.) *Times* took over the longest radio sports show in the world today.

When localites go on vacation, they just don't take their radios along, since the 1,000-watt station can only service a prescribed area, but they also take along special antennas to make sure they can pull in "The Sports Page of the Air."

Reprint of press release distributed to area media outlets by
WDRF radio in the fall of 1957

Signing off

Sports Page of the Air ran about two-and-a-half years. Matt said he was making more for his 90-minute daily show than some of the station's full-time employees.

"I asked for more money, and they said, 'No!' " Matt recalled. There was no special final program or grand farewell. "After I left, they got calls about my departure from the listeners. They eventually got someone else in there to do the job.

"I missed it immensely. Everywhere I went, even the banquets, it was a main topic, the radio show, and I missed the adulation. It wasn't pussyfooting. It was exciting."

One wondered what meaningful lesson Matt learned from his radio days. Perhaps he discovered that he could talk to anyone about any topic, or realized he had been able to master new technology in a short amount of time, or hone his organizational skills.

In response to the long question, Matt removed the unlit, freshly chewed cigar from his mouth, smiled and said, "I learned sometimes you don't ask for more money, or any money, if you love what you're doing."

CHAPTER 5

Welcome to 'The News Journal'

'I came into work,' Matt said. "People were telling me "Congratulations!" I said, "For what?" They said, "You just won a Keystone Award!" I didn't even know what it was. It was supposed to be for the best sports story for all of Pennsylvania.'

—*Matt Zabitka*

Throughout the 1950s, Matt often crossed paths with Al Cartwright, sports editor at Wilmington's *News Journal*. "He was the big mahaff of *The News Journal*," Matt said. "We would meet from time to time, and Al knew what I was doing and the stories I wrote at the *Daily Times*. I'd talk to him, and got to know him. We'd go out and play chip and putt for a nickel a hole on Spring Lake, on Rt. 202. Al was a funny guy, with a dry wit style of humor.

"He was creative. He nicknamed Delaware football coach Dave Nelson 'Admiral,' a name that stuck through Dave Nelson's coaching career at the University of Delaware. He nicknamed former *News Journal* sports scribe Larry Shenk, who later became vice president for public relations for the Phillies, 'The Baron,' after his Dutch ancestry. Al was always doling out nicknames. I became 'The Big Zee.'

"Al had a column that appeared every Monday in the paper. Delaware's football games were played on Saturday. He had a little picture of an old guy. He called him 'the old geezer who's seen them all.' He's seen every Delaware football game since they started. And Al would take the part of the geezer.

"He used to come up with the words–if he saw a guy smoking a cigar, he would say, 'What are you smoking, Army blankets?' Another favorite expression was 'I'll send my best man on it.' When he traveled, if there was anything with a Delaware angle, he would always write about it."

While working at the Delaware County paper, Matt arranged competitive golf and softball contests between employees of *The News Journal* and *Chester Times*. Afterwards, the guys would hang out and get to know each other. "Lapping ups suds at a bar after games" is the way Matt described the conclusion of the outings.

"One day, out of the clear blue sky," Matt said, "Al asked if he could come over. He said he wanted to see me. I was living in Ashbourne Hills, Claymont. I said, 'Do you want to talk about another golf tournament?' and he said, 'Yeah.'

"So, he comes over in his Volkswagen. Comes in and sits on the sofa and asks me to come to work at *The News Journal*. It was a shock.

" 'You can't afford me,' I said," recalled Matt, who was working at the Chester paper, which was a union shop, affiliated with the Newspaper Guild.

"I told him that I wasn't looking for another job. I explained that I was working for a newspaper in Chester that paid union wages. *The News Journal* reportorial staff was non-union.

"Cartwright replied, 'I don't know how much you get paid, but I'll offer you $10 a week more than what you're making at the Chester paper.' Within a week, I resigned from the Chester paper—in late September 1962—and joined *The News Journal*. Been there ever since."

Fond memories

On Sept. 29, the day before he left to go with *The News Journal*, Matt finished his assignments for the *Delaware County Daily Times*, turning in stories on two high school football games.

When asked to share some interesting stories that occurred during nearly 40 years at the Delaware newspaper, Matt said certain memories come immediately to mind.

He said he was working on the night shift and writing for two papers—the *Morning News* and the *Evening Journal*.

On Friday nights, he recalled, there were high school football games throughout the state. "We had stringers and reporters who would call in their games by phone," he said. "No laptops then. Every Friday night, the staff would take the calls. We came in early and would sit around, read comic books, talk and wait for the big flood of calls.

"This one night—when the sports staff was awaiting calls from reporters covering downstate Friday night football games—I'm on the phone with my headset on, doing an interview. This elderly gentleman, with an overcoat draped over his arm, hat in hand, comes over to me. I'm busy and he's standing there next to my desk. He wouldn't budge."

Matt explained that he was the only person in the newsroom who was busy working, and he couldn't figure out why this man had decided to single him out, bothering him while he was talking on the phone.

After several minutes, Matt said it became so annoying he tossed his headphones down, jumped up and snapped, in an obviously irritated tone, "Can I help you, sir?"

The man replied, "I'm Mr. Reese."

Matt grabbed a pen and pad and asked the man how he spelled his name. "Is it REEZ or REES or REESE?"

The man replied, "I'm Charles Reese, president of *The News Journal*." Matt was so embarrassed, he looked for a hole to jump in.

Still shaking his head at the memory of the humiliating moment, Matt said, "Mr. Reese said he made a special effort to come down and greet me personally and welcome me to *The News Journal*. I was the laughing stock of the office for weeks. I got to know Mr. Reese well over the years. He was a nice man."

Not too much later, Matt recalled sports editor Al Cartwright directing Matt to answer a waiting call.

Ed Okonowicz

At the Delaware County, Pa., Hall of Fame banquet, Matt meets with Al Cartwright, former Wilmington News Journal *sports editor, who hired Zee in 1963.*

When Matt picked up the phone, a voice said, "I want to thank you for the good job you're doing on our paper."

Flattered, Matt thanked the caller profusely.

The man making the call was Herm Reitzes, who had been a major voice in Delaware sports for decades, on WDEL radio. In retirement, he kept the scorebook at P.S. du Pont High School basketball games.

More than 35 years

later, on Jan. 30, 1997, Matt would receive the prestigious Herm Reitzes Award, named after the once famous Delaware sportscaster.

Singing cowboy

When noted personalities came through town, Matt would often grab an interview. In one of his "Delaware People" columns, Matt recalled his encounter in Wilmington with former singing cowboy and baseball team owner Gene Autry.

The News Journal

Oct. 1, 1998   Wilmington, Del.

One last tip of the hat
for cowboy Autry
BY MATT ZABITKA

The death of millionaire movie cowboy/major league baseball owner Gene Autry Oct. 2 at age 91 resurrected fond memories of a brighter yesteryear for this scribe.

It was at the Hotel du Pont in the late 1960s that I had my first and only meeting with the renowned singing cowboy who made a mint in films, recordings, radio, television and business.

Wearing a snow-white cowboy hat, shiny cowboy boots, a dark suit, white tie and white shirt, Autry had arrived at the hotel from a function he had attended earlier in Washington, D.C. He was to add decorum and glitter to the already star-studded head table at the annual Delaware (then known as Wilmington) Sportswriters & Broadcasters Association banquet.

As I escorted Autry to the huge hotel ballroom, where the banquet was to start about an hour later, he was impressed with the facility.

As we stood, chatting in the entrance to the hall, which was less than half-filled with banquet-goers at that early hour, heads turned almost in unison as word spread that Gene Autry was in the doorway.

In seconds, the small crowd already assembled in the hall rose and, looking in the direction of Autry, tendered a thunderous standing ovation, as if a conquering hero had just ridden in on a white horse waving a white cowboy hat.

Autry, chewing gum, appeared moved by the unsolicited testimonial.

Aware that he had been around horses most of his life—in movies and rodeos—I asked him if he had heard of Kelso, a five-time Delaware horse of the year, 1960 through 1964, bred and owned by Allaire du Pont.

"While I do get to a track now and then," he said, "I've never seen Kelso run. But I certainly heard of him."

Of all his business ventures that made him wealthy—hotels, radio, television, oil, ranching, rodeos, movies—Autry appeared to be tickled most by his recording of "Rudolph the Red-Nosed Reindeer."

"I really didn't want to make that record. Didn't feel it was right, not my style. I was coaxed into making the recording. It turned out to be one of my greatest. It still sells like wildfire before Christmas. I'm still collecting royalties from it."

When the banquet started and Autry was introduced by toastmaster Stan Bergstein, Phillies organist Paul Richardson broke out in a pre-arranged rousing version of "Back in the Saddle Again" as the entire assemblage of nearly 600 gave Autry a deafening standing ovation.

The practice was then to lead off with a gag gift to a guest, and *The News Journal* sports editor Al Cartwright, founding father of the WSBA as well as the Delaware Sports Hall of Fame, draped Autry with a gilded horse collar because his California Angels baseball team had led the American League in being shut out the previous season. "He loved it, and thus did not draw a gun on the MC," Cartwright quipped.

Proving he was no cowpoke, Autry drew tons of laughter when he said: "I'm glad to be back in the United States. I've been in Washington the last three days."

Reprinted with the permission of The News Journal

Into the air

Early in his sportswriting career in Wilmington, Matt had an experience traveling to an away game with a Delaware professional football team. However, the trip was by air, and, as related in the column below, not in a top-of-the-line air machine.

Upon the initial meeting with Matt to discuss the possibility of a book on his career, his airplane ride with the Comets was one of the first stories he shared. Obviously, the events of the flight left an indelible impression on his memory.

The News Journal

August 1965   Wilmington, Del.

Comet's air game
a little shaky
BY MATT ZABITKA

It was very early Saturday morning . . .

Forty-eight sleepy-eyed members of the Wilmington Comets football team goggled in frightening awe at the big plane they were about to board at Philadelphia International Airport.

"We aren't going in that thing, are we" muttered a 265-pound lineman looking at the plane and then surveying the overcast skies which threatened to explode at any moment.

"That thing" was a monstrous-winged, four-motor, DC-7, with its silver belly striped in blue and the name "Argonaut" painted thereon. It looked like a World War II reject that had been consigned to transporting turkeys. And it was this ship that was about to transport the Comets—along with the Pennsylvania Mustangs from Charleroi, Pa., some 1,000 miles away for their North American Football League openers scheduled that night in the South.

The Comets were to play the Mobile Tarpons, while the Mustangs were to take on the Florida Brahmans at Lakeland, Fla. There would be more than 22,000 pounds of humanity, plus the equipment of both clubs.

As Comets General Manager Marty Stern checked off the Wilmington group, the players walked towards the big bird with the reluctant steps of men approaching the gallows.

Adding more shock was the first thing that greeted the players as they sat down in the closely grouped seats.

In case of . . .

Sticking out of pockets on the backs of seats facing them were emergency information cards—"what to do in case of a water landing"—"over water flight procedures"–and the notation "life jacket located in seat back."

The plan started to taxi at 8 a.m., finally took off at 8:20 for Pittsburgh to pick up the Mustangs.

When the plane reached the 8,000-foot cruising level, bad weather was encountered. Time and again came the signal—"Fasten seat belts."

Every few minutes came the roller coaster bit, with the plane sinking, rolling and rocking, accompanied by scraping sounds emanating from atop the plane, as if someone was trying to scrape the paint off the ship.

"We're experiencing a turbulence," the pilot would explain smoothly.

Every time a turbulence came up—which was often—I was thankful I took out a $75,000 flight insurance policy. Then I would think about the joshing memo penned by New Journal Sports Editor Al Cartwright before the flight. "It's OK to list among your expenses the cost of a parachute." He didn't realize how sage his advice was.

As the plane taxied to a stop at the Allegheny County Airport amidst a church-like silence among the passengers, Dick Christy, the ex-All American from North Carolina State, broke up the crowd with his piercing proclamations—"Man, this is the only way to travel."

At the airport, the assembled Mustangs, waiting to board the plane, looked on in horror as the Comets filed out—staggering, weaving and bobbing like punch-drunk fighters.

Worst ever . . .

"Worst flight I ever experienced," commented Comets' Coach Jack Ferrante, former Philadelphia Eagles end, who had done much plane traveling in his time. Quarterback Jack Cummings, another frequent air traveler, agreed.

Ferrante, his shirt soaking wet and feeling chilled, was given two tranquilizers.

Two of the passengers—John J. Lesko Sr. and his son—quit the ride in Pittsburgh, decided to return to Wilmington by bus. Lesko Sr. had won two box seat tickets to the game plus a round-trip plane ride for two to the Comets' game in Mobile for winning a name-the-team contest.

"My son doesn't feel well," explained the elder Lesko.

"If that's the way he feels," quipped a Comet, "let's change our name to Argonauts . . . after this plane."

When the Pittsburgh team boarded the plane, a Mustang halfback seated next to me commented: "When we saw that plane land and then watched you guys stagger out in your shirtsleeves we got a little shaky."

The plane proceeded to Mobile—cruising at 12,000 feet at 292 miles an hour—with hardly a trace of any turbulence. It actually was a smooth ride. After landing the Comets in Mobile, where they played to a 14-14 tie with the Tarpons—the plane went on to Tampa with the Pittsburgh group, which then had to board a bus to go to Lakeland to play the Florida Brahmans, to whom they lost.

The same piggyback flight pattern was followed after the games, en route home, with the Comets landing at the Philadelphia International Airport yesterday morning at 8:45.

The entire trip home was smooth as velvet, but the players only remembered the terrifying, twilight-zonish first leg of the outgoing journey.

Seeing how shaken the players were from the experience en route, Stern, Comets' g m chuckled (when he was safely on land), "In this league, the teams that travel by plane should be classed underdogs."

Reprinted with the permission of The News Journal

Recalling that horrifyingly humorous airplane experience, Matt said, he still laughs at the fact that the father and son wouldn't get back on the plane after it landed in Pittsburgh, where they boarded a bus and went back to Wilmington. Matt added that in Mobile, he joined several members of the team and coaching staff at a nearby bar before boarding the plane—on what could be their last flight.

According to Matt, "Explained one imbibing player, 'When that plane goes down, I don't want to have any feelings.' The remedy was to get drunk as hell before going on the plane for the trip home."

Searching for 'Goose'

Newsweek magazine ran one of Matt's stories in the 1960s. Tom Malone, also a *News Journal* reporter worked as a stringer for the national weekly, covering board meetings of national companies incorporated in Delaware. He received a call to do a story on former baseball great Goose Goslin.

"He comes to me," Matt said, "and asked me if I would handle it, since I was more into sports. I said, 'Damn right!' and he told me to call *Newsweek* right away. So I talked to them and told them I could do it. They gave me plenty to go on, but they wanted it done at Goose Goslin's home, no phone interview. I asked, 'When do you want it?' They said, 'Tonight!' "

Not wanting to miss the opportunity to write for a national publication, Matt agreed and then tried to find a photographer to take with him to Bayside, New Jersey, to complete the assignment as quickly as possible.

"I rushed into photo and the only person there was Fred Comegys. He's the top man today. At that time he was just a stringer. I asked Fred to come and take the pictures. He could do it, but told me, 'I don't get through until 4:30.' "

Matt called Goose Goslin, got directions and, with Fred in tow, headed for the Garden State.

"I'm following the directions," Matt said, "into the farmlands, down dirt roads, past cornstalks, not seeing anything or anyone is sight. Then, I come to a waterfront, and see a beat-up place, with cabins on stilts above water, in a fishing village. And this guy's coming down the road, stripped down to the waist and he's pushing a wheelbarrow loaded with cement. He wanted to get dressed, put on some nicer clothes, but I told him he was fine. Fred took a lot of photos."

Matt said Goose gave them a lot of time, answered all the questions that were asked. The retired ballplayer owned a number of cabins on the water and rented them out to fishermen.

"I wrote it up, wired the story in," Matt said. "I had so much left over, I did a story for *Sporting News* on him. I sent it in unsolicited. *Sporting News* liked it. Called me at home and said if I had anything else to go ahead and send it in. I wrote for them for 13 weeks. They published my stories on Mickey Vernon, Goose Goslin, Danny Murtaugh, Whitey Witt, Shag Crawford and others. But I couldn't keep writing for them. It was a busy time for me."

Some of the material Matt got from conversation with Goose is featured in the following column that he wrote for *The News Journal*.

The News Journal

Oct. 15, 1965   Wilmington, Del.

Goslin Hits His 65th Birthday
BY MATT ZABITKA

Goose Goslin will celebrate his 65th birthday tomorrow.

Not an actual celebration, though. It will be just another day around the boats for the old American League slugger-outfielder, who played in five World Series.

The Goose is a loner. He operates an isolated fishing retreat in this dot on the South Jersey map. He lives a cloistered life in a frame bungalow, painted white with red trim.

The Delaware Bay licks at the flat scrubland of this 62 acres. He can look out his kitchen window and watch the bay traffic. Nearby are 10 cabins on stilts, joined by a narrow boardwalk. Tied to piers are 21 rowboats.

Leon Allen Goslin, who averaged .316 in 18 years with Washington, Detroit and the St. Louis Browns, affected a shudder at the mention of 65.

"It just doesn't seem like 45 years since I broke into the majors," he said. "Seems like only yesterday that I was playing in a World Series."

By his own admission, the years have been kind to him.

At 190, he is 15 pounds over his playing weight. What little hair he has is white and is a wispy crown for a weather beaten face. The Goose looks good. He is agile, physically and mentally, and fast with a quip.

"I have no regrets," he said, puffing on a cigaret. "The years have been kind to me. You might say delicious. I have no financial problems. I have enjoyed life. I have good health and can run like the devil—for two steps."

Although he rarely gets to any ballpark, he follows the game in the newspapers and on the 27-inch TV set in his kitchen.

"I rent the cabins and boats to fishermen by the season," he said. "I also do quite a bit of fishing myself. Just for pleasure. I go out in my 35-foot boat, the 'Puddin' Cake.' Good fishing here—croakers, weakfish, flounder, kings.

"Occasionally, I do some golfing. I'm a 90 player. And I have my cronies who visit me to chew the rag, watch TV, play some cards and enjoy a feast.

"I avoid the crowds. I had my fill of them when I played baseball. I enjoyed it, but that's over. I enjoy the peace and solitude here. When it starts getting too cold here—like freezing weather—I move to a home I have in Glassboro.

"A man can relax here. There's no rat race. No worry about shaving every day and getting dressed. I get all spruced up maybe once a month when I go to town—Bridgeton, Salem, Philadelphia."

The American League's batting champion of 1928 (.379) hasn't been in baseball since he managed Trenton of the Inter-State League in 1941. He left the majors in 1938, before the pension fund was organized. Goslin isn't about to make a case out of it, "but you would think that baseball would take care of its veterans, somehow."

Goslin, who was a .300 hitter 11 times and who hit .287 over 32 World Series games, still is on the outside looking in when it comes to the Hall of Fame.

"I guess my record qualifies me for Cooperstown, but I'm not concerned. I'm more proud of being elected to the Michigan Sports Hall of Fame. In that one they name only two persons a year, and it covers all sports, not just baseball."

His most satisfying year was 1924, when he hit .344, helping the Senators win the pennant in Bucky Harris' first year as "Boy Manager," and then taking the World Series from John McGraw's New York Giants.

His greatest kick occurred in the '35 series. His two-out single in the last of the ninth inning in the sixth game broke a 3-3 tie, enabling the Tigers to beat the Chicago Cubs and clinch the playoff. The late Bill McGowan of Wilmington, who had signed him to his first professional baseball contract, was one of the umpires in that game.

You might see all his heroics in book form soon. He is collaborating with "a college professor from New York" on a book about baseball. A good piece of it will be on Goslin.

In the meantime, happy birthday, Goose.

Reprinted with the permission of The News Journal

Note: Leon "Goose" Goslin, who played 18 American League seasons, was elected to the Baseball Hall of Fame in January 1968.

We need publicity

Matt knew he would receive calls from sports banquet organizers whenever their event approached. Usually, he'd get them a story, or at least a notice of some size, in the paper before the event. Newspaper publicity was, and still is (despite those who claim everyone reads news on the Internet), the best way to fill seats at these events.

In some instances, when space remains in the final days leading up to the fete, Matt is sure to get phone calls requesting "another plug" in the paper.

The following column shows how Matt handled such a request, and the rather interesting results his article caused.

The News Journal

Feb. 14, 2001   Wilmington, Del.

Timing perfect for Vermeil:
Coach scored big at banquet
BY MATT ZABITKA

For days before the annual Salesianum school sports banquet in 1977, I was besieged with calls from committee members seeking additional publicity for the gala affair scheduled for the Padua Academy.

Dick Vermeil, the youthful-looking head coach of the Eagles, was to be the main speaker.

I had written reams about Vermeil and all the other guests scheduled to attend. I had run out of words. There was nothing more to write about. Pre-banquet stories were interspersed over a two, maybe three-week period.

Everything that had to be said in print about the banquet had already been in print.

"Hey, the banquet's tomorrow. Can't you put at least a little blurb in the paper, about Vermeil coming in as the main speaker," a committee member pleaded.

"No way," I replied. "There'll be nothing else written unless there is something new to report."

"Well, this might be of interest," the caller responded. "These banquets have been running rather long. At this year's, we'll place an hourglass near the lectern. Speakers will be expected to be finished within the three minutes it takes the sand to run down from the top of the hourglass down through the neck and on to the bottom."

"Yeah, that's something new. I'll work up something on that angle," I replied.

I wrote a column about the gimmick, a column which ran the day of the banquet.

I noted in the column that the principal speaker Vermeil, after a 4-10 season in his first year as head coach of the Eagles, would be in no need of a three-minute timer to remind him of how long he should speak.

"The kind of season Dick Vermeil had in 1976, he could cover it all within less than a minute," I wrote.

The night of the banquet, Vermeil slowly approached the lectern, reached into the inside pocket of his jacket and pulled out my column of that day.

He read slowly, loudly and clearly, stressing the part where he would have no need for three minutes of speaking time in view of the Eagles' debacle of '76. As he stuffed the column in his jacket, he responded, "Here's what I think about sports writers: If I had a choice to select the brains of any person, I would pick a sports writer's. They're new and they've never been used."

The crowd howled with laughter. Many stood, straining to get a glimpse of my reaction. They wanted to see egg on my face. They didn't. I grinned, ear to ear.

Vermeil made me a cause celebre, for about 25 seconds. He pronounced my name correctly, credited the newspaper (this one) that carried the column, and registered the best laugh of the night.

No hard feelings. It was all in jest.

After the banquet, we had some laughs together.

A year later, Vermeil returned to Delaware for the annual Delaware Sportswriters and Broadcasters Association banquet at the Hotel du Pont. In the hospitality room of the hotel before the banquet, I button-holed Vermeil for an interview.

I opened up with, "You probably don't remember me," referring to his reading my column the previous year.

His retort: "I remember you very well."

Judging by the turnaround he engineered with the St. Louis Rams this season, after two straight disasters, I'm going to ask him at the next banquet whether he can attribute any of this success to the acquisition of an unused, new brain of a sports writer.

I'll save that repartee for the next banquet.

Reprinted with the permission of The News Journal

Wrestling

Matt's assignments went beyond the mainstream sports of football, boxing, baseball and basketball. During his career, he covered a wide range of lesser-followed contests, like volleyball, golf, auto racing—even professional wrestling.

Wilmington's Fournier Hall, in the heart of Little Italy just down the hill from St. Anthony's Catholic Church, hosted many a boxing and wrestling match in its day.

Serious fans would fill the building's seats to see locals match fists and muscle with out-of-town challengers, and lusty choruses of boos and cheers filled the combat hall.

Matt was there one night to see marquee performers Sergeant Slaughter and Andre the Giant.

"I didn't know what to expect," he said. "The cost was $5 a head. When I went down that particular night, there were lines in two directions, waiting for the doors to open. I was shocked to see that many people turning out for pro wrestling in Delaware."

Before the event started, Matt went into the quiet dressing room, where the wrestlers were suiting up. A doctor was there, checking each contestant's blood pressure.

"I told them I want to see Andre the Giant," said Matt, who stands 6-foot-2. "I told him, 'You're not seven feet tall!' and got him to stand back to back with me to take a measurement. Then the promoter came in. He sees me in there. It was supposed to be wrestlers only. He said, 'Who the hell are you?' I told him and he said, 'Get the hell outta here!' "

Not leaving without exhibiting some resistance, Matt said he challenged the promoter, asking his name and telling him that he would be writing up the heave-ho for the newspaper.

After being "escorted" out of the dressing room, he noticed another wrestler standing alone in the hallway, coming out of a nearby room.

"He had a Russian name," Matt said. "I interviewed him, talking to him, asking questions, and he's talking back to me. I knew some Russian, so I asked him a question in Russian. He answered, 'Huh?' I said, 'Aren't you Russian?' He said, 'I'm from North Carolina. I play the part of a Russian wrestler because it riles the fans to see a wrestler bearing tattoos of the hammer and sickle.'

"He said his life is at stake sometimes. They throw chairs at him in the ring. He has to park his car three or four blocks away because the fans will damage his car."

Matt said he got the honest impression that the guy was actually nervous. But that was to be expected, with the enraged crowd throwing things into the ring.

"I watched the people's expressions," Matt said. "They go crazy. And the wrestlers, they're athletes. They have to be in pretty good shape to go through all they do in the ring."

Golf

While meeting Arnold Palmer at the Wilmington County Club was one of Matt's shortest interviews, it also was one of his more memorable ones.

As Matt recalled, a special exhibition for the well-heeled had been scheduled at the exclusive private club. At the time, Palmer was as big as Tiger Woods is today.

Matt, who was anything but a good golfer, was interested in Palmer. In fact, a few days before the star's arrival in town, Matt had written an article sharing his thoughts on the game of golf.

"What happened is, that I wrote a column about Arnold Palmer, and I said, here you have a bunch of guys hitting a little white ball. You can't cheer, you can't breath—you can't do anything. Nobody is verbally attacking the golfers—just a bunch of guys hitting a little white ball. And the golfers demand absolute quiet as they putt or drive.

"I noted that I can't understand golfers," Matt said. "They get out there and everything has to be absolutely quiet. You can't rustle a blade of grass. They're bothered if somebody jingles change in their pocket.

"I said, 'You go to a baseball game, the guy is pitching to the batter at 90 miles an hour, and the fans are screaming. But in golf, you can hardly breathe.' "

A few days after the article appeared, Matt said sports editor Al Cartwright got a call from some "distinguished guy at the club" asking to speak to Matt. The caller, from the Wilmington Country Club, explained that Arnold Palmer was arriving, but they didn't want Matt anywhere near the event. They didn't like the column and they didn't want to see Matt anywhere near the country club.

"I went anyway," he said, smiling at the memory. "I interviewed Palmer before the exhibition in the clubhouse. He was in the locker room getting dressed. Just he and I were there. At that time, he was writing a series on golf for *Sports Illustrated.* I asked him, 'Who's your ghost writer?' He asked what I meant, and I told him I knew he didn't write the article, because he was too busy, but it had his name on it.

"When I asked him, he got mad as hell. I irritated him like hell before the exhibition. I don't know whether that hurt him or helped him on the golf course later with the slicing."

In the Hornets' press box

Covering Delaware State College football was Matt's assignment for several years. He recalled that they had a small press box with a few seats and the rest of the reporters would have to stand and watch the game.

During the off-season, the college built a larger room beside the press box. Inside the new quarters, the college president would host special guests during the game.

"I knew the president, Dr. Mishoe," said Matt. "One year, I couldn't get into the press box, so I went next door. I knocked. He let me in and I had a great seat. There was a bathroom, sandwiches, and I met the Morgan State president.

"I'm sitting there, having sandwiches and feeling important when some other reporters knock on the door. Dr. Mishoe opened it and asked, 'What do you want?' They told him they wanted to get in, explaining the press box was filled to capacity, and he said, 'This isn't a press box!' After that, whenever I went there I would never go to the press box. I was always a welcomed guest in the president's box nearby."

When the college celebrated the 100th anniversary of college football, Dr. Luna Mishoe asked Matt to attend the game.

"At half time, they called me onto the field and presented me with a plaque from Miss Delaware State for my contributions promoting college football."

Sent downstate

Part of Matt's job was to make up the paper. Sports editor Al Cartwright's column was always located on the left side. Matt moved Cartwright's column to another location.

"For my punishment," Matt said, "I was sent Downstate in August to cover high school football teams in pre-season practices."

Matt spent the time meeting all the coaches and, he said, during those months learned a lot about sports in the southern end of the state, visiting every school and writing feature stories about each.

"Usually, when you go downstate, you go to see a game and file a story. I didn't just file a straight story, I made features out of them. I went down to Laurel. I mentioned in the column that I see all these trucks coming into town on the side streets—even railroad cars—piled up with watermelons. Laurel was known as the watermelon capital of the state. The trucks led to the railroad—where there were people bidding on the watermelons.

"After the practice, I would go to the coaches' homes for coffee and things like that. I mentioned all this stuff in my stories.

"In Millsboro, after practice," Matt recalled, "the coach said, 'Come on down to my classroom. We can talk there.' He chewed tobacco constantly. I asked him if he chewed tobacco while teaching class. He was from the coal mining region of Pennsylvania. He sat at a metal desk, with drawers on both sides. He opened the bottom drawers, they were all filled with tobacco spit.

"The following year," Matt recalled, "Cartwright said, 'You did such a good job last year, you are going back down there this year.' "

When Al Cartwright was the sports editor, Matt said, his boss had a habit of coming in during the daytime, so they hardly had any contact with each other since Matt was on the evening shift.

"He would take a scrap piece of paper like this," Matt said, ripping a large paper into numerous smaller pieces, "and make little pieces, on which he wrote notes to the writers about things he didn't like.

"If he was in an angry mood, he would sign 'Al.' If he was in a good mood, he would put down something like 'Hank Aaron' or 'Stan Musial.'

"If he was irate, he would write something down, and put it in your mailbox. The scribes would come in at night and would look in their mailboxes for these notes. I came in one night, and there was a note, 'I didn't like the way you did make-up last night,' signed 'Al.'

"I took the same piece of paper, wrote on it, 'I WAS NOT ON MAKE-UP LAST NIGHT!' and put it in his box.

"I didn't say anymore. The next night I came into work, and there's the same note, back in my mailbox. Right underneath what I had written, was the reply from Al, 'That is no excuse.' "

"Izzy Katzman was make-up that night," Matt said, "but I did not reveal it. Al was dry and humorous. I don't know why people go out of town for toastmasters when they have Al. He was really good in the speaking department."

Keystone Award

Matt has been inducted into in three prestigious athletics societies—Delaware County (Pa.) Sports Hall of Fame (1978), Delaware Sports Hall of Fame (2000) and Pennsylvania Sports Hall of Fame, Delaware County Chapter (2001). On May 15, 1971, he was recognized for professional achievement by his peers, being named the best sportswriter for the best story that ran the previous year in both Delaware and Pennsylvania. (See his award-winning column printed below.)

"I came into work," Matt said. "People were telling me 'Congratulations!' I said, 'For what?' They said, 'You just won a Keystone Award!' I didn't even know what it was. It was supposed to be for the best sports story for all of Pennsylvania."

Matt and his wife, Helen, attended the awards ceremony and gathering for several days in Harrisburg. *The News Journal*, Matt said, proud of its award-winning sportswriter paid for the trip and treated both him and Helen like royalty.

The award was presented by the Newspaper Publishers Association and Pennsylvania Society of Newspaper Editors.

"It was a four-day vacation, with representatives from newspapers all over Pennsylvania. They had my columns plastered there, too. Saturday night was the climax, and they had a big banquet in this huge hall. I wasn't the only award. *The News Journal* picked up the tab."

The News Journal

March 27, 1970   Wilmington, Del.

Bombers in Finals

Son's Death Shakes Hartford's Griffin

BY MATT ZABITKA

With less than three minutes left in last night's Eastern Basketball League semifinal rubber match of a best-of-three-series, the Blue Bombers boasted an insurmountable 129-102 lead over the Hartford Capitols.

The 655 fans who came to Salesianum School were delirious in saluting the home club, which rarely looked sharper en route to a convincing 140-116 triumph.

On the Hartford bench, Caps' hefty Coach Pete Monska was as nervous as a candle flame. He was up and down. He tugged at his tie and he kept running his fingers through his hair. He ranted and raved, gnashed his teeth and made angry faces as he watched his club being carved up like a Thanksgiving Day turkey.

"What the heck's the matter with Eddie (Griffin)," Monska snarled. "He's so off his game it's pitiful."

The Hartford trainer, seated next to Monska, softly pleaded: "Don't be too hard on him, coach. He just lost a son."

Recounting the incident later, Monska said he was shocked.

"Griffin never said a word to me. I don't believe he even told any of the players. Nobody knew. I first heard about it just before the game ended. I couldn't believe it."

Griffin, a 5-foot-11, 180-pound guard, who played a key role with 16 points in helping the Caps stun the Bombers last Sunday to knot the series, ended up with 11 last night, 10 in the last half.

He was hunched over, seated on a wooden bench in front of his locker when a reporter quietly offered condolences after the game.

"His name was Michael Anthony," whispered the bearded 26-year-old Griffin without raising his head. "He died Tuesday of pneumonia in Hartford. I buried him today. He was just 22 months old."

Griffin slowly stood up, looked the reporter in the eyes.

"I thought I owed it to the team to play tonight, in spite of my tragedy. I could do no more for my son. He was dead . . . buried. I felt I had an obligation to the team. They needed me.

"Maybe the team would have done better without me. My game was off altogether. I was bad. Very bad.

"If I had to do it again I don't think I'd play. Maybe I'd watch the game from the stands, but I wouldn't play."

Tears welled in his eyes. He turned his face. The reporter walked away.

Somehow, the game, one of the Bombers' best of the season, suddenly seemed insignificant.

Somehow it was difficult to get excited about Waite Bellamy's staggering 46 points, Bobby Lewis' superlative floor play, Ken Spain's and John Savage's strong rebounding and Dave Hamilton's improved play.

For 48 minutes the Bombers were excellent. They led from start to finish as Bellamy going 21-for 27 from the field, put on quite a show.

Then there was the announcement that Bob Munion kept blaring over the public address system about the Bombers advancing to the best-of-five championship finals against the Allentown Jets. They'll play the series opener tomorrow at Rockne Hall, Allentown, 8:15 p.m., and the second one here at Salesianum on Sunday, 7:30 p.m.

But somehow all the reporter could think about was that little bearded guy in the Hartford locker . . . Eddie Griffin . . . hunched on a bench, sitting there with head in hands.

Reprinted with the permission of The News Journal

Baseball Hall of Fame

Another significant recognition of Matt's work was the acceptance of his taped interviews into the Baseball Hall of Fame in Cooperstown, New York.

Matt recalled that Norman Macht, a professor from a New England college, was interested in baseball and moved to Delaware so he could be close to Philly, where he was doing some research on Connie Mack.

After he came across several of Matt's stories in the *Sporting News,* he contacted Zee and, in conversation, asked where the sportswriter had gotten his information.

Matt explained that he had interviewed a number of old timers and also had tapes of the conversations. The professor was surprised and suggested Matt send copies to Cooperstown.

Not wanting to be bothered, Matt declined.

"Why not give me some and I'll send them," the professor suggested.

"I gave them to him," said Matt, "and three weeks later the tapes came back with a letter thanking me for them. It said they transcribed all the tapes and enclosed a lifetime pass to the Baseball Hall of Fame."

Taking the laminated card out of his wallet, Matt passed it across the table.

"Now," he said, smiling, "when I'm on a train or plane talking to a stranger, I'll flash it and say, 'Yeah, I'm in the Baseball Hall of Fame.' "

"If I knew at the time," Matt said, "that I'd be interviewing all of the famous people—some of the biggest major sports personalities of the 20th century—I'd have taken pictures of myself with the athletes. I'd have a tremendous picture gallery, and most would have agreed. And when I think back on some of these guys, and what they accomplished, it's mind boggling. Every time I see one of them on TV, I tell Helen, 'I interviewed him. I talked to him!' I got guys in every sport."

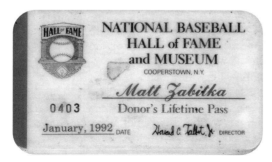

In appreciation for the opportunity to record some of his interviews for its archives, the Baseball Hall of Fame provided Matt with a lifetime pass.

Matt with Billy 'White Shoes' Johnson, at the Marcus Hook Sports Reunion Banquet in May 2001. Johnson is now a radio and TV commentator for the Atlanta Falcons of the NFL.

Hank Stram, former coach of the Kansas City Chiefs, during an interview with Matt

Matt with Al Meltzer, well-known Philadelphia sports broadcaster

At the 39th annual St. Anthony's Catholic Club Sports Banquet in 1990, Matt poses with former major league pitcher John 'Count of' Montefusco.

CHAPTER 6

Toasting and Roasting

'Then, a funny thing happened. As I started speaking, the audience got up, did an about face, and marched out of the chandeliered hall toward the Concord Pike. I'm standing there talking, and everybody's leaving. It was embarrassing.'

--Matt Zabitka

By the time he arrived at *The News Journal* in 1962, Matt had already compiled an impressive resume in the world of sports journalism. He had covered just about everything from Little League baseball to the 1960 World Series in Yankee Stadium, when the upstart Pittsburgh Pirates stunned the New York Yankees in the heyday of Mantle and Maris.

Maybe because of this background, or perhaps just for sheer orneriness, his new boss, sports editor Al Cartwright, decided the time was right for Matt to try his hand at the position of toastmaster in his newly adopted territory.

"Somebody from the Italian American Club in Kennett Square called Al Cartwright and asked him to be the toastmaster at a Little League banquet there," Matt said. "Al couldn't make it, so he recommended me."

Cartwright, who remembers having a conflicting schedule and not being able to attend the dinner, said that he told them he would get somebody to do the job.

"That somebody was Matt, who I asked just as soon as he walked into the sports department that day," Cartwright said. "I assigned him to go up and dazzle the Little Leaguers in Kennett Square and come up with a bit of a story."

Having been handed this "plum," (Cartwright's words), Matt would have no trouble turning his assignment into a story for the newspaper.

In Kennett Square, there was a guy named Fred Sinclair, who, unlike Al Cartwright, knew absolutely nothing about Matt. Apparently, the host was a little concerned about this "new guy" from Delaware County running the show at one of the premier events on the Kennett Square sports and social calendars.

Sinclair need not have worried. When it came to serving as master of ceremonies at pretty much any public gathering, Matt was quite at home, having attended and spoken at many banquets and sports affairs during his tenure at the *Chester Times* and radio station WDRF.

To Matt, it seemed the logical extension of what it meant to be a sports journalist, especially since he was on a first name footing with local athletes and sports organization officials.

"You write about people and talk about people, and they want you to be at their banquets," Matt said. "I went to football banquets, basketball banquets, baseball banquets. It just continued from there."

Before the banquet, Matt stopped in to go over details with his host at the Italian American Club, located on Pennsylvania Route 1 just on the outskirts of the place locals like to call the "Mushroom Capital of the World." When he got there, Sinclair told the toastmaster-elect that the banquet was a big deal, and that there would be tables full of influential members from the local Lions, Kiwanis and Rotary clubs—and they all wanted to be told the same thing—Kennett Square is the "Mushroom Capital of the World."

"He kept asking me if I can handle it, and I told him. 'No sweat,' " Zabitka recalled. "He probably thought that 'If this guy falls flat, my head will roll.' "

The night of the banquet came, and it seemed like the whole town, including parents, friends and kids, community leaders and businessmen, headed to the shindig at the Italian American Club.

The opening remarks went according to schedule, and all the local movers and shakers were introduced. Matt paused and caused an obvious uneasy silence at the podium. Then he looked over the audience and said something that must have made Sinclair wonder if he should head for cover or race out the door. "I told the crowd that it was time for a singing contest," Matt said. "I asked each club at each table to get up and really sing out their club song.

"They loved it. It was the highlight of the banquet. The Lions Club and the Kiwanis Club and the Optimist Club stood as a group around their tables and belted out the songs that were dear to their hearts. I was in my glory," Matt recalled with a smile. "I said to myself, 'This is going great—there's nothing to it.' "

After the singing, the guests sat down for what Matt said was a really great dinner—with the exception of the one missing ingredient—mushrooms.

As the banquet was nearing its end, and everybody was having a good time, Matt decided to put the finishing touch on what turned out to be a stellar performance as toastmaster.

"I told the crowd that this was a great dinner, with steak, mashed potatoes and peas, but not one single mushroom on the plate," Matt said. "I also told them that this was the mushroom capital of the world."

Well, several chefs, with their big white hats on—plus the servers and everybody connected with the culinary profession—went flying into the kitchen to see if they could set things right. In no time flat, the kitchen staff was proudly parading up to the podium to present a half-bushel basket full of Kennett Square's finest grade-A mushrooms to the evening's master of ceremonies.

Coordinator Sinclair, much relieved by the way the whole thing went, gave Matt a parting gift and congratulated him on a job well done.

"He came up to me after the banquet and put some money in my pocket," Zabitka said. "I never told Cartwright about that."

Maybe it was just something that Matt couldn't keep secret for too long, because Cartwright remembers hearing a lot about it in the weeks that followed that now-famous Kennett Square "mushroom" banquet.

"I'm sure he gave the crowd both barrels and was staggered when his assignment turned out to be a paying job," Cartwright said. "He talked about that $25 for weeks."

Toastmaster 101

Although he can now enjoy a load of fond memories from the days on the speaking circuit—when he entertained figures from the world of politics, business and sports—there was a time when the thought of approaching a podium caused Matt to break out in a cold sweat. Sitting back in the chair in the kitchen of his north Wilmington home, Zee recalled how he entered into the business of toastmastering.

It began during his days as an employee at the Media courthouse, promoting sports programs. He was invited to address a service club luncheon.

The invitation came from a group of businessmen at the Optimist Club in Ridley Park, Pa. He accepted, but soon had serious misgivings about what he had gotten himself into.

"I didn't want to go, and I was dying to get out of it," Matt said. "I was hoping the day would never come."

Of course, it did.

What happened at the Optimists Club banquet taught Matt a very important lesson—never, ever, ever read word for word from a prepared speech. While that approach might work fine while presenting a formal paper at a college seminar, it never comes across as anything but stiff and stale at banquets and other speaking engagements where the audience tends to want a bit of the unexpected.

"When you prepare something on paper, then start reading it, you're all right until something happens, or you hit a dull spot. That's when you get distracted, lose your momentum and start losing the crowd," Matt said. "When that happens, you're done."

And that's exactly what occurred at the Optimists Club dinner.

The speech started off smoothly enough, Matt recalled, but when he started looking around the room at all those well-dressed businessmen and political leaders, and realized that he was just a young sportswriter, he became edgy, nervous and was in serious danger of losing his audience.

"The only thing that saved me was that there was a gentleman sitting at my table named Ted Smithers, who used to coach me in basketball at Chester High," Matt said. "He saw I was fumbling around, so he got up and took some questions from the audience. He got me off the hook."

What Matt learned that day is: It's much better to prepare your material, get the gist of it, and then take it from there, off the top of your head.

"I'll never forget that day," Matt said. "But, I got over it. It's like anything else—you do it once, and you learn from the experience."

Thinking on one's feet came in handy years later, when Matt was scheduled to speak at a Claymont High School sports banquet. That year's football team had gone undefeated and the place was so crowded that they set up extra tables in the hall.

"I was the featured speaker," Matt said. "As soon as I'm introduced, two boos come across the hall from two different corners of the audience. So I looked out and said, 'I don't mind boos. I'm accustomed to boos, because people don't like what I write in the paper. But let's all boo lustily and loudly enough to shake the walls at the count of three.'

"After that boo," Matt said, "we had the biggest laugh, and they settled down and everybody was comfortable."

Friends of P.S. du Pont

As an entertainer, the legendary Dean Martin is remembered for his smooth, laid back singing style and the celebrity "roasts" he hosted during the later part of his long career. During these events, the famous—including many members of the Rat Pack such as Sammy Davis Jr., Joey Bishop and Frank Sinatra—would gather before a large television audience and pile a ton of good-natured ridicule upon the person sitting in the hot seat.

Although Matt would never consider himself a celebrity, he has, through the years, become a familiar figure to readers considering sports their favorite part of *The News Journal*. It was only a matter of time before it was Matt's turn to be roasted by some of the people who had appeared in his columns over the years.

A group of those folks who brought about a Matt Zabitka "roast" had organized themselves quite by chance some years before. It occurred when a few ex-jocks from the old P.S. du Pont High School got together for lunch. They had such a good time talking about the good old days when they were playing sports that they decided to meet the next year. Word spread and the group grew. The regulars finally decided to hire out a hall to hold an annual walk down memory lane.

It didn't take long before alums from other schools—like Brown Vocational, Archmere, Salesianum and Wilmington High School, folks who had become friends while playing against each other—were asking for an invite to the annual get-together.

And that's how the Friends of P.S. du Pont was born.

After a while, the group moved the site of the shindig to the Talleyville Fire Company, just north of Fairfax, and they added a new dimension to their event.

"One of the features is that they roast somebody every year," Matt said. "And they never tell who the person is beforehand--it's a big secret."

Finally, the Friends of P.S. starting asking Matt to come out to Talleyville and meet some of the people he had written about through the years. But it seemed like there was always a reason why he couldn't attend.

"I would tell them that I couldn't get out of the office at night," Matt said. "I also told them that the editors figured it wasn't really news—just a bunch of guys rehashing old times."

To their credit, the Friends of P.S. would not take no for an answer.

It wasn't long before Matt got an assignment call from his boss at that time, sports editor Rich Luna, to go to Talleyville to cover the banquet. In typical Zabitka style, Matt listed all the reasons why he couldn't go.

"I didn't want to go, and I kept telling my boss that," Matt recalled. "Finally, the boss told me it was an order. I had to go."

When Zee got there, he found a *News Journal* photographer on the scene. Matt's

Matt conducts a phone interview at the News Journal *building at Ninth and Orange streets in Wilmington.*

instincts as a reporter told him something was up, but he couldn't quite put his finger on it.

Meanwhile, the hall began to fill up, and Matt saw many of the people that he had come to know during his days at *The News Journal*. And all of these folks knew who Matt was.

"I had gotten to know them, and you don't forget people just because they are not playing sports any more," Matt said. "It really means more to people when you write about them after they are out of the limelight."

Matt, who thought that he was on the clock as a reporter, figured he'd better get busy, so he got out his notebook and took down page after page of notes, interviewing ex-athletes before the banquet. Meanwhile, everyone else had settled in for the evening to have a good time.

When he figured he'd gotten enough material for his next column, he leaned back on his chair and got ready to listen to the evening's speakers, and, of course, try to figure out who was going to be roasted.

Mike Walsh, who for many years was sheriff of New Castle County, got up and made the announcement. The person being roasted was none other than Mr. Matt Zabitka!

"That's the first I had heard of it," Matt said. "I was flabbergasted—especially about the fact that everybody knew it but me."

As the roastee, Matt had to sit there and take it as speaker after speaker blistered him with demeaning jokes and gave him a bunch of "awards," including an old frame with no picture or glass—just a beat up hunk of wood with a hole in the middle.

With each new speaker, Matt pleaded with his friend Mike Walsh for a chance to say something to the crowd. But he was told to wait, "his time would come."

When Matt finally got his chance to talk, Matt told the audience, "I'll get you guys back for this somehow.

"Then, a funny thing happened. As I continued speaking, the audience got up, did an about face, and marched out of the chandeliered hall toward the Concord Pike. I'm standing there talking, and everybody's leaving," Matt said. "It was embarrassing."

Facing this incredible shrinking audience, Matt decided to try something that had worked wonders for the Philadelphia Flyers and the late Kate Smith. He started belting out the well-known national standard, "God Bless America."

It worked.

Those who hadn't reached the exit did another about face, and started back laughing and cheering. It was like a chain reaction, and those who had left the hall were climbing over each other to get back in.

Maybe he didn't get a recording contract, but it made for a nice evening and another Matt Zabitka column.

"It was a big hit—especially my response," Zabitka said. "They had never had anything like that before."

Terror on the back nine

Getting a good story for a column while having a good time is a Matt Zabitka trademark.

While writing such stories seems to come naturally to the veteran sports reporter, the legwork can be a little exhausting, and you never know where your next assignment is going to land you.

In his early days at *The News Journal,* Matt's boss Al Cartwright would have him write a weekly column about whatever sport seemed to be the most popular among readers at the time.

"We were getting all kinds of bowling results, so Al Cartwright told me to write a bowling column," Zabitka said. "After I started doing that, we got even more stuff coming in."

It just kind of went from there, Matt remembered. Before long, he was turning out two, three, even four bowling columns a week.

Eventually, the boss got to thinking that was a bit too much attention being given to one sport.

"Cartwright told me that he only wanted one column a week, and now I was writing one every day," Zabitka remembered. "So, he told me to switch over and start writing a column about golf."

Matt made the switch, but the result was the same. The columns generated still more interest as golf stories and statistics continued to pile in. Once again, Cartwright had to remind his prolific reporter that he was only looking for one golf column a week—not a half dozen.

While Cartwright wasn't looking for any more golf columns, he was looking for a golfer from within the sports department of *The News Journal* to play in a prestigious local event.

Each year, the golf pros and country club presidents put on a big tournament, with some of the best golfers in Delaware competing at a location that rotated annually.

The fact that he was earning a reputation as a golf columnist, who had interviewed the likes of legend Arnold Palmer, must have made Matt seem like the perfect guy to represent the paper in this well-known tournament.

Up to that time, Matt had played some chip and putt, but now he was being asked to match shots with some of the area's best golfers.

"I had a starter's golf bag, the kind a kid would use," Matt recalled. "I did have a good pair of golf shoes."

Not wanting to look like a novice in front of the golfing elite, not to mention the horde of spectators expected to show up at the Brandywine

Country Club, Matt sweated it out, praying for rain and thinking about quitting the job he loved.

Mother Nature and Al Cartwright must have wanted Matt to show up, because the day of the tournament turned out to be one of the nicest of the season. The good weather brought everybody out, including the reluctant reporter.

"There were so many golfers participating that they had to have a staggered start, with guys teeing off on the 1st and 9th holes," Matt said. "When the guys saw me they told me to hurry to the 9th hole where my gang was ready to get started." Lugging his well-worn golf bag to the teeing area, Matt looked up at the crowd of people peering out from the windows of the huge dining room behind him. They wanted to see if their favorite golf columnist could golf.

"I hit a rocket that stayed about five inches off the ground," Matt said. "Still, it went almost 60 yards. I did a little better on the greens."

When play was finished for the day, Pat Schwab, who was then golf pro at Rock Manor Golf Course, took home top honors. As for Matt, he was able to finally laugh and congratulate himself on surviving the event with his dignity intact.

When the award ceremony took place that night, there were two things that struck Matt as a surprise.

First, his boss, Al Cartwright—the guy who couldn't make the tournament—managed to show up for the award ceremony.

Second, there were to be two awards given that night, one to Pat Schwab for his stellar play, and the other to Matt, whose score turned out to be the highest of the day.

When Matt walked up to get his prize, a dozen spanking new golf balls, he was greeted with gales of laughter and a round of good-natured applause. Not wanting to let the crowd have the last word, he turned his attention to the audience that seemed to be having just a little too much fun at his expense.

"I told them to wait just one minute," Matt said. "I reminded them that out of 120 or so golfers, only two could say they took home a prize—me and ex-PGA touring golfer Pat Schwab. It broke up the crowd."

While sportswriters in most instances are not as skilled as the athletes they cover in playing a particular sport, there are certain things such reporters do when it comes to preparing for interviews or speaking engagements.

For Matt, it depends on the person being interviewed or honored and the type of banquet where such awards are being presented.

"You can't just waltz in and ad lib a bunch of remarks," Matt said. "Unless you know the person and can talk off the top of your head. You have do a little research, so that when the time comes for you to speak or ask questions, you know what you are talking about."

For example, Matt said, if the guy's being honored for a performance as an Olympic swimmer, you find out as much as you can about the sport and the person as you can. It shows you are interested and that you have done your homework.

The bottom line, according to Matt is "be prepared."

Herm Reitzes Award

Nothing could have prepared Matt for the 1997 Delaware Sportswriters Awards Banquet where he was presented with the Herm Reitzes Award.

With his gravelly voice, Reitzes was one of the top broadcast sports journalists in Delaware, and he covered the Fightin' Blue Hens football team when they played their games at the old Frazer Field, just behind the present day Carpenter Sports Building on the UD's North Campus area.

"As he got older he stayed in sports, doing volunteer work at sporting events," Matt said. "He also kept score at P.S. du Pont High School athletic events."

The award, given in Reitzes' honor, recognizes contributions made by the recipient in all areas of athletics, including print and broadcast journalism.

All Matt was told about this particular banquet was that it was going to be held at one of Wilmington's premier banquet settings, the DuPont Country Club—and that he'd better be there.

"When I got there, I joined a bunch of guys seated at a big table, so I sat down and got ready to enjoy the banquet," Matt said. "I didn't know anything about the Herm Reitzes Award, or even that it was to be given that night."

That's why Matt was probably the most surprised person in the ballroom when he was called to center stage to receive the coveted award. When he began to make his remarks upon receiving the award, his thoughts turned to his wife, Helen, and his family. He wished they could have been there to share in the celebration of his lifelong efforts on behalf of sports in the First State.

"I told the crowd that it's too bad that I could not have my family here with me tonight," Matt said. "I think they are on their way to Virginia to visit our granddaughter who is at Radford University."

That's when the fellow who had given Matt the award pointed to a table where his family, including wife, Helen, and daughter, Shirley, were seated.

Matt went over and gave his wife a kiss and then told the crowd, "I know I saw them packing. They even set the suitcases out." But it had all been planned to fool the award winner.

Before Matt relinquished the microphone, he told the crowd a rather unlikely story.

Seems, he said, he was driving by the country club on his way to pick up some cat food at Kmart, when he decided he needed to stop and use the men's room.

As he came inside the lobby, he ran into some guys from *The News Journal,* who asked him if he was hungry and if he would like to sit down and grab a bite to eat.

The cat was going to have a late supper that night.

Matt summed up the situation for the crowd by saying, " I was going out to get some cat food, and now I'm getting an award like this. Only in America!"

CHAPTER 7

Keeping Former Athletes in the Spotlight

'These people, they're forgotten. You brighten their whole life. For one or two days, they will get calls. They're on top of the world again, in the limelight. It really makes them happy, means a hell of a lot to them.'

—*Matt Zabitka*

Relatively few athletes, whether they were national figures or state champions, earn enough to live out their days in luxury. Bad investments caused even some of the greatest of the greats to end up in nursing homes or turn into unknowns, living out their lives in modest homes in quiet towns.

After their careers in the minors or majors were finished, lack of benefits and small salaries in the old days caused ball players to take "real life" jobs in factories and companies. Often, they worked alongside colleagues who had no idea about what their coworker had done in his glory days on the diamond, in the ring or on the field or court.

No idea, at least, until they happened to read one of Matt Zabitka's articles.

Whether Zee's story appeared in his Monday-morning "Delaware People" column, in Thursday's *Crossroads* supplement or in the daily "Sports" section, the reading public was kept informed of the whereabouts and status of those who had, at one time, made sports headlines.

On his desk at *The News Journal* rests a stack of 3" x 5" metal file cabinets. Long and narrow, these containers are dented from overuse and mismatched in color—a few light gray, others black. To their right sits a solid, medium green, IBM typewriter, with the label "Z Best" taped to its front.

Matt Zabitka: Sports

Inside the small metal boxes, known as the "Zee Files," are Matt's contacts—a treasure trove of names, addresses, phone numbers and brief notes detailing what each particular athlete had done to deserve recognition or a story in the newspaper.

These, and a modern computer and keyboard, are Matt's tools. The files make up his depository, a vault of sports people and contacts. Most had screamed or cried with delight at their particular moment of victory. Many more weren't as fortunate and became might-have-beens or almost-weres. But they all tried and were, at some point, deserving of some column space or "ink," as Matt sometimes says.

But Zee's handprinted records only supplement a sharp mind that can still rattle off dates and scores of the games he covered, plus anecdotes and descriptions of the folks he interviewed decades ago. Many of them had outstanding careers, on and off the field. Others, he said, have enjoyed seeing their children and grandchildren play the same sports. Often, Matt's written about several generations of athletes in the same family.

In addition to Matt being on the writing or giving end, his work also has placed him on the receiving end—and usually with pleasant results.

Matt, in the office with his personal card index, known as the Zee Files, which he uses to keep track of current and former athletes and coaches. Pat Williams, senior vice president of the Orlando Magic and a frequent subject of Zee's columns said, "Matt has the best Rolodex in the world."

In Matt's home office are stacks of plastic bags, the kind you get to carry out your purchases at the drug store or supermarket. These are filled with thank-you cards and letters, and they number well over a thousand.

From grandparents and corporate executives, from coaches and students—written on store-bought, Hallmark-style cards, beneath embossed letterhead and on sheets of simple, loose-leaf paper—their message is the same: "Thanks."

Following are a few examples of the notes and messages in the cards and letters Matt has received (actual names have been deleted):

Notes of appreciation

Dear Mr. Zabitka,
Re: Our daughter, a Tower Hill graduate
I am still grateful for the article you did on (our daughter). She was down in her senior year and this lifted her greatly. People in the community and her church gave her recognition.
My husband and I will always remember your support and kindness.

Dear Matt,
Just a note to say thanks for the article. It was well done, also thanks for all the help you gave us for the (team). Kids and players need guys like you to spread the news they deserve.

Dear Matt,
Just a short note to thank you for the superb article you wrote in this past Sunday's paper. As always you are very kind to me and you know it is greatly appreciated.
I had many congratulations from various people due to your most informative story.

Dear Matt,
I just want to thank you for the kind article that you wrote about Dad after he passed away. I enjoyed your description of Dad's semi-pro baseball and high school basketball days; he was always very modest about all of his personal and athletic successes, so many people didn't realize how great an all-around athlete he was.
We are all most proud of Dad for how well liked he was and for how many friends he made throughout his life. We are still in shock that he died so suddenly at a time when he was looking and feeling great. My family and I are very grateful for your nice tribute to Dad.

Congratulations

> *Delaware Sports Hall of Fame! Look out! Here comes Matt Zabitka!.*
>
> *Matt, We are both very proud of you! This should have happened years ago!*

From an older gentleman

> *Dear Mr. Zabitka, the best to you . . .*
>
> *I've meant to drop you a few words, for lo these few days now. What brought this about is a piece you composed, "Old Days of College Gridiron." In that I am in my 82nd year on earth, and too, that I was in attendance at the same U of Penn game as Mr. . . . . , I've seen some of the very same players of whom he speaks. However, I must question . . . . .* (The writer offers numerous anecdotes about old time football.)
>
> *I could go on and on, Matt: oh, what good old days! For now, I enjoy reading of them. Thanx for all your columns. . . I enjoy them.*

"I make a point to answer them all," Matt said. "Even if it's a short note."

Zee said he knows his articles have positive effects on those about whom he writes. "They call and tell me that after the article comes out their phone starts to ring, they get notes in the mail. They get people coming out of the woodwork to contact them," Matt said, obviously pleased with those results.

"These people, they're forgotten. You brighten their whole life. For one or two days, they will get calls. They're on top of the world again, in the limelight. It really makes them happy, means a hell of a lot to them."

So many times after an article, Matt said, he's heard an expression of thanks, followed by the words, "Matt, you made me famous!"

"I do a lot of that. Once a guy or a girl's playing days are over, that's when they need a lift. That's when it means the most."

Black ballplayers

Over the years, Matt wrote a number of articles about athletes who played in the old Negro National Baseball League. Their careers on the diamond occurred during a time when blacks were barred from playing in the all-white major leagues and they received little recognition for their achievements.

More than personal local profiles, these articles offer noteworthy historical glimpses into the way league and hometown sports were conducted, and the important role black athletes played, during the first half of the 20th century.

"I think I did stories about every living ballplayer who played in the Negro National League in Delaware," Matt said. "What I liked best about those interviews was learning what it was like for them. It's history. You learn so much about how things were.

"They traveled by bus everywhere they went. Traveling through the countryside. When they had to go in a store, they nominated one guy to go inside. Sometimes, they wouldn't serve them. They let them use the hose outside for a drink, but wouldn't serve them in the store.

"They barnstormed, weren't paid much. Had their own league teams and World Series. The players' box scores often weren't reported in the white newspapers."

When Matt would meet with these former athletes, he also discovered that many of their friends and coworkers never knew what they had accomplished.

"It was something they kept in the closet," Matt said. "Many people in their community didn't know what they did in the past. Their neighbors didn't know that they had played ball years ago. I met them in their homes and got their stories."

Matt's columns show his ability to provide readers a very clear picture of his subject and the setting where the interview takes place. He is able to establish a trusting relationship during these brief and very private encounters. As a result, he essentially makes the reader an invisible observer in the room, listening to Matt converse with the aging athletes.

This descriptive talent is apparent in many of Matt's columns and has become one of his trademarks. Interestingly, he is able to draw these wonderful word pictures, whether describing an intimate one-on-one conversation or reporting on a celebrity's remarks at a large banquet gathering.

The portraits of four Negro League baseball players from Delaware are spotlighted in the following Matt Zabitka columns.

JUDY JOHNSON

The News Journal

May 6, 1989   Wilmington, Del.

Judy Johnson, 89, can't cry, but his face reflects sadness

BY MATT ZABITKA

I put my right hand in the limp, open palm of Judy Johnson's right hand, urging him to squeeze if he recognized me.

His other arm lay stiffly outstretched on the white linen bed sheet.

"He has no movement at all in his left arm or his legs," nursing assistant Bonnie Lowry said quietly.

All the time I was urging him to squeeze my hand to indicate there was a mental contact, I kept up a steady stream of chatter. I recalled the many Parkway baseball banquets we had attended together, my visit to his Marshallton home where he proudly showed me his many baseball mementos, the many telephone conversations we had pertaining to baseball.

I recalled the time he was named Delaware's Athlete of the Year for 1975 and the standing ovation he received. I talked about his induction into the Baseball Hall of Fame at Cooperstown, N.,Y., on Aug. 18, 1975, when he was so overcome with emotion he twice broke down and cried. I talked about his induction into the Delaware and Maryland sports halls of fame.

I kept up a nonstop line of chatter, hoping to create a spark in the former baseball great, who has been a patient at the Tilton Terrace Health Care Facility, 8th and North Rodney streets, since Oct. 30.

All the time while I was talking, Johnson's eyes, wide open, were riveted on my face, but his face was expressionless.

Just as I was running out of words, it came. He squeezed my right hand with his right hand once. Then again. And again.

The emotion of it all got to me. I almost cried.

Then, as I picked up again on the one-way conversation, his right hand held my right hand loosely up until the time I left, about 15-30 minutes later.

Johnson, who was inducted into the Cooperstown Hall of Fame two months before his 75th birthday, will be 90 years old in October. But he doesn't look his age. There are flecks of gray in his short-cropped hair, but his face isn't a road map of wrinkles.

Now in his seventh month at the health-care facility, he shares the room with another patient.

In the small room, there are four potted plants on the sill of the small window that looks out onto 8th Street. The bathroom door at the foot of his bed is plastered with photographs, several showing him wearing a New York Yankees' cap with smiling nurses at either side of his bed. An 8-by10 black-and-white photo reveals a young Judy Johnson in a baseball uniform. It's from another time, another era.

Hanging from a metal bar at the foot of his bed is a small white, stuffed panda, trimmed in maroon.

"World's best grandpa," reads the lettering on the panda's chest.

Also on the bar, next to the panda, is a miniature red and white Christmas stocking, a stale piece of red-striped candy cane peeking over the top. "To my favorite ballplayer," the inscription on the stocking reads.

A guest book in the room contains about 120 names, some with an added comment. "Jesus is Lord," wrote Marion Marshall. "This time a smile, next time a hello," wrote Bob Michel. "Just to talk baseball with my buddy," Henny Cooper wrote.

Johnson spends most of his time lying in bed. Occasionally, he watches sports or soap operas on the TV set that juts from the wall in the middle of the room.

During my visit, Johnson didn't utter a word. He never smiled. He just stared.

Although advanced in age, he had been in good spirits up until the time his wife, Anita, died in November 1985, a month before they were to mark their 62nd wedding anniversary.

In a 1987 interview, I asked him how he passed the time since the death of his wife, who had been the anchor in his life. "I just sit here and cry," he said softly, his voice trembling.

Today, the Hall of Famer doesn't cry. There are no tears left. But there's deep sadness in his soul. It's etched on his face.

Reprinted with the permission of The News Journal

The News Journal

Feb. 22, 1999   Wilmington, Del.

Memories of Judy Johnson

BY MATT ZABITKA

Judy Johnson was among the most unpretentious, gentle human beings I ever met during my tenure with the *News Journal.*

We'd sit on a settee on the porch of his Marshallton home, a porch that was a veritable museum with memorabilia of his illustrious baseball career, covering almost every available space on the walls enveloping us, and Judy would talk about the Negro leagues, about people he played with and against—Satchel Paige, John Henry Lloyd, Ray Dandridge, Cool Papa Bell, Oscar Charleston, Leo Day, Josh Gibson and others. Never, not once, did I ever hear Judy talk about himself and his exploits in baseball. He always talked about and lauded teammates and opponents. There wasn't a braggadocio bone in his body.

Yet, he had so much to talk about. It was all there on the wall of the porch—a photo showing him with Baseball Commissioner Bowie Kuhn, a plethora of other photos posed with baseball VIP's, autographed baseballs, dozens of plaques, a silver baseball bat, a huge photo of himself in baseball uniform, a glove on left hand, right hand on knee, posed at third base as if in anticipation of a ground ball coming his way.

One large poster advertised a game featuring the greatest Negro baseball players ever assembled, with photos of each. Of course, Judy was pictured. So was Satchel Paige and others.

Remembrances of Judy surface at this time, as February is Black History Month.

Memories of Judy, the man, spill over like the Niagara.

There were the annual Parkway baseball banquets, for one. Judy would call a day or two before the banquets and ask if I was going. "I love John Hickman [owner and manager of the Parkway team]. He's a wonderful man," Judy would say, "but I can't stand all the speeches. They're too long." But Judy would be there at the head table, rarely wanting to speak.

At his induction into the Baseball Hall of Fame at Cooperstown, N.Y., Aug. 18, 1975, he was unable to talk beyond a few words. He was emotionally overcome. He walked away from the lectern in tears and sat down.

102

In 1976, at the annual Delaware Sportswriters and Broadcasters Association banquet he was honored as Delaware's Athlete of the Year for 1975. There were a lot of eyebrows raised by the selection before it was finalized. A man of 75 was to be named Delaware's Athlete of the Year! Sounded preposterous.

The honor was coming 50 years too late. It was meant as a belated honor in view of his induction in the major Valhalla in Cooperstown.

Night of the banquet, the big question was how the capacity crowd of 500 would react—to a 75-year-old man as Athlete of the Year.

When Judy's name was announced, there was polite applause. And as he slowly walked to the lectern, the house erupted with thundering applause, every one in the room standing at attention, in respect to a genuine legend.

Of course, Judy was too overcome to speak. He tried. Then he cried, and to another round of thundering applause he tearfully made it back to his seat.

Although advanced in age, he has been in fairly good spirits until his wife Anita, whom he referred to as "The anchor of my life," died in November 1995, a month before they were to mark their 62nd wedding anniversary.

In a 1987 interview, I asked how he passed the time since the death of his wife. "I just sit here and cry," he said softly, voice trembling.

Judy Johnson died Thursday, June 15, 1989, at age 89, while a patient at the Tilton Terrace Health Care Facility on North Broom Street. He had been admitted after suffering a stroke, his left side paralyzed.

Nurses at the hospital were aware of my friendship with Judy, were happy to see me. They were concerned. Judy wasn't eating, wasn't speaking. Not to anyone.

As Judy laid in bed, eyes closed, I held his hand and spoke a torrent, recalling happier times. He understood what I was saying. He squeezed three times. I left, wiping tears . . . after I had left the room.

For this Black History Month, February of 1999, I bless and burn with memories of Judy Johnson.

He was black.

He made history.

Reprinted with the permission of The News Journal

ARTHUR C. "RATS" HENDERSON

The News Journal

Feb. 22, 1981   Wilmington, Del.

Born too soon

BY MATT ZABITKA

Seated in his favorite high-backed, simulated-leather chair in the living room of his Vandever Avenue home, Arthur C. "Rats" Henderson kept drumming the arm of the chair with the fingers of his over-sized right hand.

With his left hand, he kept trying to make a fist. It was difficult. "I had a stroke a couple years ago," he explained, extending his left arm. "Can't do much with this hand."

Next to his chair was a cane which he uses to get around, like when he takes a laboring stroll to the park one block from his home. But strolls these days are infrequent because mobility is difficult. Usually Henderson can be found in his favorite chair, watching television. He loves to watch baseball, especially Phillies' games.

His fluffy white hair is accented by his dark skin. He sounds like Ray Charles when he speaks and, although Henderson is 83 years old, he looks like a younger, more handsome Redd Foxx.

Sixty years ago, while pitching for the Bacharach Giants of Atlantic City, "Rats" Henderson was the terror of the Eastern Colored Baseball League, which included such teams as the Baltimore Black Sox, Cuban Stars, Harrisburg Giants, Brooklyn Royal Giants and Hilldale, a team which featured Delaware's Judy Johnson at third base.

The Bacharach Giants also played teams outside their league, against clubs like the Pittsburgh Crawfords, Homestead Grays, West Phillies, Ed Boldens's Philadelphia Stars and the Brooklyn Bushwicks.

"I used to have a very fast ball and a curve with a lot of speed on it," Henderson recalled with a laugh. Holding up his right hand, with a long index finger extended, he explained how he threw his curve.

"This finger was always pointed out over the ball when I threw my curve," he said. "The batters could easily tell when a curve was coming by looking a the way I held the ball. But I threw that curve so fast that the batters, even though they knew it was a curve, had a difficult time hitting it."

Judy Johnson, Delaware's only member of the Baseball Hall of Fame at Cooperstown, attests to Henderson's pitching prowess.

"He was one of the best," Johnson acknowledged. "He was a tough man to hit. The Bacharach Giants always saved him for the Sunday games when they played us (Hilldale)."

That Johnson had a tough time hitting Henderson is all there among Henderson's yellowed newspaper clippings in a tattered scrapbook that keeps falling apart at the touch.

During his tenure with the Giants, Henderson pitched the Atlantic City club to two straight league championships. And in a poll conducted by a newspaper to select an All-Eastern black baseball team of that era, Henderson was one of five pitchers picked.

The others were Nip Winters, Phil Cockrell and Rube Currie of Hilldale, and Oscar Levis of the Cubans. Judy Johnson was a solid selection at third base. Henderson was the second highest vote-getter in the balloting with 209, topped only by Harrisburg's aggressive playing manager Oscar Charleston, a center fielder, with 212 votes.

Henderson's pro career stared when he was in his early 20s, pitching for a sandlot team in his native Richmond, Va.

"The Bacharach Giants were on their way back to Atlantic City from a spring training trip and they stopped over in Richmond to play our team," Henderson recalled. "I pitched against them and beat them. They signed me up after the game. They gave my mom $10.

"I packed a suitcase and left with the team, while my mom was crying something awful. I had never seen much water before I got to Atlantic City and, when I got there and saw the ocean, I was stunned. I had never seen so much water in all my life."

Playing for the Giants, Henderson was paid $275 a month, plus 75 cents-a-day meal money.

"We traveled in an old, rickety school bus," he recalled. "With 18 people and all that equipment aboard, it was very cramped on the bus, which broke down regularly, sometimes forcing us to miss a game. Sometimes we'd be on the bus 15-18 hours and when we got off we could barely walk.

"I remember playing with the Giants in Wilmington several times, usually against Hilldale. Played at the old Harlan field and at the Third Street field."

Henderson, who picked up the nickname "Rats" as a pre-teen in Richmond, used to play winter ball in Cuba and Mexico.

"One winter in Cuba, I out-pitched Adolpho Luque in a game," he said. "I believe Luque was then a pitcher with the Cincinnati Reds. After the game, John McGraw, then the manager of the New York Giants, came out of the stands to shake my hand.

"He told me, 'If you were anything but a colored player, I'd give you any amount of money to pitch for the New York Giants.' I never forgot that."

Henderson, who was a 5-foot-7, 195-pound right-hander, pitched for the Bacharach Giants from 1923 to 1928. Later he pitched for a team in New York, laid off from baseball for two seasons and returned to Atlantic City to pitch for the Johnson Stars.

"I used to tell my players wherever I pitched to get me two runs and I'd protect that lead," he said, breaking into a chuckle. "In those days, when you started a game you were expected to stay in there all the way, no matter how hard the other team was hitting you. You stayed in there and took your punishment."

During his playing career, Henderson played with and against some of the greatest black players in baseball, people like John Henry "Pop" Lloyd, Bizz Mackey, George Carr, Oscar Charleston, Oliver Hazzard and, of course, Judy Johnson.

Many of today's players who pass as major leaguers couldn't hold a candle to the great black stars of the past. But the Majors in those days barred blacks.

"I was born too soon," said Henderson. "I watch big leagues on TV today and I know I could pitch faster and better than some of the guys I see. Nobody can tell me that 'Pop' Lloyd, for example, couldn't have made it big in the major leagues."

In a faded newspaper clipping from Henderson's scrapbook there was a story about Lloyd, a former Bacharach Giants teammate who died at age 79. The story mentions Lloyd was without a doubt the country's greatest Negro player.

The article goes on to say that one St. Louis baseball writer was asked by an *Esquire* magazine sportswriter who he thought was the greatest player of all time. His reply was: "If you mean in organized baseball, I'd say Ty Cobb or Babe Ruth. But if you mean in all baseball, the greatest player I ever saw was a colored man named John Henry Lloyd."

Henderson migrated to Wilmington in 1944 and gained employment with Continental Can through the intervention of Judy Johnson, then the company's shipping platform supervisor. He remained a Continental employee 18 years, receiving a clock radio on his retirement. "I still have it," he said, chuckling, "and it still works."

Henderson idolizes Judy Johnson. "He was a wonderful ball player, a wonderful third baseman. I was really happy to see him inducted into the Hall of Fame."

On the wall in Henderson's second-floor den, overlooking his backyard, is a large photo of a smiling Judy Johnson, proof of Henderson's admiration for his adversary on the diamond during another time, another place.

Despite his physical condition, Henderson maintains a rosy outlook on life. He's quick to laugh, seems to have kind words for everybody and doesn't dwell on his infirmities that for the most part keep him glued to his favorite chair.

Today, his career behind him, Henderson and his wife Hazel, a former Howard High grad, live in a white-painted row house with a neat-as-a-pin interior. Religious pictures and sayings can be found hanging on walls throughout the house. There's even a large photo of Pope John Paul II pinned to a facing that covers the unused fireplace.

If Henderson were 23 today and blessed with the same baseball talent he displayed in the Roaring '20s, he'd probably be in the majors, commanding a six-figure salary and living in a mansion in the suburbs.

Like so many great black athletes of his era, Henderson was an innocent victim of the times, but he harbors no animosity towards anyone. He survived the long bus rides in rinky-dink buses, the one-meal days (usually a hot dog or a hamburger at a roadside hashery), the humility of being deprived of an opportunity to play in the majors, and all the frustrations that came with being a black man in a predominantly white society during one of America's darkest periods.

That Arthur C. "Rats" Henderson was a truly outstanding player of his era is chronicled in the newspaper clippings that are in his brittle scrapbook. Practically every story recounts his mound heroics. And there are multitudes of such stories.

"I just can't tell you enough about Henderson," said Judy Johnson. "There's no doubt in my mind that he ranks with the best of the black baseball players."

Reprinted with the permission of The News Journal

WILLIAM "BUBBY" SADDLER

The News Journal

July 3, 1985   Wilmington, Del.

Saddler remembers
baseball during '30s
BY MATT ZABITKA

Satchel Paige, Josh Gibson, George Scales, Wild Bill Wright, Happy Evans, Chaney White, Judy Johnson, Roy Campanella, John Beckwith, Ray Dandridge, Cool Papa Bell—all legendary baseball players from a past the white establishment never truly recognized.

William "Bubby" Saddler of Delaware City played either with or against them all, as a shortstop with the Philadelphia Black Meteors, Philadelphia Stars, Newark Eagles and Bacharach Giants.

Saddler, now 76, a lifelong resident of Delaware City, is a tall, spare man, with a thin white mustache and a fringe of white hair surrounding the bald spot on the top of his head. He wears glasses and is a little hard of hearing, but his mental capacity is amazing.

He used to ride a bike all over Delaware City. It was his only means of transportation. Kids on the streets, seeing him coming on his bike, would shout greetings. "Uncle Bubby" is what they called him. But there'll be no more bike riding for the former National Negro Baseball League veteran.

He fell off his bike June 15, fracturing ribs and sustaining lacerations and contusions. He was hospitalized seven days at St. Francis Hospital.

Two days out of the hospital, relaxing in the living room of the Delaware City home of Mr. And Mrs. Harry Portlock, where he lives, Saddler appeared none the worse for his ordeal.

Baseball talk did something for him no medication could. It made him laugh, reminiscing about the old days when he rode rickety team buses, played night games under dim lights, wondered from payday to payday whether there would be anything in the envelope, and generally being ignored by a white press.

That was in the days when blacks were barred from playing in the majors and formed their own league.

"Oh, I have no regrets," he said, flashing a wide smile, hand-slapping a knee. "I've got baseball to thank for a lot of things. It was through baseball I had my first ride in a Cadillac, was able to stay in a hotel for the first time in my life, and got to own my first suit of clothes—$55 at Wanamaker's.

"If it wasn't for baseball, I probably would've never gotten out of Delaware City. The first trip I ever took out of Delaware was to Philadelphia, to play with the Philadelphia Meteors. Later, I played in Canada, Cuba and in a Puerto Rico winter league. I got to see a slice of the world."

Stroking his chin and always smiling, Saddler recalled that he was part of a baseball team formed in Delaware City in 1920, the Monarchs. Saddler's career began in 1932 and spanned the '30s. After beating all area competition, Saddler's team challenged the top black teams in Wilmington, then took on Wilmington's top white teams, including the Chicks.

What Saddler didn't know was all the time he was being scouted by the Philadelphia Black Meteors.

"I'm resting at my home one day and there's a knock on the door. It's two men from the Black Meteors. One was an undertaker, and owner of the club. They offered me $150 a month to join the team. Heck, I was never out of Delaware and they wanted me to go to Philadelphia.

"They picked me up at my home in a Cadillac. The undertaker told me to buy a suit and charge it to the club. Bought the suit at Wanamaker's in Philadelphia. First suit I ever owned.

"On paydays, sometimes I got the money, sometimes I didn't.

"Halfway through the season, the Black Meteors let me go to the Newark Eagles for $350. Played with them one season, including a winter league in Puerto Rico. We won the league championship there. We had some great players: Leon Day, Eddy Stone, Ray Brown, and Ray Dandridge, who I felt was one of the best third basemen in the National Negro League. I put him up there on a par with Judy Johnson, and Judy's a real good friend."

Saddler played briefly with Ed Bolden's Philadelphia Stars before joining the Bacharach Giants for a five-year tenure as shortstop.

"It was tough traveling everywhere in a bus that wasn't built for comfort," he winked. "I remember a night game we played on a Friday in Iowa and we had a double header scheduled that Sunday in Chicago, 500 miles away. About 250 miles this side of Chicago, the bearings burned out of the bus. We arrived in Chicago on Sunday night, with just enough time to make it to the park.

"Then there was the time we had a series of games in Canada. It rained just about every day. We couldn't play and we had run out of funds to cover meals and hotel. The owner of the club had to wire his wife in Philadelphia for money.

"We were supposed to get paid on the 5th and 20th of each month. Some paydays we might get part of our salary. We never got it all. Use to be so bad players had to pitch in to cover the fare of some teammates to get them to their home after the season was over.

"When we traveled by bus I never slept. I watched the bus driver so he wouldn't fall asleep."

Saddler recalled Hall-of-Famer Roy Campanella, later to play with the Brooklyn Dodgers, as one of his Bacharach teammates. "We roomed together. Of course, Campy was just a kid when he came with us. He was signed because they saw so much good in him. He started with us as a third-string catcher.

"My first year in the league, I remember being told not to play Cool Papa Bell [also a Hall-of-Famer] deep at short because he was so fast. All the infielders played in close, he used to steal second and third standing up."

Saddler noted that it was Judy Johnson who taught the great Satchel Paige how to pitch a curveball. "Before that, all Satch knew was to rear back and fire bullets. He needed more than that because the batters were all waiting for that fastball. I hit Satch, but he had more success with me than I had with him.

"I played with and against a lot of great players in Delaware, but they never went away. They saw no future in baseball. I took a chance and went away. I never regretted it."

Saddler, who is reputed to have more runs at Wilmington's Pennsy Field than any other player, white or black, never made more than $200 a month. Today, he talks of his experiences as if they were worth millions. And, after all, you can't put a price tag on memories, which evolve only through experience.

Reprinted with the permission of The News Journal

HOWARD LEROY "TOOTS" FERRELL

The News Journal

Aug. 12, 1985   Wilmington, Del.

Ferrell lived a baseball dream
BY MATT ZABITKA

As a teen-ager, Howard Leroy "Toots" Ferrell made frequent trips from his New Castle home to the old Wilmington Ball Park, home of the Wilmington Blue Rocks. Sometimes he rode a trolley car. Other times he'd pedal his bike or hitch a ride.

For Ferrell, the lure wasn't the Blue Rocks. It was the great, touring, black baseball teams that played games there.

In 1947, two months after he graduated from Howard High, where he was an outstanding athlete in baseball, basketball and football, Ferrell decided to make his move. He very much wanted to play in the National Negro Baseball League.

"This particular night, the Newark (N.J.) Eagles were playing the Philadelphia Stars. I went to the park carrying my $3 glove," said Ferrell, a big (6-foot-3, 266) strapping man with a booming voice and gregarious demeanor.

"I asked the Stars' manager if I could pitch batting practice before the game. He said they had their own pitcher for that. So I asked the Eagles' manager, Bizz Mackey.

"Mackey gave me an Eagles uniform to put on, then took me to the bullpen and had me pitch to him for maybe 20-25 minutes. I was really popping the ball.

"Afterwards, Mackey wanted to know all about my parents, where I had played baseball, where I lived, whether I'd be interested in leaving home to play ball.

"After the game was over, I joined the Eagles on the team bus. Mackey had me direct the bus to my home in Hamilton Park in New Castle. This was around 11:30 p.m. While Mackey and I went inside my home, there was this big bus with all the baseball players in it, parked outside.

"Mackey talked to my mother (Hilda), a great baseball fan. He told her I had good potential, that he'd like to have me join his team.

111

My mother said, 'Take him. Go ahead, take him. He loves to play baseball.'

"I packed six pairs of khakis and six pairs of gabardine slacks in a couple of suitcases, joined the team on the bus outside and was off. No salary had even been discussed.

"The very next night, before about 5,000 people at Shibe Park (later to be known as Connie Mack Stadium), here I was an 18-year-old kid starting for the Eagles against the Stars. I pitched four innings; gave up a couple of hits and hit two batters with pitched balls.

"After he took me out, Mackey told me, 'I don't care if you hit 90 batters, just keep going. Keep popping that ball.' My fastball was clocked at 90 miles an hour."

That was the start of Ferrell's professional baseball career, which later saw him playing with the Baltimore Elite Giants, Montreal Royals, Pueblo, and joining Jackie Robinson's barnstorming all-stars.

He played in most of the major league stadiums of that era— Shibe Park, Yankee Stadium, Briggs Stadium, Fenway Park, Memorial Stadium, Forbes Field, Griffith Stadium, Polo Grounds, Comiskey Park, and Ebbets Field—pitching against such teams as the Kansas City Monarchs, Cleveland Buckeyes, Memphis Reds, Homestead Grays, Birmingham Black Barons, Philadelphia Stars, Brooklyn Bushwicks and New York Black Yankees.

He played with or against a raft of outstanding black players who made it in the previously "all-white" major leagues; players like Luke Easter, Junior Gilliam, Monte Irvin, Wes Covington, Sam Bankhead, Sad Sam Jones, Joe Black, Larry Doby, Hank Thompson, Curt Roberts, Roy Campanella, Gene Baker, Satchel Paige, and Jackie Robinson.

"My first year with the Newark Eagles I had a 6-2 record. Monte Irvin played second base, Larry Doby shortstop, and Ray Dandridge was the third baseman on that club."

Lighting up a Kool cigaret, Ferrell reached into a desk drawer and pulled out his first pro baseball contract he ever signed. The ink is faded on the contract but still legible. From August 1, 1947, until the end of that season, the contract specified the Newark Eagles were to pay Ferrell $200 a month.

"I remember the first paycheck I ever received for playing baseball. It was the most money I ever seen in my life," said Ferrell, taking a long drag on his cigaret and watching the smoke swirl towards the ceiling. "I went out and splurged. Bought me a pair of white buck shoes. Always wanted a pair. Never could afford them. Paid $11 for 'em."

Ferrell's stay with the Newark Eagles was short-lived. The following year, 1948, he was traded to the Baltimore Elite Giants and played with them through 1950.

"When I was with Baltimore, we played many games in the Wilmington Ball Park. I was making $300 a month then. All three years I was with the club, my roommate was Junior Gilliam (later to go on to an outstanding, lengthy career with the Dodgers, in Brooklyn and in Los Angeles). Gilliam and me, we were like brothers. I used to bring him to my New Castle home. And he just loved to eat the chicken my mom prepared for him.

"In 1951, Gilliam and me were sold by Baltimore to the Brooklyn Dodgers. And they threw in pitcher Joe Black (later to play with the Dodgers, Cincinnati Reds and Washington Senators) for added measure. The Dodgers paid $12,000 for my contract."

But Ferrell's debut into the "white" organized baseball structure had to be put on hold.

"The very next season the Dodgers bought me, I went into the Army for two years. Was in Special Services, based in Fort Campbell, Ky. All I did was play baseball, basketball and football with the base team. Hurt my shoulder real bad playing football there as an end. Never healed properly.

"First year out of the Army, I pitched for the Dodgers' Montreal Royals club in triple-A ball. Had a 2-6 or 2-7 record. The following year, the Dodgers sent me to St. Paul in the triple-A American Association. Halfway through the season, my arm was acting up pretty bad. I was sent to Johns Hopkins Hospital in Baltimore for treatment. I had a feeling my career as a pitcher was shot.

"When I got out of the hospital, I was assigned to Pueblo, Colorado, Class A ball, where the Dodgers wanted to make a first baseman out of me. But I couldn't hit a curve ball. I came home. My pro career was over."

Playing with Montreal, Ferrell recalled that among his teammates were Tommy Lasorda (current Dodgers' manager), Dick Williams (present San Diego pilot), Don Zimmer (Chicago Cubs coach), plus Sandy Amoros and Chico Hernandez.

Barnstorming with Jackie Robinson's all-stars throughout the South after the regular season was over, Ferrell pitched batting practice at $150 a game. On the team were such top players of that day as Harry Simpson, George Crowe, Luke Easter, Sam Bankhead, Wes Covington, and, of course, Robinson at second base.

"Jackie Robinson was a gentleman-type guy," said Ferrell, lighting up another Kool. "But he'd raise hell if things were going wrong. He liked to win. I used to play him regularly in pool and checkers. I beat him in pool and split even in checkers.

Attesting to Ferrell's proficiency as a pool player are two trophies and two plaques displayed prominently in the living room of his one-story home on Kiamensi Road, in the shadows of Delcastle High School. "Pool's now my favorite sport," he said, flashing a big grin. "One time I pocketed 46 straight balls." He competed in the World Pool Championship in St. Louis two years ago.

His ton of wonderful baseball memories includes striking out Monte Irvin three times in one game and belting one of Satchel Paige's blooper pitches for a near home run at Wilmington Ball Park. "The ball hit the top of the left field fence and bounced back into the park," he said. "I had to slide into third to make a triple out of it."

Chuckling, Ferrell noted that he was the first black from Delaware to ever make it to spring training with the Brooklyn Dodgers at Vero Beach, Fla.

His pro baseball career over, Ferrell played locally with Frank Crawford's All-Stars and Alco Flashes. "I was 37 when I played my last baseball game," he said.

He also played semi-pro football in the area, with Adams A.C., the first integrated team in Wilmington, and in the late '50s for $20 a game with Tinicum A.C., where his teammates included Dick Christy, former North Carolina State star and one-time Wilmington Clipper.

For the past 22 years, Ferrell has been employed at the Delaware State Hospital. He's a security attendant.

Looking much younger than his 55 years, Ferrell, in his white tennis shoes, blue jeans, and sleeveless navy-blue tee shirt accenting his bulging muscles, looks like he could still belt a few out of the ball park. "But I can't throw," he said, rubbing his shoulder. "Got Ben-Gay on it now. Hurts something fierce when it rains."

Reprinted with the permission of The News Journal

Note: Toots Ferrell was inducted into the Delaware Sports Hall of Fame in 2000, the same year as Matt Zabitka.

Local greats in the ring

With boxing one of Matt's favorite sports, it's not surprising that he would track down and chronicle Delaware's ring greats. In the following two columns, Matt captured the careers of Johnny Aiello and Al Tribuani.

JOHNNY AIELLO

The News Journal

February 1976   Wilmington, Del.

'Little guy' Aiello part of boxing's golden era

BY MATT ZABITKA

It was fight-training night in dimly-lit Fournier Hall gym.

Bob Yearicks, a 210-pounder, clad in white shorts and T-shirt was running laps around the darkened basketball court, where the stands were folded against the walls.

In one corner, 175-pound Mike Vannicola, part-time student at Delaware Tech-Stanton, was skipping rope.

To one side of the ring on the more brightly lit stage, heavyweight Bill Cycyk, a good-looking guy with a Fu Manchu adorning his face, was punching the heavy bag.

Cycyk, a former Dickinson High athlete who is an apprentice bricklayer, is in his third month of training. He's scheduled to make his ring debut Feb. 12 in the same place where he trains.

As Cycyk, with determined look, punched the big bag, a small guy with iron-grey hair and a slight paunch watched intensely from inside the nearby ring.

"Move around, move around," the little guy quietly but firmly kept telling Cycyk, "Throw a little chop in there . . .lean into it."

Cycyk is 23 years old. When he was born, the little guy giving the orders had already been retired as a boxer about 10 years. Cycyk said he had heard so much about the great reputation of the little guy as a boxer and a trainer that he sought him out, wanted to work under the best. The best, he heard, was the little guy.

The "little guy" is Johnny Aiello. But nobody ever calls him "little guy" to his face.

When Aiello was in his 20s he was already retired from a boxing career that stretched from 1936 to the early 40s.

"Must've had 300 amateur fights," said Aiello, a bulldog of a man who said his amateur record was around 294-16.

115

Few amateurs in the history of the state amassed the honors Aiello did when he was a 5-foot-2, 115-pound scrappy battler taking on all comers.

He won the New York Golden Gloves bantamweight titles from 1938 through 1940, the National AAU championship in 1938, and before that, both the Diamond Belt and Silver Gloves titles in Philadelphia.

In 1937 he was named to the Pan American boxing team, which toured successfully through South America where he won all his five fights.

He fought against the best of his day, the likes of Billy Speary, Angie Ambrosano, Eddie Giosa, Frankie Donato, Phil Terranova, and the Forte brothers, Tommy and Johnny.

One night in Madison Square Garden, in Golden Gloves elimination, he fought and won five fights.

He tried pro boxing for one year. Had 17 bouts. Won 15, lost one, drew once. "George Gainsford, he was then managing Sugar Ray Robinson, was my trainer," Aiello recalled. "I used to train at Greb's gym, 118th and Lennox Ave. in New York.

"I gave up on pro boxing because there was no money in it. Times were tough. Most I ever got for a pro fight was $1,200. That was for an eight-round semi-windup in the Garden. Sugar Ray was in the windup. I fought a guy named Rodriguez. Won a decision."

Aiello, now in his sixth year as a plumbing code inspector for New Castle County, after having been a Wilmington fireman 20 years, claims he never suffered any serious ring injuries. "Never had a broken bone. Not even a cut. I credit that to good conditioning. I was also a very good, clever boxer. I was knocked out only once, by Frankie Donato."

Aiello said Speary, of Nanticoke, Pa., gave him the toughest fight of his career. "That was up in Boston, for the National AAU championship. I guess I fought Speary maybe six, seven times. We finished about even. Speary was then fighting almost every night. He hardly ever trained. He was a very good strong boy. Classiest I ever fought. He wasn't a knock-out type. Neither was I."

Aiello labeled Al Tribuani as "one of the greatest fighters to ever come out of this town. Him and I and Lou Brooks, we all won Golden Gloves championships in New York the same time, in 1940. That was really something for a small state like Delaware."

For Aiello, a baseball catcher, first at High School, as the old Wilmington High was called, and then at P.S. du Pont, his boxing career started through an ad in the newspaper.

"I was going to school then and there was this ad in the paper saying they were going to run a boxing tournament. I went over and saw a fellow named Tom Crumlish and signed up.

"First fight I ever had was against Jimmy Lancaster at the old auditorium back of (old) Wilmington High. I lost, but I thought I was robbed. Two weeks later I fought Lancaster again and beat the heck out of him. I was on my way."

In his early days as a fighter, his parents were dead set against his being a boxer. "I used to have to sneak out of the house to go to fights. Stan Winterick, I'm not sure if that's the right spelling of his name, well he's the man who first taught me a lot about boxing."

During Aiello's amateur days, winners would get clothing, rings, trophies, money orders, etc. Never money.

"The first prize I ever got was a sweater," he chuckled in remembrance. "I was the best-dressed kid on the block. I wore that thing to shreds. I guess the prize I most value to this day is a ring, which I still wear. I'm very proud of it. Got it for winning the National Golden Gloves (118) title. It has a diamond setting in the center with boxers on each side."

Reprinted with the permission of The News Journal

AL TRIBUANI

The News Journal

Aug. 7, 1973   Wilmington, Del.

Tribuani: He needs a good word
BY MATT ZABITKA

Five days before the European phase of World War II was to end in 1945, Al Tribuani was holed up in the mountains in Czechoslovakia with the 90th Division Infantry.

"We got ordered to dig out some S.S. troopers, also holed up in the mountains," recalled Tribuani. "All hell broke loose. In close combat I took two machine gun bullets in my left arm."

Al spent more than six months in hospitals and was honorably discharged with numerous medals—Bronze Star with cluster, Purple Heart with cluster, Silver Star, five battle stars, Victory Medal, European Theatre of Operations.

117

Two bullets shattered his arm and ended his life's dream of becoming welterweight boxing champion of the world.

Al has plenty of time these days to think about the tragedies, the heartaches and the suffering he has experienced. He also has time to think about wonderful years in his past, years when he starred in football for Salesianum and then at Wilmington High his senior year. He smiles faintly when he recalls his boxing career as a teen-ager winning the National Golden Gloves championship at 16 in Madison Square Garden, and again at 17 in Chicago, when he knocked out Bob Satterfield in the first round.

Hospitalized

Al Tribuani, 52, has been a patient for two weeks at the Veterans Administration Hospital, Elsmere. He underwent a nose operation last week and they're doing a lot of exploratory work on his body that took punishment through some nearly 200 fights during a 10-year ring career. He's also being checked for emphysema.

Al is on the 7th floor. He can look out the window and get a beautiful panorama of Wilmington, a city he once ruled as "king" in his role as a red-hot world boxing champion prospect. Those were the glory years for Al, who first started boxing competitively at age 15 in 1936.

Al followed his fantastic Amateur successes into the pro ranks in 1941. Twice he defeated Al (Bummy) Davis at the Philadelphia Arena.

"The second time I beat him," said Tribuani, "he broke my cheek in about 20 places." Both times Tribuani came off the canvas to beat Davis, then a leading contender for the world title. Tribuani called those two bouts with Davis "The two toughest of my career."

En route to his goal of becoming world champ, Al Tribuani also defeated Lew Jenkins, a former world lightweight titleholder, and lost a close decision to world champ Henry Armstrong in Philadelphia's Convention Hall, before what was reported as "the third largest indoor crowd ever to see a fight in Philadelphia."

Army braked rise

Just as Al's star was rising, he had to leave for the service.

Then there was that shattered arm suffered in the mountains of Czechoslovakia. All his hopes and dreams went down the drain.

He tried to make a ring comeback in 1947 when he left the service, but his bullet-ridden arm wouldn't hold up. He gave up the ring in 1948.

One time, as king in Wilmington, Al Tribuani couldn't walk down Market Street without being mobbed. He was "Mr. Big" in the local sports world. Reporters hounded him, fans fought for the privilege of buying him a drink, he was toasted wherever he went.

Today, in his loose-fitting, drab, hospital robe, war hero and ex-boxing champ Al Tribuani looks out the window from his 7th floor room at the Veterans Hospital. There's a big city below. But to him it's just a vacuum, the ashes of a kingdom he once ruled.

Today, Al Tribuani is a lonely, forlorn figure. Today is when he could use some of the adulation that he was inundated with during his glory years. Today is when he could use a kind word from friends; just a get-well card or letter, or even a phone call. Today is when it means the most to Al Tribuani to be remembered.

Reprinted with the permission of The News Journal

Semi-pro baseball

Matt's article about a testimonial banquet for John Hickman, a major figure in the Delaware Semi-Pro Baseball League, captures the high level of community interest in the sport and the audience's affection and respect for the honoree.

The News Journal

Nov. 16, 1990   Wilmington, Del.

Surprise tribute leaves Hickman speechless

BY MATT ZABITKA

John Hickman pushed aside the crème de parfait on the table in front of him and asked for a cigarette as his fingers nervously drummed the table.

"I'm dying for a smoke," said the longtime Parkway manager and patriarch of the Delaware Semi-Pro Baseball League.

Doris, his wife who was seated on his right, looked perplexed. "Jack [she always calls her husband Jack] hasn't smoked in three years."

But it was the kind of night when a guy needed some type of an outlet to ease his pent-up emotions and anxieties.

In front of Hickman, seated on the dais in the auditorium of the Sheraton Brandywine Inn on Concord Pike, were 260 friends, relatives, admirers, longtime associates, umpires and rival managers, along with guys who played for his Parkway teams from the 1940s to the present.

119

The surprise tribute, three months in the planning, to the legendary manager was spearheaded by former minor-league and Parkway pitcher John Shew, athletic director at Delaware Technical and Community College. He was assisted in the planning by a host of other Hickman supporters.

Shew drove Hickman and his wife to the hotel on the ruse that Ted Turner, owner of the Atlanta Braves and CNN, would be there to address the advisory committee that's trying to bring minor-league baseball to Delaware.

"When they pushed me through the front door of the hotel and I saw the hundreds of people massed throughout the lobby area, people I know, I fell apart. I mean hook, line and sinker," Hickman said. "I still wasn't fully aware what was going on, but I had an idea."

Listening to speaker after speaker heap adulation and praise on the venerable manager, a stranger entering the packed auditorium might've gotten the impression the gathering was either a retirement party or a wake. Maybe a celebration or fiesta.

Actually, it was all those and much more throughout an affair that started at 6 p.m. on Saturday and concluded at 12:30 a.m., Sunday.

There were proclamations from Wilmington Mayor Dan Frawley and Gov. Castle designating Nov. 10 as "John Hickman Day." And there were at least a half-dozen other citations and presentations, including a plaque listing Hickman's year-by-year managerial record in the Semi-Pro League, from 1956 to 1990. It showed that his 35-year regular-season record was 733-312, with 16 pennants, including eight straight from 1965-72; that he won 13 playoff championships, and that 10 times he won the pennant and playoffs in the same year.

Among the highlights was a videotaped message Ed Lawrence sent from St. Petersburg, Fla. Lawrence, now in charge of all umpires in minor-league baseball, set an all-time Semi-Pro League record for most career wins (78) while pitching 13 years for Parkway. He lost only 23 times.

Seated behind his desk at his Florida office, Lawrence delivered a passionate talk, which was played for the audience on a VCR. Lawrence took the word "testimonial," and letter by letter he projected what each letter meant to him concerning Hickman.

Hickman stood up during Lawrence's talk to better see and hear the TV monitor. All through the talk, Hickman kept dabbing at his eyes with a handkerchief and wiping his nose. The tears wouldn't stop. His wife, emotionally overcome, couldn't watch. She sat with her head bowed.

At 12:15 a.m., it was time for Hickman to cap the evening.

"I can't talk; I'm all choked up," said Hickman, a man who has never been known to be at a loss for words. "It has been a great evening, one I'll never forget. I don't think there's ever been a night like this in Wilmington. I won't be able to sleep tonight. I'm not deserving of all this, but I thank you all.

"I could not have lasted all these years without my wife at my side," he added, tears welling in his eyes.

A standing, 40-second ovation answered Hickman as he sat down.

Reprinted with the permission of The News Journal

Reporters on the air

In a 1989 column, Matt spotlighted three well-known sports broadcasters. Because of their long-time association with University of Delaware football, and each's distinctive voice and style, these on-air personalities developed a following that tuned in each Saturday afternoon to listen to their reporting on the Fightin' Blue Hens and their opponents.

The News Journal

Oct. 28, 1989   Wilmington, Del.

Reitzes, Kelley, Pheiffer voices of UD football

BY MATT ZABITKA

They were the voices of University of Delaware football.

They did the play-by-play over radio of Blue Hen games, from the late 1930s to the present.

A flock of people have served as color commentators over the past half-century, but there were only three play-by-play announcers.

Gravel-voiced Herm Reitzes, who died in 1987, was the first.

The late Bob Kelley, whose animated voice inflections mirrored the exciting action on the field, was the second.

He served the longest stretch. He started in 1950, which was Bill Murray's last year as head coach, and called 378 games before being stricken with leukemia the fourth week of the '87 season. Kelley never returned to the mike and died in 1988.

WDEL's silver-haired Bill Pheiffer, whose voice is as smooth as the top of a pool table, has been calling the plays since Kelley passed away.

There was some question whether there was another play-by-play man after Reitzes and before Kelley. Dick Aydelotte, who retired from WDEL in August 1987 after 45 years with the station, recalled that he was a 20-year-old student at Delaware when he joined Reitzes as a color commentator doing home games at Frazer Field that paralleled the B&O railroad tracks, two or three football fields from Old College.

"I think it was around 1947, I believe, that Atlantic Refining Co., which sponsored Delaware games on radio, fired Reitzes," said Aydelotte. "It broke his heart. If I recall correctly, they brought in a guy from Harrisburg to replace him."

However, Mario Stalloni, Delaware fullback from 1946-49 who is now living in Wallingford, Pa., remembered that Reitzes was still doing Delaware games in '49. "That was my last year of football at Delaware and I remember Reitzes interviewing players before we boarded a plane for an away game."

If Stalloni is correct, Delaware has indeed had only three play-by-play announcers in some 50 years.

During that long stretch, the voices doing the commentary have been almost as many as Heinz 57 varieties. They have included, in addition to Aydelotte: Harvey Smith, who retired from WDEL in June 1978 after 50 years of service; Harry Themal, current general news columnist for *The News Journal*; Tom Mees, now in his 10th year with ESPN, the all-sports TV station in Connecticut: Ted Youngling, 1948-49 Blue Hen football letter-winner; Todd Kalas, son of Phillies broadcaster Harry Kalas; and Len Holmquist, who put in a 10-year stint.

Also: Gorm Walsh, Dan Casey, Peter Booker, Jack Lee, John Warner and Don Voltz. Pheiffer also served as color man for Kelley.

Broadcasts of Delaware home games originated at Frazer Field. The last game played there was the fifth of the 10-0 season of 1946, after which the Blue Hens played their home games at Wilmington Hall Park until 1951 before moving to their own stadium on campus in 1952.

Without a doubt, Reitzes was the most colorful of all Hen announcers.

"He was horrendous with his inaccuracies," recalled Mario Stalloni. "Sometimes he'd call me Tony Stalloni. Other times he'd say the ball was on the 52-yard line. But everybody loved the guy. He was a real nice guy. He had a distinct voice, one which you could recognize anywhere, even in a blackout."

Reitzes once told me he never used a spotter. "Hell, there was no room for a spotter in the small press box. Besides, I didn't need one. Delaware carried only about 25-28 players and I got to know them all by their moves on the field."

I asked Reitzes if he was the best sportscaster in Delaware during his era.

"Hell [a word he used often to preface his response], I was the only sportscaster in the state."

Indeed he was, and he became a legend.

Reprinted with the permission of The News Journal

Delaware Sports Hall of Fame

In 1976, Delaware inducted seven members into the first class of its Sports Hall of Fame.

Barbara Viera, Delaware Sports Hall of Fame official and former University of Delaware volleyball coach, congratulates Matt at the awards ceremony.

Of the 194 male and female athletes recognized through 2001, Matt has written about practically every one. In 2000, he was selected one of the few writers inducted into Delaware's premier athletic honor society—joining Izzy Katzman (1993 inductee), Herm Reitzes (1990) and Al Cartwright (1980).

It's also amazing to realize that Matt has written about all of the persons named Athlete of the Year by the Delaware Sportswriters and Broadcasters Association, all the persons voted High School Football Coach of the Year, all the players named Most Valuable Player in the Delaware Semi-

123

Pro Baseball League and all those inducted into the Delaware Baseball Hall of Fame.

Frequently, Matt has been asked how many articles he has written.

Determining even an approximate number would be impossible, considering he's written for more than a dozen publications. But with the help of computer records from a system installed in *The News Journal* eight years ago, it's possible to determine a rough number of Matt's output during the last several years.

"I checked once," said Matt, "and I've done about 7,500 since 1994. There were times I had 18 stories in one week for all the *Crossroads* (Thursday supplement) sections, plus the regular paper. But when I first came to Wilmington, I used to write as many as four columns for the *Morning News* and *Evening Journal*, different stories for each paper."

During dinner at the June 2001 ceremony when Matt was inducted into the Pennsylvania Sports Hall of Fame (Delaware County Chapter), his former boss Al Cartwright mentioned that one of Matt's trademarks was using a lot of names of local people in his columns.

Describing Matt as a "runaway writer," Al also said Matt was very conscientious. One day at *The News Journal*, Matt approached Al and handed him a stack of columns, which Matt had prepared prior to going on vacation.

Al said he took the papers, and replied, "Matt, let's give the readers a vacation, too."

CHAPTER 8

Comments about the Greats

'If you were to invent a name for a sportswriter, you couldn't do better than Matt Zabitka. He would be a wonderful character for a TV sitcom. He is the classic newspaper guy. You can see him with a brimmed hat, trench coat, spiral notebook—not a pen but a thick pencil—and a press pass stuck up in his hat. These guys aren't around anymore. They're either gone or they've gotten tired of the business and quit.'
—Pat Williams, Senior Vice President, Orlando Magic

Getting the scoop from the big names that passed through town was one of Zee's specialties. Whether the sports star was in the First State to appear at St. Anthony's Sports Banquet or the Wilmington Sportswriters and Broadcasters Association annual dinner—or any other reason—Matt would appear with pad, pencil and tape recorder in hand.

Following are some complete columns, as well as some excerpts from others, featuring a few of the many VIPs of the sports world Matt has interviewed.

TED WILLIAMS

When Ted Williams visited Wilmington, Matt wrote two stories about the famous baseball player. One appeared in Feb. 11, 1983, and a subsequent article appeared on Feb. 24.

Notice how Matt developed two different articles from the information he secured during one interview with the batting champion.

The News Journal

Feb. 11, 1983   Wilmington, Del.

The Kid still hits, but as a speaker
Ted Williams wows Tonies' guests

BY MATT ZABITKA

They used to call him Tempestuous Ted, Terrific Ted, Splendid Splinter and The Kid.

That was in the days when he blasted rival pitchers all over the lots as a Boston Red Sox outfielder during a fabulous major league career from 1939 until he retired in 1960 at age 42.

Theodore Samuel Williams is no longer tempestuous, no longer a splinter, weighing 235 pounds, and he's no longer a kid. He'll be 65 on August 30.

But he's still terrific as ever, as was evidenced by the response he evoked from the 900-plus crowd at Thursday night's 32nd annual St. Anthony's Catholic Club's sports banquet at the Padua Cafetorium.

As a closing speaker, he socked a grand slam. And, as a goodwill ambassador for baseball, he proved to be the super hero in civies that he was in the Red Sox uniform.

From the moment he showed his face in the pre-banquet hospitality room right up until the start of the gala affair, Williams was besieged for autographs and requests from folks who just wanted to shake the hand of the most remarkable hitter baseball has ever seen.

Tieless, wearing a Navy blue sports jacket and gray pants, Williams seemed to be thoroughly enjoying himself amidst all the attention and adulation being heaped his way.

Requests for his autograph became so heavy that an announcement had to be made before the start of the banquet, requesting fans to stay clear of the dais until the affair was over.

With both hands in his pockets, ample shoulders squared, Williams addressed the audience clearly and articulately.

"I'm always being asked if I had a chance to do it over again would I've liked to be playing baseball today instead of the days when I did play.

"I can honestly say I think I played in a great era. I personally think the greatest era. I played against some of the greatest players who ever lived and played in this game. And I look back and I say, gee, I wouldn't give that up for anything.

"I got to see Willie Mays, Hank Greenberg, Bob Feller, Newhouser, Jackie Robinson. I could keep going on and on.

"And who was the greatest player I ever saw? Well, I'm going to tell you.

"With all due respect to Hank Greenberg, Hank Aaron, Willie Mays, Mickey Mantle, Jackie Robinson. I could keep going on.

"But I have to say, in my heart, if anybody was better than Joe DiMaggio I don't know who the hell it was."

Naturally, Williams' choice of DiMaggio at an Italian-oriented banquet produced a wild outburst of applause and cheers.

Williams opined that one thing that has changed baseball today is AstroTurf.

"With AstroTurf I'm sure there's more emphasis on defense, of the coverage in the outfield, balls rolling faster in the infield and speed on the bases.

"With those things in mind, I have to think the game is played just a little bit differently.

"I would have to say this, in my opinion of the modern player, that certainly I think the defenses are better, with stress on speed and a little more emphasis on pitching.

"But I don't quite see the hitters today playing baseball. And it is certainly no criticism of them because there are great players playing today. But I don't think it's quite the era of hitters that there were 20-30 years ago."

Before the banquet, in the quiet of a Padua classroom, I asked Williams if there was any goal that eluded him during his career that was to get him inducted into the Hall of Fame in 1966.

"One thing I will always be sorry about is that I didn't get a chance to play in more World Series. I only played in one (in 1946) and we came so close three or four times. I didn't do very well in the only Series I played (he was 5 for 25 in seven games). That was the one thing I'll always regret the most, that I didn't play in more World Series."

Asked if there was one memento from his lengthy and illustrious career that he cherished the most, he shot instantly, "Yes, there was one. What I prized more than anything else was an autographed baseball from the one and only and forever will be. It was a baseball signed for me as a rookie.

"I went to Babe Ruth. He was in our clubhouse. I went up to him and got a ball signed by him. On the ball he wrote, 'To Ted Williams, your pal, Babe Ruth.' "

Reprinted with the permission of The News Journal

The News Journal

Feb. 24, 1983   Wilmington, Del.

'Splendid Splinter' wows them at St. Anthony's

BY MATT ZABITKA

Phillies manager Pat Corrales was there. So was Ed Lopat, a former New York Yankees pitcher. And Dan Marino, the University of Pittsburgh quarterback . . .

The roster was a who's who of sports, including Philadelphia Eagles quarterback Ron Jaworski, Salesianum grad Paul Soares, now a Navy lineman, and Lou Moser of Chalfonte, an Atlantic Coast Conference basketball referee.

But the man who stole the show at the recent St. Anthony's Catholic Club's 2nd annual sports banquet at Padua Academy was Ted Williams, the "Splendid Splinter" of Boston Red Sox baseball.

Still blessed with ample hair, Ted's now thick-waisted, jowly in the face and has a little sag in his ample shoulders. But there was no problem recognizing that this was indeed the legendary Ted Williams, the man who drilled 521 home runs and had a phenomenal .344 batting average over 19 major league seasons.

He spoke clearly and articulately, and honored every one of the hundreds of requests for an autograph. Long after the banquet ended, he was still seated at a table signing autographs.

I asked Ed Liberatore, chief scout for the Los Angeles Dodgers, who was responsible for Williams' presence at the affair, how that person was able to pull strings and get the Hall-of-Famer to come to Wilmington.

It's no secret that Williams abhors banquets. He had admitted earlier that he attended only five banquets in the last five years, and this one was only his second this winter.

Liberatore smiled as he reached into his pocket, pulled out his wallet and tapped it. That told the story.

Whatever St. Anthony's paid Williams, it was worth it. Williams, once know as "The Kid," turns 65 on Aug. 30, but he wowed the audience of 900.

Before the banquet, during an interview in the privacy of a Padua classroom, I found the six-time American League batting champ and four-time home run king far from the tempestuous reputation that haunted him as a super star. He was gracious, courteous and most cooperative, answering every question put to him.

Williams said he was proudest of the year he batted .406, in 1941. "That was something that was most outstanding that I was able to achieve in baseball. I think the fact that I hit for as high an average and I couldn't run that fast is an achievement," he said. "As you get older, I think you forget about the little specifics and you think more about the overall and I hope that as I go on and carry on, I'm going to live about 20 more years, and if I do, I'd like to be remembered as someone who really contributed to the game."

Of course, he added, "The Hall of Fame is a culmination of everything you've done over the years and certainly that's the end prize, to be voted into the Baseball Hall of Fame. That's what every major leaguer hopes for."

Williams agreed that today's baseball uniforms look more like softball outfits, but "they're better though. I don't like too much jazz on them myself. But, I tell you, they're comfortable and they're easier to play in, I think. Although the light flannels, remember the big balloons, they didn't look as good either."

I questioned Williams about the final game of his career. It was on Sept. 28, 1960, at Fenway Park in Boston against the Baltimore Orioles. After going hitless in his first two official at-bats, in the eighth inning he belted a titanic 450-foot homer, the 521st and final one of his career, into the right-center-field seats behind the Bosox bullpen. As the crowd of 10,000 stood and applauded, Williams circled the bases, then headed straight for the bullpen, through the tunnel and to the locker room.

For many minutes, as the game was held up, the standing fans cheered wildly and applauded, wanting Williams to come out to take a bow. He never did. I asked him now, almost 23 years later, why he didn't come out to acknowledge the thunderous standing ovation.

"Well, that isn't quite accurate," he said. "I did make an appearance [a little later]. Mike Higgins [then Bosox manager] was pretty smart about this. I had to go out to the outfield the next inning [bottom of the eighth]. As I was running out, [Higgins] has somebody right behind me. I was being replaced. So I did go back on the field. It was a great moment for me. I have to admit that. Here it is 23 years later and I still remember it as a great moment for me."

The Sox still had a series ahead at Yankee Stadium before completing the 1960 season, but Williams never suited up again. I asked him why?

"I already told them [after the final home series with Baltimore] that this was it for me. I told them that. I've always been just a little bitter about that because they knew I was not going any place after that day."

Williams said he was happy and satisfied with his career.

"You know what, I don't want to go back to yesterday. Yesterday was a tough day for me. I signed autographs [the night before at a kids' baseball clinic in York, Pa.] until my right arm about fell off. I didn't sleep too well the night before. I'm going to sleep better tonight. I'm going to feel better tonight.

"No, I wouldn't go back one day. I've been very lucky in my life. I know how lucky I've been where I could've been wiped out like that [while serving as a pilot in World War II and the Korean conflict] and it didn't happen. And chances I took that certainly I wouldn't do them again.

"But I wouldn't go back one day. I'm living for the future. I'm projecting good things for me ahead and that's the way I feel, really."

When Williams closed his career in 1960 he was 42 and still able to bat .316 over 113 games during which he hit 29 homers and drove in 72 runs.

Only once in his 19-year career did he bat under .300. That was in 1959 when he finished with .254.

He holds the Red Sox all-time record for games, at-bats, runs, hits, doubles, homers, total bases, RBIs, extra-base hits, batting average, slugging percentage.

He holds the distinction of being the oldest major league player to win a batting title when he hit .388 at age 39 in 1957, He was 40 when he captured his last batting crown the following year with .328.

Reprinted with the permission of The News Journal

BILL VEECK

The News Journal

Jan. 3, 1986   Wilmington, Del.

Veeck was no wreck:
Owner was talker, charmer, entertainer
BY MATT ZABITKA

A bottle of beer in one hand, a cigarette in the other, a wide smile creasing his craggy face, Bill Veeck hobnobbed with the celebrities and hangers-on in the Phillies' hospitality room on one of the upper floors of the Hotel du Pont.

At every pivot on the wooden stump that served as his right leg, there was someone vying for his attention, wanting to talk to him.

Fifteen minutes remained before the 15th annual banquet of the Wilmington Sportswriters & Broadcasters Association (at which Veeck was to speak) would start on the lower level of the hotel in the main ballroom and I was chomping at the bit.

I had been assigned to write a column on Veeck but I couldn't get to him. I couldn't separate him from his well-wishers. This was in January of 1964, shortly after I had joined the sports staff of *The News Journal* papers.

In desperation, I forced myself on Veeck, explaining my predicament.

"Sure, I'll be glad to talk to you," he said, taking a swig of beer right out of the bottle. He apologized to the people surrounding him, the ones with whom he had been conversing, then told me he'd be right back. He first wanted to fortify himself.

He peg-legged it to the small bar in the room, returning with three full bottles of beer. "OK, where do you want me to sit?" he asked.

I pointed to a large, over-stuffed chair in one corner of the room. He put his three bottles of beer on a small end table, plopped in the chair, propped his wooden leg on an Ottoman, then pulled out several packs of cigarettes, tossing them on the table.

I asked him how many cigarettes he smoked a day? With a wave of a hand, he replied, "Oh, I've cut down quite a bit. I'm down to five packs a day."

Between puffs on ciggies and drinking beer, Veeck turned out to be one of my most memorable interviews. The interview continued long after all the room occupants had left for the banquet hall below.

Not once during the interview did he talk or even hint of his heroics with the Marines. It was during World War II, on Bougainville, an island in the Solomons, when he suffered an injury that later led to the amputation of a part of his right leg. Rather than wear an artificial limb, he chose a wooden stump, explaining that it enabled him to move about much faster and easier.

He told me his talents as a promoter first surfaced in 1941, when he and Charlie Grimm, an old pal, bought the Milwaukee Brewers. They paid "over $100,000," half of which was their own money, for the franchise, an eighth-place club on the day of the sale.

Veeck, then 28, said he immediately jacked-up attendance by nightly showings of a "screwball show" called "Veeck's Varieties."

"It wasn't unusual at all," said Veeck, "for Brewer patrons to win prizes like a 200-pound cake of ice or a live lobster." He also gave fans something else—a winner—and via such tactics boosted attendance from approximately 75,000 in 1940 to 273,589 in 1942.

Asked what he regarded as his biggest mistake in baseball, he laughed heartily, slapping a leg with a hand.

"Which one?" he asked. "I've blown so many major decisions I wouldn't dare go over them. It would take too long."

Of all the gimmicks he pulled off during his illustrious and colorful association with baseball, he was hesitant about naming his favorite.

As for Eddie Gaedel, the 43-inch-tall midget he sent up as a pinch-hitter when he had the old St. Louis Browns in 1951, Veeck laughed loudly over that episode.

"He had a strike zone of about an inch-and-a-half when he hunched over and bent his knees," Veeck continued, laughing all of the time. "That was the first time anything was done to put entertainment zip into the sport [on the major league level] and I was condemned by some for doing it."

Next he talked about Satchel Paige, whom he described as "my favorite ballplayer," and baseball in general. Veeck enjoyed discussing his newest vocation, that of a syndicated sports columnist.

He noted that it took him at least eight hours to write his weekly 800-word column.

"I write laboriously," he said. "But I can afford to, since I have the time. I find that getting a good lead is the toughest part. I keep writing and re-writing until I find something that reads fairly well. I just don't have the natural writing ability.

"I don't know how in the world sports writers can write so rapidly. I've always held the highest esteem and admiration for sports writers. They cover an event and in a few minutes have a complete story written. That boggles my mind."

Veeck was modest. He was a gifted writer, a trait he probably inherited from his father, who was a sports writer. His father quit the newspaper business to become general manager and later president of the Chicago Cubs.

Veeck, who at 28 was one of baseball's youngest magnates, became a columnist as a result of a book he authored—"Veeck, As In Wreck."

In his column, he reviewed and critiqued sports books. To keep abreast of happenings, he said he subscribed to seven daily newspapers and subscribed to five other dailies for two-week periods.

When we both left the room for the banquet hall, Veeck had consumed all the beer, but not all the smokes.

Veeck was a familiar figure on Delaware's rubber chicken circuit.

In February 1968, he drove up from his Easton, Md., home to address the Hercules Men's Club at the Hotel du Pont. In February 1972, he was the toastmaster at St. Anthony's Catholic Club's 21st annual sports banquet at Fournier Hall. And in January of 1973, at the 24th annual banquet of the Wilmington Sportswriters & Broadcasters Association, I, as president of the association at the time, had the honor of introducing him as the toastmaster for the evening.

Wherever he went, Bill Veeck always guaranteed a good show in every walk of life, at every level.

He was one of a kind.

Reprinted with the permission of The News Journal

CAL RIPKEN JR.

The News Journal

Sept. 21, 1995   Wilmington, Del.

Fond memories of Cal the rookie: A young Ripken feted in Delaware

BY MATT ZABITKA

On Sept. 6, Calvin Edwin Ripken Jr. broke Lou Gehrig's all-time record of 2,130 consecutive games. To add to all the hoopla, I'd like to inject a local angle.

On Jan. 17, 1983, a few months after he was named the American League Rookie of the Year, Ripken surfaced as one of the VIPs at the annual banquet of the Delaware Sportswriters and Broadcasters Association at Padua Academy in Wilmington.

He was 22, and unlike today, had a full head of hair, with not a strand of gray showing.

And as he still is today, he was cordial and somewhat shy as I taped an interview with him in a far recess of the Padua cloakroom, a spot I chose to get him away from autograph-seekers and well-wishers.

Used at shortstop and third base in his major-league debut with the Baltimore Orioles in 1981, Ripken never dreamed at the time he would go on to eclipse Gehrig's streak 14 years later.

He had played in only 23 games, batted .128 and had but five hits (all singles) in his first year in the bigs. He didn't have enough at-bats to be considered for any honors.

"I'd like to play 20 years in the big leagues. I'd like to have good seasons most years. I don't think you can improve every season, but I'd like to have 20 solid seasons," he told me at Padua.

"I really look up to guys like Pete Rose [that was before Rose was banned from baseball] and Carl Yastrzemski, who go out and play until they're 42, 43, and keep their bodies in shape. That's ultimately what I'd like to do."

On being named Rookie of the Year in '82, he said he was "very pleased and honored" because there was such a good crop of rookies that season.

"At the start of the season, I didn't look to go out and try to be Rookie of the Year. I went out to try to help our team get into the World Series. Making Rookie of the Year is a big honor because you get only one shot at winning it."

He noted that in his rookie year, two pitchers he hated to face were Len Barker of the Cleveland Indians and Goose Gossage of the New York Yankees.

"Barker was a big guy who had a 90 mph fastball, and Gossage threw hard and was wild enough to be intimidating."

Then, it was Ripken who idolized major-league baseball players, followed their accomplishments religiously, sought their autographs.

Today, the shoe is on the other foot. It is Ripken who is idolized and hounded for his autograph and sought for personal appearances.

"When I broke in the Orioles in '81," he recalled, "I was in total awe of the other players.

"That was part of my problem. You watch these players while you're growing up, players like Reggie Jackson and Goose Gossage. You watch them on TV and all of a sudden you're with them, and you say to yourself, 'I'm in the big leagues with these legends who've been playing for such a long time.' I really didn't think I could compete with them at first. It was part of a mental problem.

"But then I decided, 'Well, I'm here, and I can play in the big leagues. They're here and they're good ballplayers, but I am too.' Once I decided I could play here, it became easier. But being in awe of my contemporaries was my big problem at first."

Ripken said that when he was a kid, his idol was Brooks Robinson (a 23-year major-league third baseman, 1955-1977, all with the Orioles).

"I used to love to watch him play because he was so exciting," Ripken said. "As a third baseman, he made diving plays and all kids like to see the extra-tough plays made successfully."

Today, kids, some of whom may be big-leaguers of the future, are mouthing the same things about Ripken.

Ripken has come a long way since he broke into pro ball in 1978 at 18 with Bluefield of the Rookie Appalachian League. He batted .264 and tied for the league lead by participating in 31 double plays as a shortstop. That was the same year he committed 33 errors. But he never gave up on his ultimate goal—to play in the majors.

Signed by the O's in the second round of the June '79 free-agent draft, he said the bonus he received was nothing to speak of.

Money wasn't paramount with him at the time. What was paramount was getting a chance to play in pro baseball.

Playing with Miami of the Class A Florida State League in '79, he was paid $500 a month with no additional expense money.

"It was very hard to live in Miami on a salary like that. The rent and cost of living was very high."

When he made it big with the O's, among his managers was the controversial, bellicose Earle Weaver. "Mine was a good relationship," Ripken said of Weaver. "I think he liked me as a player and I liked him as a manager. He never got real personal with any player. It's hard for me to describe him as a person. But as a baseball manager they call him a genius and I can see why."

These thoughts and many others came to mind as I went down the tail end of the road with Ripken, counting off the days/games until he broke Lou Gehrig's all-time streak.

In attitude, demeanor and focus on home and family life, Ripken doesn't seem to have changed one iota from the teen-ager who earned $500 a month in Class A baseball to the 35-year-old today who rakes in millions.

It was all so much in evidence on national television Sept. 6—the love and emotion expressed by the fans and the manner in which Ripken responded.

It was a lovefest.

Reprinted with the permission of The News Journal

JOE MONTANA

The News Journal

Jan. 29, 1989   Wilmington, Del.

Montana got chance he wanted

BY MATT ZABITKA

Ten years ago, in a vacant classroom at Padua Academy, seated behind a desk too small for his 6-foot, 200-pound frame, Joe Montana contemplated his future.

Just five weeks earlier, on New Year's Day 1979, the former Ringgold, Pa., High athlete sparked a second-half rally that gave Notre Dame a 35-34 victory over Houston in the Cotton Bowl.

In Wilmington for the 28th annual St. Anthony's Catholic Club's sports banquet at Padua, Montana wondered how high he would be picked in the NFL draft three months away, or if he would be drafted at all.

"I'm looking forward to the draft," he said. "I'm very excited about it. I just want to play professional football and I'm just waiting for the chance. It's kind of killing me, waiting until May."

Asked how high he expected to go in the draft, he shrugged his shoulders. "I have no idea. A lot of people told me I'm going to go high, but you can never tell. The draft is so funny that one minute you could be going high and the next minute you're pushed down to the fifth or sixth round.

"Now that I'm out of school [he graduated from Notre Dame in December 1978], I'm planning—if everything goes well for me in the draft—to move out to the West Coast. Buy a home there.

"If pro football doesn't work out for me, I'll probably get into some type of marketing field. Maybe try getting into motion pictures."

Montana noted that he hailed from the same section of Pennsylvania—Monongahela—as Joe Namath, but they had never met.

"He lived about 45 minutes from my home," he said. "The football coach I had in high school coached against Namath when he played high school football."

Montana confessed that he had dreamed of attending Notre Dame ever since he first started playing competitive football, at age 8. "Notre Dame was always on TV, always in the news. I just thought it would be the best place to go."

After his spectacular career at Ringgold, where he was an All-State and All-American high school quarterback and earned letters in basketball and baseball, he said he received "more than 100 college offers." But his mind was already set. He was going to Notre Dame.

At Notre Dame, he played only six seconds as a freshman and was listed dead last on the depth chart, even behind some walk-on quarterbacks.

His sophomore year, he twice rallied Notre Dame to victories in come-from-behind situations. That's when Coach Dan Devine started to take notice.

His junior year (1976), he sustained a separated shoulder and sat out the entire season. "That was the first and only injury I had in college," he said. "That probably was the biggest disappointment of my collegiate career."

While in Wilmington, Montana made it a point to phone a former Notre Dame teammate, Mark McLane, former Salesianum School All-State running back. They were teammates on the 1975 Irish team that finished 8-3.

At the banquet, when Montana was introduced, shrieks like those reserved for rock stars greeted him. In his brown suit with a double-vent jacket and flared pants, looking like a younger version of Namath, Montana felt right at home.

Memories of that interview with Montana surfaced as I watched Montana rally the San Francisco 49ers to a 20-16 victory over the Cincinnati Bengals in Super Bowl XXIII.

For Montana, it was the third time in this decade that he quarterbacked the 49ers to the Super Bowl championship. Against the Cincinnati Bengals, he was 23-for-36 passing, for 357 yards and two touchdowns. And in the three 49er Super Bowl wins, he passed 93 times and was never intercepted.

In the 1979 draft, he was picked by the 49ers in the third round, the 82nd player selected overall.

Reprinted with the permission of The News Journal

ELMER F. LAYDEN
(one of the Four Horsemen)

The News Journal

March 5, 1963   Wilmington, Del.

<u>Layden Says Here</u>
Rockne's Chemistry Skill
Equaled Coaching Ability
BY MATT ZABITKA

Thirty-nine years ago, Elmer F. Layden, as a member of the storied "Four Horsemen" backfield at Notre Dame, helped to write one of the most inspiring football chapters in American history.

Last night, this same Layden—now gray-haired, older and slower, and 30 pounds heavier—appeared in the flesh at the Hotel Du Pont, where he served as toastmaster for the 32nd annual dinner of the Traffic Club of Wilmington.

Suave and debonair, and looking more conservative than a blue serge suit, Layden had the mien of a professor at a swank girls' college than the rugged, spirited competitor that he was.

For this reporter, seeing Layden had the same effect as if Notre Dame's fabulous coach Knute Rockne had suddenly come to life.

Layden played three years for "The Rock" (1922 through 1924) along with the other "Horsemen"—Harry Stuhldreher, Jim Crowley and Don Miller.

"Knute Rockne was a great man, a great coach," said Layden in a voice that was just above a whisper.

Layden punched out his filter cigarette stub in the ash tray then reflected some more.

"You know, most people remember Rockne as a great coach, which he was. But too, few know that he was equally as great a chemist and a professor. He would have been an outstanding success in any field that he chose.

"He was a kind man, a man who possessed feeling and compassion for others. In all my years of association with him I never heard him use profane language—never—neither on the field or in the locker room.

138

Oh, maybe he would utter an occasional profane word but nothing more than that.

"All those stories credited to Rockne—you know—the ones like "Win this one for the Gipper," etc.—they're all true. That's one thing Rockne was great at—psychology. He was a master psychologist. That was the secret of his fantastic success as a football coach at Notre Dame where he posted a record of 105 wins, 12 losses and five ties from 1918 to 1930.

"Sure, we had tremendous records at Notre Dame when I played, going 8-1-1 in 1922, 9-1-0 in 1923 and 10-0-0 in 1924, when we won the national championship. But it wasn't because we were such phenomenal players. We actually were not. Rockne's psychology made us better players. He extracted from us every ounce of energy we could muster."

Lighting up another cigarette, Layden continued: "I can recall being berated by Rockne on two occasions, but never in blasphemous terms. In 1922, against Purdue, I fumbled after gaining 15 yards. Rockne took me aside later and let me have it, accusing me of carrying the ball like a loaf of bread. Fortunately, we beat Purdue, 20-0.

"In 1924, in our 13-6 win over Northwestern, I fouled up the signals. Rockne waited until he got me in the locker room before he gave me the dickens."

As for the present situation at Notre Dame, under Coach Joe Kuharich, Layden refused to pour any blame on Kuharich's shoulders for the nose dive of Irish football supremacy.

"It's just the law of averages," he commented. "Teams have cycles. They win a lot of games, then they lose a lot. Notre Dame just happens to be experiencing one of those 'off' cycles. But they'll be back, occupying the high position in national football that they once held."

As for the rumors that there's alumni pressure on the powers-that-be at Notre Dame to fire Kuharich, Layden smiled. "I doubt it very much. However, you must realize that while I do still avidly follow Notre Dame football, seeing 4-5 games every fall, I'm not as close to the situation as I used to be. I can say that when I coached at Notre Dame (1934-40) I never encountered any pressures whatsoever, whether from the alumni or from the school administrators."

Perhaps it should be pointed out that the reason there was no cry for Layden's scalp was because he was just as successful as a coach as he was a football player. In the seven seasons he piloted at N.D., Irish teams won 47 games, lost 13, tied three, for a .783 mark, the third best in the school's history, surpassed only by Rockne and Frank Leahy.

139

Layden explained that the famous Four Horsemen backfield averaged only 160 pounds, but the group's average speed for running 100 yards in football gear was 10.4 seconds.

"I recall the weights vividly because in 1924, prior to the start of our game with Princeton, we were all weighed."

At 5-11, Layden was the tallest member of the Four Horsemen.

"Those who were part of the Four Horsemen backfield keep in pretty close touch," said Layden. "We visit each other, write to each other, and occasionally phone each other."

The fondest memories Layden carries over from his football days are not the victories. "It's the friendship from one another," he said. "I'll always remember the wonderful friends made through football. While the Four Horsemen received much adulation, we who carried the ball in those days never forget the boys up front—the Seven Mules—who made it all possible. Adam Walsh, the center, was the team captain; Chuck Collins and Ed Huntsinger were the ends; Rip Miller and Joe Bach were the tackles; and Nobel Kizer and John Weibel were the guards."

Layden said that the question most often asked of him in his travels, as a representative of General American Transportation Corp., is to make comparisons between then and now.

"That's difficult to do," he added. "Times and situations have changed so much."

Just one more question the fellow with the pad and pencil implored.

What kind of athlete were you in high school?

"Want me to brag?" he chuckled. "Really, I made All-State at Davenport, Iowa, High, in basketball, football and track. It was my high school coach, a brother of Chicago Bears' owner George Halas, who interested me in going to Notre Dame. My coach, who has since died, left Davenport High to serve as a football aide at Notre Dame. After he located in South Bend, he came back and never let up on me until I decided to go to Notre Dame. For me, that was the turning point in my life. It was the greatest thing that ever happened to me."

Reprinted with the permission of The News Journal

RALPH KINER

The News Journal

Feb. 11, 1985   Wilmington, Del.

Slugger Kiner reflects on Hall of Fame career
BY MATT ZABITKA

A funny thing . . . strike that. It should read "an embarrassing and humiliating thing" happened to me on the way to St. Anthony's 34th annual sports banquet Thursday night at Padua Academy.

En route to the sellout affair, I visited with Baseball Hall-of-Famer Ralph Kiner in his Hotel du Pont room, where he was laboring over notes to be used later that night in his role as toastmaster at the Tonies' affair.

We talked baseball for maybe 15-20 minutes as my tape recorder busily whizzed away, recording our conversation, or so I believed.

Elated with what I thought was a very good interview, I wanted to play back the last couple of minutes for Kiner to hear. Nothing came out of the recorder except the whirl of the spools. My black box, which had been so good to me all these years, had malfunctioned. There was nothing on the tape.

Instead of blowing his cool for taking up his time, the one-time National League home run king calmly flicked the ashes off one of the three cigars he says he smokes a day and suggested, "Let's do it all over again," adding, probably to assuage my feelings, "Hey, the same thing's happened to me a number of times."

A repeat interview followed, this time recorded, for insurance's sake, with pen and paper.

Kiner, still 6-foot-2, but appearing slightly leaner than the 195 pounds he weighed when he set a National League record by leading or tying for the lead in home runs in his first seven years in the majors, this season will be his 24th year as broadcaster of New York Mets' games.

"I really love what I'm doing," he said, settling back comfortably in his chair. "The only bad part is the traveling. I had enough of that [in] my 10 years in the majors."

As an expert on the Mets, he painted Dwight Gooden, National Leagues' Rookie of the Year in '84 as "the best young pitcher I have

141

ever seen, and that goes back to the days of Bob Feller. He has as much ability as any pitcher of 19 ever had. He has better control than Feller had."

And Kiner, who drilled 369 home runs during his big league career with the Pittsburgh Pirates, Chicago Cubs and Cleveland Indians, knows all about pitchers—the good, the bad, and the in-between. He faced enough of them.

"The one pitcher who gave me the most trouble was Ewell [the Whip] Blackwell. He was the toughest any right-handed batter ever faced. His delivery had a lot to do with that. In my opinion, there was no one in the majors comparable to him."

Kiner, who belted 12 grand-slams and hit two or more home runs in 34 games, attributed part of his homer-hitting success to playing in Forbes Field, then home of the Pirates.

"Forbes Field was tailored for me. The wind blew toward left field, which is good for a right-handed home run hitter. Having the prevailing winds blowing out was even better than having a shorter fence.

"I would say that if I had one park that I would've liked to play in as a home player it would've been Ebbets Field in Brooklyn. I think that would've been the easiest park of all to play in."

I pointed out that during his first two years in pro baseball, with Albany of the Eastern League in 1941-42 (he also spent six weeks with Toronto of the International League in '43 before going into the service), he really never showed signs of developing into the great home run hitter that he was to become in the majors.

"I hit 11 home runs in the Eastern League my first year and led the league the next year with 14. That may not seem like a lot of home runs, but there's an answer to that. It [Eastern League] was an extremely tough pitching league. They used a very dead ball and the parks were big. But when I hit my 11 homers, I was still among the leaders and led the league the next year.

"When I went into the service [1943-45] I was a skinny kid. I was very young, weighed about 160. Through maturity in the service, I was in the Navy Air Force program, I went through a very rigid program and probably was in the best shape of my life when I went through that program.

"When I came out of the service, I was a mature, grown man, weighing about 195, all muscle.

"In the service, I went to St. Mary's Pre-Flight School in California. I got my wings and graduated out of Corpus Christi, then went to the Hawaiian Islands in the Pacific where I flew planes in sea rescue work mainly and things like that.

"In the 2 1/2 years I was in the service, I maybe played 10 baseball games. I was never in the right place at the right time to play baseball. So I missed those years of playing baseball."

Evidently, being away from the game didn't hurt the Santa Rita, N.M., native.

His first year in the majors (with the Pirates in ''46) fresh out of the service, he led the N.L. in homers with 23. The following year he drilled 51 round-trippers, followed by successive seasons of 40, 54, 47, 42 and 37 homers. In one five-year stretch, he belted 234 homers, more than anyone else for that period.

His rookie year, when he led the N.L. in home runs, he was paid $5,000. Randy White of the Dallas Cowboys makes about four times as much for playing one football game.

After the '52 season, in which Kiner socked 37 homers and the Bucs had their worst record in history, winning only 42 games, Pittsburgh boss man Branch Rickey, a notorious penny-pincher, was determined to prune salaries. Kiner, N.L. home run leader seven straight years, expected a salary cut, but was stunned when Rickey wanted to dock him 25 percent, the maximum amount allowable.

"He was a brilliant operator, but had no compassion for baseball players," Kiner said of Rickey.

Of the mountain of batting records he amassed, Kiner said he is most proud of being the N.L. home run leader seven successive years.

The one record that escaped him was Babe Ruth's home run mark. "But that was never in my reach," he said.

And of all the managers he played for in the majors, he said Al Lopez rated No. 1, "as good a manager as I've ever seen."

He described Stan Hack as "a very nice man but not that much of a leader." Frankie Frisch was "extremely difficult and tough." Fred Haney, "very competent." And Billy Herman, "a non-descript type."

And what is Kiners' most-prized and cherished memento from his illustrious 10-year major league career?

"I was never a saver. I really didn't save anything."

Holding up his left hand and making a fist to accent the huge ring on his ring finger, Kiner took a slow drag on his big cigar and smiled. "This is my most prized possession. This is what it was all about, for me."

It was the ring he received for being inducted into the Baseball Hall of Fame at Cooperstown, N.Y., in 1975.

Reprinted with the permission of The News Journal

MICKEY VERNON

Matt's long-time, Delaware County, Pa., hometown friend Mickey Vernon has been the subject of many of Matt's columns. When speaking about the former American League batting champion, who once was described by President Dwight Eisenhower as "my favorite big league player," Matt said that he is amazed that Vernon has not been inducted into the Baseball Hall of Fame.

Ed Okonowicz

Matt chats with longtime friend and former American League batting champion Mickey Vernon, at the Pennsylvania Hall of Fame, Delaware County Chapter, banquet.

Vernon said he and Matt met at a social affair about 55 years ago. At a tribute to Vernon in Washington, D.C., while he was with the Senators, Matt traveled to the event and participated in the ceremony at Griffith Stadium.

"I always thought he was a good writer," Vernon said. "He always gave a lot of exposure to local athletes and the community."

The News Journal

Aug. 11, 1990   Wilmington, Del.

Vernon missed big bucks
from baseball pension

BY MATT ZABITKA

Ray Ford of Hockessin, a long-time baseball buff, was puzzled by something he read in the fully revised 8th edition of The Baseball Encyclopedia, the complete and official record of major-league baseball.

It's a 2,781-page, 3 1/2-inch thick hardback, costing $49.95, which Ford had received as a Father's Day gift from one of his granddaughters.

"Is it true 10-year veterans of the major leagues could expect a pension of $91,000 a year?" he asked, expressing surprise.

"No way," I replied. "That has to be absurd. I can't fathom a retired major-league baseball player getting a pension that amounts to almost half as much as what the president of the United States makes while still active."

Ford let it be known that he wasn't joshing.

"Look in the top of the second column on page 12 of the Baseball Encyclopedia," he said.

Sure enough, Ford was correct. It states that a 10-year veteran of the major leagues could expect a pension of $91,000 a year. That averages to about $1,800 a week for being idle. Gulp.

Mickey Vernon, two-time American League batting champion and a 20-year major-league veteran (1939-60), emitted what I took was a sarcastic chuckle when asked if he was pulling down $1,800 a week in retirement.

Vernon, a native of Marcus Hook, Pa., with strong ties to Delaware—his sister, Mrs. Edith Cushman, lives in The Timbers, and his father-in-law, Dr. Albert Firth, lives in Northcrest—noted that the annual $91,000 pension probably applied to today's players, not of his era.

"The pension program got started at the end of the 1946 season," recalled Vernon, who was a smooth fielding left-handed first baseman with a classic batting swing. "Each player was asked to put up $250. It became an official plan in April of 1947, when club owners agreed to match what the players contributed.

"The players contributions were deducted each pay day.

"When the plan first started, a player could expect $100 a month when he reached the age of 50."

Pensions kept spiraling with the passing years as did salaries.

But Vernon isn't grumbling. "It's a sign of the times," he said. "All I can say is more power to the players, to get all they can." He noted there have been a number of different groups of his era trying to upgrade the pensions of players of the years when the play first started. "But nothing has happened," he said. "It's tough to change it now."

In Vernon's last year in the majors (1960), he got into nine games with the Pittsburgh Pirates, all as a pinch hitter. The following three years, he managed the Washington Senators. This was followed by 13 years managing minor-league teams and coaching at the major-league level. He then hooked on with the New York Yankees as a minor-league batting coach in 1979 when he was hired by Al Rosen.

145

In 1982 he was called up by the Yankees to be batting coach. "That was the year, George Steinbrenner had three managers, five pitching coaches and three hitting coaches," Vernon said. "June 4 that season, I was reassigned. Steinbrenner didn't really fire people, he reassigned them. Bob Lemon was let go that year as manager after 20 games into the season."

But you won't get Vernon to badmouth Steinbrenner. No way.

"I didn't get rich, but he paid me well," Vernon said.

He was with the Yankees organization from 1979 until he retired in 1987. When he was dropped as batting coach in 1982, he was made a scout, spending a lot of time at Veterans Stadium checking over talent and making nightly reports. "And when the Phillies were on the road, I'd sometimes get assignments to go elsewhere, like New York or Cleveland.

"The only reason I decided to retire was because the Yankees were going to reassign me to a job that would've entailed a lot of traveling."

Reprinted with the permission of The News Journal

PAT WILLIAMS

Today, Pat Williams is senior vice president of the Orlando Magic basketball team and resides in Florida. But the Tower Hill School graduate said that he never feels far away from Wilmington, thanks in large part to Matt Zabitka.

Although Williams had left Delaware by the time Matt arrived at *The News Journal* in 1962, the Delaware sportswriter has been chronicling the sports executive's career in his hometown newspaper for about 40 years.

"I find it interesting that he has plugged into me as a Wilmingtonian," Williams said, then added, he's not surprised, since Matt has a bulldog reputation for relentlessness and diligence.

As a person, Williams said Matt exemplifies honesty and integrity. "As a worker," Williams added, "Matt had

Orlando Magic, Ltd.

no equal. He has to be the hardest working newspaper man in America.

"If you were to invent a name for a sportswriter, you couldn't do better than Matt Zabitka. He would be a wonderful character for a TV sitcom. He is the classic newspaper guy. You can see him with a brimmed hat, trench coat, spiral notebook—not a pen but a thick pencil—and a press pass stuck up in his hat. These guys aren't around anymore. They're either gone or they've gotten tired of the business and quit."

When asked why he has remained in touch with Matt for all these years, Williams laughed at the other end of the phone. "You can't help but be in contact with him. He has to have the best Rolodex in America. He just wrote an article about my recent book."

Pausing, Williams stressed the value of old-fashioned reporters.

"Every city of any size," he said, "needs a Matt Zabitka, who I respectfully call a chronicler, someone who has a history and picture of the past. You need someone with deep roots in the community. Wilmington is fortunate to have that in Matt."

The News Journal

May 5, 1987   Wilmington, Del.

Williams worked a real Magic trick

BY MATT ZABITKA

The day he graduated from Wake Forest University in June of 1962, Pat Williams' father, James W. Williams, was killed in an auto accident returning home from his son's graduation [and NCAA regional baseball tournament].

It was a devastating blow to Pat, who had visions of playing pro baseball, with his dad in the grandstands cheering him on.

The urge to play pro ball stayed with Pat, former three-sport star at Tower Hill School.

"The day after my dad's funeral, I visited Bob Carpenter [then owner of the Phillies] at his Montchanin home," recalled Williams in a telephone interview from his Orlando, Fla., home. "I told him of my great desire to play pro ball.

"The next day, Bob phoned from Shibe Park [the home of the Phillies]. He asked me to meet him at the ball park the next day.

147

" 'I have a job for you,' he told me. 'You're to report to the Miami club of the Florida State League.' As I was leaving his office, he asked if I was broke. Then he handed me $500 as a signing bonus and said, 'Keep your eyes and ears open at all times, on and off the field.'

"When I arrived in Miami, I checked the report sent to the club by Carpenter. I'll never forget one of the comments in the report. It said, 'Has a future in front office.' "

Williams never made it to the front office of a major league baseball team, which was his life's ambition after failing to make it as a player. Somewhere along the path he hoped would take him to the Phillies' front office his express train was derailed. No matter that *The Sporting News* in 1967 had named him Minor League Executive of the Year for his outstanding work with the Phillies' Spartansburg, S.C., club of the Class A South Atlantic League.

But Bob Carpenter's evaluation of Pat Williams 25 years ago—"has future in front office"—turned out to be most prophetic. But in a basketball front office, not baseball.

Today, after successful NBA front-office stints in Chicago, Atlanta and Philadelphia, Williams has moved to Orlando. In 10 months he produced a miracle, spearheading a successful drive to secure an NBA franchise for a sports-starved area better known as the home of Disney World and Epcot Center.

On Wednesday, April 22, the official word was given; the Orlando Magic would be part of the NBA starting with the 1989-90 season.

"For 10 months, up until the official word was out, I was in a state of suspension," said Williams. "Then came a great feeling of relief, followed by a numbing feeling. It took a week to sort out the emotions.

"For 10 months I worked 10-12-hour days, usually seven days a week. I must've made at least 150 speeches in front of organizations throughout central Florida."

Added his wife, Jill. "I think Pat addressed every service club in Clearwater, St. Petersburg, Daytona Beach and Orlando, spreading the case. Then he'd come home and continue to talk some more. I don't think there's one person in central Florida who hasn't heard Pat make a formal speech.

"The day after Orlando was awarded a franchise, he started to work frantically. He hasn't stopped since," added Pat's wife.

Williams sees the Orlando franchise as a can't miss operation.

"We have a drawing base of around 7 million people. Already 14,500 fans have paid $100 each as a deposit for season tickets," he explained.

Construction on the Magic's $89 million arena, which will seat 15,500, started the early part of January. Scheduled to be completed by the fall of 1988, it's located about 15 miles from Disney World, in a complex that already has a convention center, a hotel and other facilities.

Williams, vice president and general manager of the 76ers at the time he bolted to do the spadework in Orlando in June '86, admitted it was a huge gamble.

"At every point in life you get one opportunity to do something to get to a higher level," he explained. "This was my opportunity. It was time for a new adventure. I didn't want to look back, years from now, and have misgivings about not giving it a try.

"The way things have worked out, it's a dream come true." . . . . .

Despite the hectic pace that was his life the past 10 months, Williams somehow still found time, assisted by his wife, to write his sixth book. Titled "Keep the Fire Glowing," the book, geared to married couples, is due out this fall. And the past week, the Williams' adopted 6-year-old Korean twin boys, expanding their family to eight. The guy is a human dynamo. . . . .

Bob Carpenter recognized Pat Williams' role in life 25 years ago when, in his report, he wrote, "Has future in front office."

Reprinted with the permission of The News Journal

RANDY WHITE

When asked to provide an article about a Delaware-born football star, Matt pulled out two notebooks and immediately offered a selection of stories he had written about Randy White, Dallas Cowboy defensive tackle, four-time Pro Bowl selection and member of the Professional Football Hall of Fame.

The former McKean High School football player is considered by many as Delaware's most well-known member of the National Football League. Matt added that he had just spoken to White on the phone a week earlier, needing material for a column he was writing about the Dec. 24, 2001, death of Dallas Cowboy defensive end Harvey Martin.

When a telephone call was made to White's home in Texas, the answering machine invited the caller to leave a message. While explaining that the call was from Delaware and the writer was seeking a few comments about Matt Zabitka, White picked up the phone and enthusiastically began to talk about Zee.

"I think Matt is a great guy. He was the big guy at *The News Journal* when I started playing sports. He covered my entire career, from high school to being inducted in the College Football and Pro Football Hall of Fame. Matt not only covered sports," White said, "but he cared about the people he wrote about. He is the kind of sportswriter that whenever he calls, I know that I will call him back. Matt has always been straight with what he wrote. He would never take what you said and twist it this way or that.

"He made you feel comfortable, and he made me feel important. He's been kind to me and he's always covered my career in a positive way. That means a lot to me. He's a really good guy."

The News Journal

April 19, 1989   Wilmington, Del.

White proved that All-State doesn't mean everything

BY MATT ZABITKA

Practically every year after the scholastic All-State football selections are announced, you can count on one, two or three calls from disgruntled parents, wanting to know why their sons weren't on the first team. This is usually followed by a litany of statistics.

"How's my son going to get a college football scholarship when you don't put him on the first team?" the concerned parents usually ask.

I usually point out to callers the case of Randy White, who recently announced his retirement from pro football after 14 years with the Dallas Cowboys. He was an eight-time all-pro defensive tackle.

White never made All-State first team during his years at McKean High. His last three years in high school, the Highlanders had an overall record of 13-16-2. Yet White's potential didn't go unrecognized. He went on to the University of Maryland, made first-team All-American his last two years, won the Outland Trophy and Vince Lombardi Award as college football's top lineman in 1974, and was Dallas' No. 1 pick in the 1975 NFL draft, the second player selected overall.

The way college scouts scour the nation for talent these days, no way can you hide talent, even if it surfaces on second team or honorable mention in All-State selections. There have been instances where high schoolers who didn't get any All-State mention went on to illustrious college careers.

Earl Batten, now in his third year as a government and history teacher at Alexis I. du Pont High, was an assistant coach at McKean during White's sophomore and junior years, and he had White as a senior in '70 when he succeeded Blaine Tanner as head coach.

150

"Randy showed talent the first day of practice in 1968 when he was a sophomore," Batten recalled. "It was just the way he walked. I was standing with the defense in the secondary practice, when the quarterback handed Randy the ball. When he barreled into the secondary, you could almost feel the ground shake.

"He was a starter from the first day of practice, playing fullback, line-backer, and some defensive end.

"His junior year [2-7-1 team record] he just got better. He even snapped for punts and extra points.

"His senior year [4-6 team record], he was captain and a natural team leader. He was so strong and powerful he was afraid of going full steam in practices. He always had this fear of hurting someone."

Batten noted that White also had a strong throwing arm.

"If we had been smarter as coaches, we would've made Randy a quarter-back.

"There was this one game against Dickinson in '70 when we had been run-ning a lot of sweeps. On one of the sweeps, the ball was lateraled to Randy and he fired a 45-yard touchdown pass. We beat Dickinson, something McKean was unable to do for the next seven-eight years.

"Randy never got his degree from Maryland, but he could probably buy the university. I have a master's [degree] and I'd gladly trade my degrees and a year's teaching salary for what Randy made in a month.

"Randy proved more of a success than a guy with a long list of degrees."

White was also a standout in baseball (first baseman) and basketball at McKean. His tape measure home runs are still talked about.

"I always hoped Randy would stick with baseball," LaVerne White, Randy's mother, revealed. "I felt a career in baseball would last longer than football and he wouldn't be subjected to all the injuries with which he's now plagued.

"Long before the officially announced his retirement from football, I had wanted him to retire. I thought, health-wise, it was the best thing to do. But he wanted to get in at least one more year.

"I told him if he'd retire now, he would probably be a sure bet to make the pro Hall of Fame on the first ballot five years from now. I wanted that to hap-pen while I'm still alive and would be able to attend the ceremonies."

Reprinted with the permission of The News Journal

Years ago, Matt said, Randy White's name came up in conversation with another NFL personality at a local sports banquet. When asked about including the incident in the book, Matt smiled and said, "Sure. Randy will probably enjoy it."

"I remember Mike Ditka, of the Chicago Bears," Matt said. "I saw he was alone at St. Anthony's banquet and he had a drink in his hand. He had a negative reputation. I went over to him and, just to make conversation, said, 'You know you're in Randy White country?'

"He snapped back, 'What am I supposed to be, afraid?' "

STAN MUSIAL

The News Journal

Feb. 12, 1982   Wilmington, Del.

Musial a hit at St. Anthony's banquet

BY MATT ZABITKA

"I feel tough with a bat in my hand but not with this mike." Stan Musial explained his uneasiness at the microphone as he addressed a sell-out crowd of 800 at Thursday night's 31st annual St. Anthony's Catholic Club Sports Banquet in the Padua Academy Cafetorium.

The baseball Hall of Famer, one of the sport's all-time greats, let it be known that he wasn't much of a public speaker and went on to prove it.

Still looking in great physical condition for a man of 61, "Stan the Man" orally sparred around, jumping from subject to subject, at times with no continuity.

But who cared?

Just the sight of this baseball immortal was enough to add great importance and glamour to this bash. The baseball romanticists gawked in awe at one of the best all-around players ever to play baseball.

The seven-time National League batting champion and three-time Most Valuable Player could have delivered a dissertation on the mating of tsetse flies and the audience would have listened to every word.

"When I think of Wilmington," said the Donora, Pa., native, "I think of Bob and Ruly Carpenter who live in this area. I was sorry to see them leave baseball.

"I remember once coming to Wilmington to play an exhibition game (against the Blue Rocks at the old Wilmington Ball Park).

"When I was 17, I was offered a basketball scholarship to Pitt and also a chance to sign a baseball contract with the St. Louis Cardinals. My dad didn't want me to go into pro ball. He wanted me to go to Pitt.

I got my mother to change my dad's mind, and the third time the Cardinals' scout came to my house my dad relented and signed for me. He had to sign the contract because I was only 17 then."

Among other things, Musial, who amassed 3,630 hits and 1,951 RBI during his illustrious career from 1941 to 1963, revealed that he once aspired to be a fighter and rooted for Paul Waner of the Pittsburgh Pirates and Carl Hubbell of the New York Yankees as a youngster. He also described Phillies pitcher Robin Roberts as one of the greatest right-handers of his era, said he had a hard time hitting against Phillies pitcher Curt Simmons, remembered Phillies third baseman Willie "Puddin' Head" Jones as a player who always had trouble with his feet, praised Philles outfielder Richie Ashburn and discussed briefly the "palm ball" Phillies pitcher Jim Konstanty relied on.

"I don't make too many appearances such as this," Musial admitted. "But when I was in the limelight, I was all over the country (attending banquets)."

Toastmaster Harry Kalas, the TV/radio voice of the Phillies, announced that this was only Musial's second banquet in the last 10 years.

Musial was greeted with a 20-second standing ovation when introduced. Before and after the banquet, he was mobbed by youngsters and adults for his autograph.

In an interview before the banquet, I asked him if he liked the clean-cut All-American image that followed him throughout his major league career. Wasn't there at least one time in which he was thrown out of a game or was involved in a fight?

"I can't say that I was ever evicted from a game or involved in a fight," he said, smiling. "I was brought up to respect authority. The umpires were the authority. I didn't argue with that. Something might be missing from the game today, with people always wanting to challenge authority."

He recalled that he received $65 a month when he broke into pro baseball as a 17-year-old southpaw pitcher with Williamson of the Class D Mountain League in 1938.

"I wasn't much of a pitcher. I had no confidence," he admitted. "I was wild. I'd walk a lot of guys.

"My second year in the minors, also with Williamson, I dove for a ball and hurt my shoulder. I couldn't throw, so they made me an outfielder."

He was to spend almost two more years in the minors before cracking the Cardinals' roster and going on to great heroics in the ensuing 23 years.

Flashing a king-size diamond ring on the pinkie of his left hand, Musial remarked, "This is a Hall of Fame ring. It takes care of a lot of other rings. This is the one I cherish the most."

At his height, Musial earned $100,000 a year. Today, fringe players pull down more than that, players who couldn't carry his glove.

"No. I don't begrudge players for getting all they can today," he said. "More power to them. Everything is relative. The players of today just happen to be in the right place at the right time. Today the clubs have larger ballparks and there's TV revenue, plus concessions and parking. There's more money coming in today than when I played.

"I guess if I'd be playing today I'd be an I M—instant millionaire."

I asked him if he wasn't a millionaire now. "You said that, I didn't," he responded, breaking into a grin.

"I am doing well. I'm part owner of two restaurants, a bowling center, a Hilton hotel and have banking interests in St. Louis, and own a couple of hotels in Florida."

Of all his multi-accomplishments in the majors, he said he was most proud of his 3,630 hits, an all-time record that stood until the Phillies' Pete Rose broke it last year.

The evening's comic relief was provided by double-talk artist Jack Edelstein, introduced by Kalas as "The chairman of the National Football League rules committee." Edelstein's non-stop patter had the audience howling in their napkins. In some of the stuff that could be understood, Edelstein said, "I really didn't want to come here. I had the option of coming here or attending an autopsy in Philadelphia." And "I talk Philadelphia. I took speech lessons sitting in on Philadelphia council meetings." And "I coulda been an All-American football player, but I come from a Jewish Orthodox family and wasn't allowed to touch pigskin."

A surprise guest speaker was Foge Fazio, new head football coach at Pitt, who subbed for his quarterback, Dan Marino.

"Dan couldn't be here tonight and asked if I'd speak for him," said Fazio. "And when Dan Marino asks you to speak for him, you speak for him."

Ray "Boom Boom" Mancini, 20-year-old National Federation lightweight boxing champ (22-1, 17 knockouts) who has a world lightweight title match coming up April 17 against Arturo Frias, received a resounding ovation when introduced, and another one after he completed his well-received animated speech.

Other speakers included Gorilla Monsoon (Bob Marella) former professional wrestler, Steve Watson, Denver Broncos' wide receiver, Bob Crable, Notre Dame's All-American linebacker, John Spagnola, Philadelphia Eagles' tight end, Dick Ruthven, Phillies' pitcher, Rollie

Massimino, Villanova's basketball coach, and William McLaughlin, Wilmington mayor.

Among those introduced were Eddie Davis, Delaware's world champion harness driver, Ed Liberatore, chief scout for the Los Angeles Dodgers, Bob Mattei, top bowler in the St. Anthony's League, and Joe Garagiola Jr., son and namesake of the former major league catcher turned sportscaster.

Reprinted with the permission of The News Journal

'BOOM BOOM' MANCINI

The News Journal

May 11, 1982   Wilmington, Del.

'Boom Boom' Mancini a hit in the ring and out

BY MATT ZABITKA

Instant combustion. That's what Ray "Boom Boom" Mancini was after his surprising first-round TKO victory over World Boxing Association light-weight champion Arturo Frias in Saturday's nationally televised bout from the Aladdin Hotel in Las Vegas.

The 21-year-old, 5-foot-5-1/2, 135-pound buzzsaw from Youngstown, Ohio, leaped over the ring, blew kisses, hugged and kissed everybody in sight, and unabashedly shed tears of joy.

In the post-fight interviews, he spoke with machine-gun rapidity, excitement oozing out of his every pore. He spoke reverently and devotedly of his parents, whom he kept hugging, squeezing and kissing, and he attributed much of his ring success to God.

The graduate of Youngstown's Cardinal Mooney High had much to be thankful for, much to celebrate. He had won a world title and earned the fattest payday of his ring career—$100,000.

Three months ago, I interviewed "Boom Boom" at St. Anthony's Catholic Club's 31st annual sports banquet at Padua Cafetorium. Even then, as he was after Saturday's fight, he displayed the same emotional characteristics that have endeared him to a large segment of fight fanatics.

155

Numerous times he bounced off the chair to greet persons who had wandered into the little classroom where he was being interviewed.

"Hey, there's Stan the Man," he shouted, leaping off his chair to greet Baseball Hall-of-Famer Stan Musial, the banquet's principal speaker, who had wandered into the room with a beverage in hand. Returning to his chair after embracing Musial, he said, excitedly, "We were together last week (at a banquet). He's one heckuva man."

A little later, Ed Liberatore, top scout for the Los Angeles Dodgers, sauntered into the room. The effervescent Mancini again rocketed off his chair to embrace Liberatore. Returning to his chair, he remarked, excitedly, "I love Ed. I've adopted him as my grandfather. There's nothing phony about him. We were together at three banquets last week. He's the guy who asked me to come here tonight."

There was also a warm—and excitable—Mancini greeting Bob Marella (a.k.a. Gorilla Monsoon), the 6-foot-6, 355-pound professional wrestler.

Anything and everything Mancini did was with emotion and excitement. He bubbled so much I had a difficult time containing him during the interview.

Mancini was a surprise guest at the banquet. His name wasn't even listed in the printed program. He came only because Liberatore asked him to tag along. But it was evident that the little guy, attired in a black pinstripe suit and wearing spats, was the hit of the banquet with his down-to-earth speech.

Explaining his wardrobe, which made him look like a character straight out of Damon Runyon's "Guys and Dolls," he told the audience, flashing that infectious grin, "Somebody told me that where this banquet was to be held is 99 percent Italian."

With his left hand in his jacket pocket and using his right hand for emphasis as he spoke, Mancini brought a hush among the audience of 800, followed by thunderous applause when he confessed that "I kiss my father on the lips after every fight and every night. I never thought anything of it. I see nothing wrong. Don't be ashamed to kiss your father in public."

This he demonstrated before a national TV audience after Saturday's fight when he planted not one but numerous kisses on his father's lips. His father, Lennie, now white-haired and slightly stooped, had been an outstanding pro fighter in his own right. He had signed for a world title bout for February of 1942, but was never to realize his dream. Drafted into the Army a month before the fight, he got shot in France, as a front-line infantryman, ending his career as a fighter.

Earlier, Mancini had told me the main reason he got into boxing was to win the world title for his father, which he did Saturday. He said he had his first fight, as an amateur, at age 15 in April 1976, in Cleveland.

"It was a Junior Olympics Tournament and I won the three-rounder and went on to win a gold medal," he recalled. "I was 126, a featherweight, then.

"I fought three years as an amateur (43-2, 23 knockouts) and have been fighting pro 2 1/2 years."

He said he played three major sports in high school—tailback and defensive back in football, point guard in basketball, and pitcher and centerfielder in baseball.

"The Toronto Blue Jays offered me a shot to go to one of their baseball tryout campus, but I didn't go," he said.

Closing the talk at the Tonies' bash, he referred to his upcoming title bout with Frias. "I'm very sure about this fight. Bet your house, your kids, everything. I'm going to win."

No truer words were ever spoken.

Reprinted with the permission of The News Journal

Worth reading

Matt selected the following excerpts from several of his columns. They are reprinted with permission of *The News Journal.*

CHRIS SHORT was regarded as the best left-handed pitcher the Phillies ever had until Steve Carlton surfaced.

"I nearly quit school at Sanford in the seventh grade, and again as a 10th grader in Lewes [now Cape Henlopen High School]. I was really a wild pitcher then. I hit this kid in the head with a pitch and I felt real bad. The boy's father, who was the umpire, made me quit pitching and go to first base. After the game, I decided if I ever played baseball again, I would never pitch.

"A few years later, in 1954, as a soph at Lewes, because of my size and speed, I was asked by the school coach to pitch. I refused. I was finally coaxed into pitching. I lost my first start, 1-0 in 11 innings. Later, in another game, in about the 6th or 7th inning, I hit a batter on his temple. Even though he was wearing a protective helmet, the pitch knocked the kid cold. As the batter laid unconscious on the ground, I nearly broke out into tears. I didn't want to pitch anymore. But my high school coach urged me not to give up. He said it wasn't my fault. After that experience wore off, I came back to pitch and never stopped."

Short went on to pitch 15 years in the majors, with the Phillies and Milwaukee, compiling a career record of 135-132. In 1967, Short was the first Phillies southpaw in 50 years to win 20 games. He died Aug. 1, 1991.

JOHN P. (COUNT OF) MONTEFUSCO pitched in the majors for 13 years with the San Francisco Giants, Atlanta Braves, San Diego Padres and New York Yankees. He was Rookie of the Year in 1975.

"When I got traded by the Padres to the Yankees in 1983, I had a 5–0 record with the Yankees, 14-4 combined with the Padres and Yankees that year. And I didn't pitch for six weeks that season. So my record could've been much better than it was. I had a chance to become a free agent, but the Yankees offered me a three-year contract for over $2 million with an option year on it, worth $2.7 million. And I signed it. I made probably over $700,000, most I ever made.

"I saved every uniform I ever played in, in the majors. The entire uniform. Also saved baseballs. I also saved the no-hit ball with which I struck out my 200th batter, who happened to be Johnny Bench. But my dog, Henry, a black lab sheep dog, chewed up the ball. I also saved baseballs from all the shut-out games I pitched. I never asked for autographs. Now I wish I had. My mother threw out my entire baseball card collection, which would probably be worth about $250,000 today. I must've had 20 Mickey Mantle rookie cards. Mantle was my idol. I had dresser drawers full of baseball cards. Had to be over 100,000. I have no cards today, except my cards.

"I wish I would've saved more money than I did. I made almost $5 million in baseball. I really never worried about money. I mean I spent what I had coming in and always thought baseball would be there the rest of my life, that when I would quit as a player I'd be a coach."

HOWARD ESKIN is a Philadelphia sportscaster on radio and TV, with a reputation for telling it like it is.

On a scale of 1-to-10 among fellow Philadelphia sportscasters (radio and TV), Howard Eskin, sports talk host on WIP radio, is probably 11.

There have been documented feuds with Bill Campbell, Al Meltzer, and I don't know how many others.

On the air, Eskin, who looks like a well-groomed Prince Albert with his neatly trimmed beard and mustaches, is precocious, pretentious, opinionated, brash, abrasive, obnoxious, and at times sophomoric.

He is both hated and loved by his legion of listeners, who number many in Delaware.

But Eskin is also a live wire, a hustler who goes after the news. He probably has more personal contacts with professional athletes than any other sportscaster in Philadelphia.

One thing Eskin is not is bland. He speaks his mind, and lets the chips fall where they may. This quality has made him probably the best known and most listened-to Philadelphia sportscaster. . . .

Asked if he deserved that label of "obnoxious," he broke out in a chuckle.

"People say they don't want to hear opinions. But they really do. If you say the Phillies are great, the 76ers are great, the Eagles are great, after a while people will say, 'What the heck is this guy talking about?' I learned early in my career you've got to be yourself." . . . .

BOB COSTAS is considered one of the brightest award-winning sportscasters on the scene today.

"First paying job I ever had as a sportscaster was doing minor league ice hockey. Got paid $30 per assignment.

"I worked three years on a campus radio station at Syracuse University before becoming a radio announcer, first at WSYR, a 5,000-watt station in Syracuse. I went to KMOX in St. Louis. Was there seven years. That's where I got my first big break, after sending a tape to the station manager. . . . . From KMOX I went to NBC. . . .

"Baseball is my favorite sport. There's time between the pitches and the pace of the game allows an announcer to establish his own style and become conversational as well as calling the plays. . . .

"Now in TV sports, unlike radio when the play-by-play man was supreme, the color men are often the bigger stars. And rightfully so because since you can see the picture and the technology is so advanced, it's not so much the person who tells you what happened, but the guy who explains why it happened.

"In this way the color man is more essential to a television broadcast. Color men like John Madden, Tim McCarver, Tony Kubeck, Al McGuire and Billy Packer, these guys become stars in their own right."

159

Costas, definitely a star in his own right, said he'd rather do what he's doing than be president of the United States, and that he would be in some form of communications if he wasn't with NBC Sports.

"The pay wouldn't matter, as long as I made enough to live on," he concluded.

BOSH PRITCHARD was "Mr. Outside" and Steve Van Buren was "Mr. Inside" with the Philadelphia Eagles in the 1940s.

"I was a 10-year starter for the Eagles and made $10,000 a year. When I came up in 1942, they didn't have jet planes. It would take us 14 hours to get to the West Coast for a game. We went to Pittsburgh for a game by train.

"Our coach, Greasy Neale, hated to fly. He was superstitious. Greasy was one of the all-time great coaches in pro football. He was the type who kept the morale up. And when we went on the field, it wasn't a question of whether we'd win or lose, but how much we'd win by. He instilled that type of confidence in us. He was a great morale builder when you played with players like Steve Van Buren, Jack Ferrante, Peter Pihos, Joe Muha, Al Wistert, Russ Kraft, Alex Wojiehowski and quarterback Tommy Thompson, you know you were in solid company. Our tackles during those days were lighter than our tackles on two world championship teams. Wistert and Sears each weighted 220, compared to today's heavyweights."

JACK FERRANTE is one of the few players who ever made the transition from high school and semi-pro football to the NFL, with the Philadelphia Eagles, without the benefit of any college experience. He later coached the Wilmington Comets.

"I was signed by the Eagles for $2,500. That's 10 games, at $250 a game. The Eagles had to pay me whether I played or not.

"My last year with the Eagles (1950), I was getting paid $7,500 for the entire season (12 games). We also played two exhibition games, and if you were a veteran you got paid $50 for each exhibition game, and $25 if you were a rookie.

"When I played with the Wilmington Clippers of the American Association, in 1941-42, I got paid $75 for home games, $50 on the road, because they had to feed us and pay for train travel to the away games."

Reprinted with the permission of The News Journal

CHAPTER 9

Friends and Colleagues

'He's stayed in the job so long because it's his true love and passion. He's doing what he loves doing and gets paid for it. He just loves to write stories. You don't see that in today's world. If he retired, he'd get a job as a sportswriter.'

—Robert McCreary, Matt's grandson

Having worked in the newspaper business for so many decades, Matt has made connections with and impressions upon people of every level of sports.

Some of the people who Matt has met through his columns have become his friends. Others, who know him less well, still respect his talents and appreciate his work and the pride and attention his columns have generated among the subjects and the readers.

To those that have worked with Matt, or spoken to him for even a short time, or heard him on the banquet circuit, it's obvious that he likes telling stories. And even though he tends to repeat his favorite tales, it's enjoyable to experience first-hand the enthusiasm that the gruff-voiced, cigar chomping sportsman demonstrates in the telling.

Following are comments from some of the folks who have known or worked with Zee. And, yes, each of them has a special Matt Zabitka story or two to share.

Ron Fritz

**Sports Editor
News Journal**

Ron Fritz, 35, and Matt's current sports editor at *The News Journal*, came to the Wilmington paper in 1994 and became Matt's boss in 1999.

"I knew going in that Matt was a legend," Fritz said, adding that he was savvy enough to tap into Matt's immense knowledge of Delaware sports.

"He knew Delaware like no one," Fritz recalled. "I was fortunate to have five guys on the staff with more than 25 years of experience. It was a wealth of knowledge. And as far as local stories, Matt was the source."

Sitting across a section of Matt's desk in his second-floor cubicle are nearly a dozen file boxes jammed with 3"x 5" index cards, each containing the name, address, phone number and related bio and sports information about people he has interviewed. This contact file is a treasure trove of information on past and present sports scene stars residing in the Delaware Valley.

"With Matt," Fritz said, "you're dealing with a professional. It's a joy. You don't have to tell him what to do. He's just a pro. He and I are in the office a lot during the day. I get to listen to him conduct interviews on the phone. He asks people to spell their name, give their height and weight. You don't just see that these days.

"You can tell, once he latches onto a lead, he zeroes in on it. You can tell the exact moment it happens."

One time, after asking a person for his height and weight, Fritz heard Matt inquire, "What did you eat for breakfast?"

At first the sports editor was puzzled about the question, but he soon realized that

Sports editor Ron Fritz and Matt at The News Journal

Ed Okonowicz

Matt's inquiry was related to the athlete's illness during football practice.

Fritz said when he gets an intern or young reporter who needs to learn the ropes or find out about the area, he sends them to Matt.

"He's a walking encyclopedia, just a special guy. Everybody on the staff looks up to him. He's entirely helpful and he's funny. He's a good personality to have on the staff. At least once a day he makes me smile or laugh, especially if I'm having a bad day."

Fritz mentioned hearing several of Matt's favorite stories nearly a dozen times—particularly the one about Matt being nabbed by President Kennedy's Secret Service agents at a Washington Senators baseball game (see column on the next page).

Then there are the stories about Matt, ones that each person who's worked with him is eager to relate. In Fritz's case it occurred when he and his wife, Lisa, were on a cruise in the Gulf of Mexico.

While chatting with people on a sunset cruise, the Fritzes found out that another vacationing couple was from Middletown, Delaware. When they asked Ron where he worked, he told them *The News Journal*.

They immediately asked, "Do you know Matt Zabitka?"

According to Fritz, "I said, 'It so happens that I'm his boss.' And they told me to say hello to Matt. When I got back and mentioned it, Matt said he remembered writing about their sons."

"But here I am, 500 miles from Delaware, on a cruise, and people want to know if I know Matt Zabitka."

To many long-time readers, such an incident is not a great surprise, because—in a fair number of instances—Matt has written about three generations of athletes in the same family. One major joy of working with Matt, Fritz said, is that Matt's stories are essentially correct and the editors rarely need to correct his copy. Attention to detail is inherent in Matt's strong work ethic.

"If Matt is going to go on vacation," Fritz said, "he's sure to have finished the stories for his column in advance. That's the way he is. I get worried when I don't see him. If he were gone, we would miss more than his work. He's the spirit of the sports section. He's the soul. Every one of us would feel his absence. People look for what he writes.

"He's a humble guy. When he went into the Delaware Sports Hall of Fame, he didn't want recognition. He just wants to write about the kids and athletes. He's not happy being in the spotlight."

Fritz smiled when he recalled the night at a Wilmington Blue Rocks baseball game in Frawley Stadium when Matt was invited to throw out the first pitch.

Fritz and his wife sat with Matt's family, which included his wife, Helen; daughter, Shirley; and son-in-law, Jim McCreary; plus several grandchildren and friends.

"We were sitting up in one of the boxes they have, and that's where I really saw the love his family has for him," Fritz said. "It's a really tight knit family, they have a lot of admiration for him.

"I kidded him after his pitch rolled across home plate. Matt told me the sun was in his eyes."

Pausing, Fritz said, "I can't imagine putting out the sports section without him. I know we'll come to that one day. But that will probably be under another sports editor. He'll probably outlast me. You feel lucky to work with someone like him, and I'm his boss."

The News Journal

Nov. 23, 1988   Wilmington, Del.

JFK: Up close,
but not quite personal
BY MATT ZABITKA

Marking the 25th anniversary of the assassination of President John F. Kennedy in Dallas, Texas, there has been, and still is, an outpouring of recollections—on TV and radio, in newspapers and magazines, in private conversations.

Everybody seems to have a story, an opinion, and a recollection. So do I.

I never met JFK. But, because of him, I almost "earned" cell space in a D.C. jail. Who knows, it could've been a federal pen.

It happened in April 1963, seven months before the president's life would be snuffed out.

I had just joined *The News Journal* sports staff a few months earlier and was assigned to cover the 1963 baseball opener between the Baltimore Orioles and Washington Senators at what is now Robert F. Kennedy Stadium.

The president was scheduled to be there to throw out the ceremonial first pitch.

Portable typewriter and binoculars in hand, I arrived at the stadium early. I wanted to catch batting practice and interview Washington manager Mickey Vernon, who was a two-time American League batting champion during his playing days.

I parked my gear in the press box and proceeded to the area behind the Washington dugout, where the president and his entourage were to be quartered for the game. All the seats in that restricted area were still not occupied. It was like two hours before game time.

I had no official field pass. The one I was to have received in advance of the game never arrived.

It didn't matter. I was going to get on the playing field, pass or no pass.

As I was going over the fence to get on the playing field, an "army" of blue coats pounced on me. They rushed in from the east, the west, the north and the south. I guess they thought I was planting a bomb in President Kennedy's private box.

I was nabbed in the act, still astride the fence.

There was a big commotion. Batting practice grinded to a halt. Reporters already on the field, official field passes pinned to their jacket lapels, zeroed in on the action. Me.

As I was frantically pleading my case to the gendarmes, ready to run me in, this well-dressed gentleman approached. He asked one of the officers what the commotion was all about.

That "gentleman," I noticed by his lapel pass, was Bob Addie, veteran sports columnist for *The Washington Post*. I had never met Addie, but knew him by reputation. I had read his stuff in *The Sporting News*. Addie was in charge of issuing field passes for the game. Addie was a "big name" in D.C. Everybody knew him, even the officers.

I explained my plight to Addie. With a wave of the hand, he instructed the officers, "Let him go. He's okay."

I got my interviews, thanks to Addie, and I got to see the game from the press box, about 25 yards from the president's box.

About 15-20 minutes before the start of the game, President Kennedy, sporting sunglasses, strode to his box while an Army band on the field played "Hail to the Chief." It was quite impressive.

Throughout the game, during the lulls, I had my binoculars glued on the president. He seemed so close. I felt like I could reach out and touch him.

After an inning or two, off came the president's jacket. Later he loosened his tie.

Through the first several innings, he kept score in the official program, shelling peanuts all the time. About the fifth or sixth inning, he gave up keeping score, pushed the sunglasses over top his bushy hair and soaked in the sunshine.

Who would have thought that seven months later, on Nov. 22, 1963, that such tragedy, with worldwide repercussions, would befall one of the most popular presidents of the 20th century?

Reprinted with the permission of The News Journal

Robert "Bob" McCreary
Matt's Grandson

Robert "Bob" McCreary, 32, is Matt's grandson. Also a mover and shaker in the First State, in January 2001 *Delaware Today* magazine named Bob "Delawarean of the Year" for his charitable work in a number of areas, including his role as executive director of the Delaware Human Rights Project's National Campaign to Fight Crimes Against Children.

When Bob isn't performing random acts of human kindness for complete strangers, he's traveling the world as a member of President George W. Bush's advance team. In that role he has visited such distant locales as Poland, China, Latvia, Italy and Albania.

For a number of years when he was growing up, Bob lived with his grandfather. He recalled what a thrill that was.

"I used to think he was my best friend," Bob said. "I would always hang around with him, but later I found out he was my grandfather."

The feeling is mutual. So often, during sessions with Matt, he'd refer to his grandson, Robert, and how he had called the Zabitka home from Washington, D.C., during the inauguration of President George Bush. Matt also has souvenir White House passes and stamped government travel documents that were given to him by his grandson following his return from presidential trips abroad.

Bob smiles when he shares his memories of accompanying Matt on some of his interviews, particularly one with Billy "White Shoes" Johnson in Chester, Pa., and getting into Eagles practices—big thrills for a youngster in elementary school.

Matt enjoys a moment with his grandson, Robert McCreary, at the Pennsylvania Hall of Fame banquet. Bob originated the idea of having a book written about his grandfather.

Ed Okonowicz

166

"He's one of the last of the old timers to maintain a great work ethic," Bob said. "When we would go to a Phillies game, he would never let anyone give him anything. He wanted to write what was happening without feeling any sense of obligation. He never took free tickets or anything that would affect his job."

Matt had to work at the paper until close to midnight, and Bob used to wait for this grandfather to arrive home.

"I was about five years old, and when he came home we would go down to the basement and play pool until three in the morning," Bob said. "I'd stay up until he came home from the paper, and we'd play pool for hours. How many five-year-olds stay up and play pool all night? I used to live for that."

Bob recalled a day when the two of them visited Atlantic City. While strolling the Boardwalk, Matt told Bob to stand outside a store while he went inside to buy some cigars.

As any eight-year-old would, Bob began to roam and went into the store next door.

When Matt exited the store he had been in, Bob was not standing at the prearranged spot.

"I was looking at comic books," he said. "I saw my grandfather come out and running back and forth, looking all over for me. After a while he found me, grabbed me by the shoulders and asked, 'Are you all okay?' When I said I was fine, he starts spanking me on the Boardwalk. People are yelling at him, shouting child abuse. We were both crying and then hugging. He was just worried about me."

Matt's reputation has spanned many generations, and no one realizes it more than his relatives.

Bob met a man who proudly told Matt's grandson that "Zee" had written about him, about his father and about his son who was going off to college.

"When they find out I'm his grandson, people come up to me or call me to pass on stories to him," Bob said. "When I run into people, they don't ask how I'm doing, they say, 'How's your grandfather?' I love bragging about him because he's my hero. He's a soldier of the sports world. Every great of all the sports, he's not just done their stories, he's become friends with some of them.

"He doesn't do it because it's a job. He loves it. I think he'd do it for free. Joe DiMaggio commended my grandfather because he didn't ask about Marilyn Monroe (see column below) when he interviewed him. DiMaggio didn't like reporters asking him about his ex-wife."

And what about the book idea?

"It's important because my grandfather has such wonderful stories to tell, and he's met all these famous sports people like Jessie Owens, Ted

Williams, Yogi Berra, Joe DiMaggio. I think that's incredible. Also, he should get accolades from the public for all he's done. He's touched the lives of thousands of people. He's stayed in the job so long because it's his true love and passion. He's doing what he loves doing and gets paid for it. He just loves to write stories. You don't see that in today's world. If he retired, he'd get a job as a sportswriter."

Nick Grossi   Committee Member
St. Anthony's Sports Banquet

Nick Grossi's barbershop on Lincoln Street in Wilmington's Little Italy is a sports fan's museum, with photographs, posters, memorabilia and trophies spotlighting many of the stars who have passed through the shop's doors.

For a half century, the annual St. Anthony's Sports Banquet was one of the premier sports events for stars and fans alike, and Nick was in the thick of the arrangements and hosting.

He worked with Matt closely over the last several decades.

"I met Matt in the 1960s, I think," Grossi said. "We became friends. He always wrote a beautiful article for the banquet. He was very good, and well known around the state. He's a Chester boy, and I got a lot of friends up there. I used to mention a few names, and he knew them. We knew people in common, and we hit it off right away."

Grossi smiles with pride when asked about hooking up Matt with DiMaggio, a star they had been trying to get to the banquet for many years.

"We wrote letters, but never got a response," Grossi said. "Then, one year, Rudy Rubini was knocking on my door at 10 o'clock at night and said, 'Guess what, Nick! We got Joe DiMaggio next year!' We were all excited. That was in 1980.

"I called up Matt and said, 'You got a special interview with Joe DiMaggio tomorrow.' And he said, 'Where?'

" 'Come to my barber shop at 12 o'clock.' When we went to lunch at the St. Anthony's Club dining room, somebody else was sitting next to Joe DiMaggio. And I said, 'This is Matt Zabitka from *The News Journal.*' And Joe said, 'Move over, pal. Come over here, Matt, sit right here.' "

Matt's recollections of the meeting are reprinted in his 1980 column.

The News Journal

Feb. 8, 1980   Wilmington, Del.

Joe DiMaggio
Yankee Clipper still
the All-American Boy at 65

By Matt Zabitka

There was a gallon of wine in the middle of the rectangular table, around which were seated 12 men enjoying an early afternoon repast in the privacy of the otherwise unoccupied lounge.

This was yesterday at St. Anthony's Catholic Club, Scott and Howland Streets.

It was a very special lunch, one that will be remembered and recalled for as long as the St. Anthony's Club exists, because the guest of honor was "the Yankee Clipper" himself—Joltin' Joe Dimaggio, who was in town to address the annual St. Anthony's Sports Banquet at the Padua Cafetorium last night.

In Wilmington's Italian community, DiMaggio, the former New York Yankees center fielder who is in the Baseball Hall of Fame, is probably better known than George Washington, more admired than Babe Ruth, more popular than Pete Rose. If Joe's paisanos had it their way, they would nominate him for sainthood, which is probably the only honor that hasn't as yet been bestowed on him.

I sat at the table between DiMaggio and Los Angeles Dodgers' scout Ed Liberatore, the man responsible for bringing DiMag to Wilmington. I paid close attention to Joe's eating habits. Maybe, just maybe, I could spot DiMag reaching for the "red sauce" in the gallon jug in the middle of the table.

He didn't. "Joe didn't even have a sip of the wine," whispered Rudy Rubini, vice president of the club, who also does the food purchasing for the lounge's restaurant.

It wouldn't have been any big deal if DiMag imbibed. It's just that throughout his entire illustrious playing career in the majors (1936 to 1951, all with the Yankees) he had this Jack Armstrong All-American Boy image. He was never involved in fights, brawls, scandals, drinking bouts or carousing. He was always Mr. Clean, Mr. Good Guy, Mr. All America. And that's exactly how I found him to be yesterday.

169

Impeccably attired in a Navy-blue sports jacket with gold buttons, blue shirt, maroon tie, gray flannel slacks and black shoes, his white hair trimmed short and face exuding a healthy glow, DiMag projected the image of a perfect gentleman. But he did shatter two images I had of him.

First, there was this symbol I always had of him as a big coffee drinker. After all, didn't he make "Mr. Coffee" nationally famous via the TV ads in which he was featured?

Surprise!

"Mr. Coffee" passed up coffee at yesterday's lunch. He ordered a low calorie soft drink.

Surprise No. 2 was his demeanor. He had always been painted as a very private person, low key, not given to a lot of talk. I found him exactly the opposite.

DiMag was not only very talkative, but most cooperative and exceedingly warm. Three times he slapped me on the lap and asked me not to leave.

The American League's Most Valuable Player in 1939, 1941 and 1947 displayed a voracious appetite. He had two helpings of scrambled eggs with pepper and sausage, plus a piece of lasagna.

This it the first time I've eaten today," he confessed between bites. "It's a combination breakfast-lunch for me."

I asked him if this was his first trip ever to Wilmington?

"I don't have that much recollection of Wilmington," he frowned. "If you don't have a recollection of a place after a long time, you must've had a bad day."

I had been told that DiMaggio was here in 1943, appearing with Gypsy Rose Lee at the old Armory, 10th and Du Pont Streets, during a War Bond Drive. He was a sergeant in the Army then and auctioned off a baseball. But he couldn't recollect that occasion, explaining that he has visited so many places that it is difficult to recall any particular place.

Did he ever play an exhibition game with the Yankees at the old Wilmington Ball Park, as one long-time Wilmingtonian recalled?

"It's possible, but I'm not sure. It could've happened when we were coming north from Florida after spring training."

Asked what memento from his baseball career he cherished the most, he said it was a glove which he no longer has, but wished he did.

"It was a small glove, not much larger than the type you use to keep your hands warm in the winter. I had that thing sewed by a shoemaker at least a dozen times. I used it when I played in the (Pacific) Coast League and when I first went up to the majors. It was practically a rag. I wish I had it now. I could never find it. I don't think anyone would want to steal it. If anything, they'd want to throw it in the rubbish.

"My last days with the Yankees I used a glove that was pretty big, almost similar but not quite as big as the large gloves used today. What they use today, well they need something like that on the AstroTurf infields because the ball scoots awfully fast."

He said that he had never been thrown out of a game throughout his entire career and never was in any baseball-related brawls.

But there had to be at least a couple of brawls behind the scenes, which were never reported in print. Huh?

"Nope," he replied.

Well how about at least a violent argument with the manager, a coach or a teammate? Maybe just once?

"Nope," he shook his head and smiled.

And who was it that said, "nice guys finish last?" He'd better check out DiMag, who played in 10 World Series, won the American League batting championship twice and led the league in home runs twice (46 in 1937 and 39 in 1948).

Were there any questions asked by reporters that would gall him after a game?

"No, no," he waved his hand slightly. "During the time I was playing we didn't have that type of person (reporter) that you are talking about today, if you're talking about the present day. We had fellows (reporters) like Sid Murcer, Joe Williams, Hype Igoe, Jimmy Cannon. These fellows did their homework. We had so many guys (reporters) that knew their work and they didn't ask the embarrassing questions.

"These fellows were top writers at the time. Sure, they looked for little things to make stories more newsworthy. To me, they reported more of the game than today. Today, they probe more on the personal side, trying to get another angle."

DiMag wanted it made clear he wasn't taking a swipe at today's type of journalism, explaining: "It's completely all right. Times change, so do styles of reporting."

He gave high marks to friend Billy Martin, the battling manager who has made more pit stops in the role of skipper than A.J. Foyt during a 500-mile auto race.

I asked DiMaggio how he would rate Martin the Mauler as a manager on a scale of 1-to-10.

"As a strategist, I would have to say he is as good as anybody managing today. I'd have to put him at the top of the list, but if anybody tops him, they'd have to be even."

Did he regard his 56-game hitting streak as the No. 1 highlight of his career?

"There are so many things to think about, to pinpoint one achievement would be very difficult to do.

"Being in 10 World Series and on nine championship teams in 13 years, that to me is a great achievement. That is one of the most outstanding things, to be on championship teams. You know, some fellows play a whole lifetime without even smelling the roses."

And how would the Yankee Clipper like to be remembered?

"As it is right now," he said, a glow creasing his ruddy face. "As it has been going on for me for the last 28 years that I have been retired. It's nice to know people remember you. Kids come up to you and ask for autographs, saying they heard of me through reading books and from their fathers and grandfathers. Being well-received wherever I may be going. That's nice. That's the way I like to be remembered."

Still fit at 65, with not a trace of a protruding belly, DiMaggio said he keeps in shape through a rigorous schedule that keeps him constantly criss-crossing the United States "to keep business appointments, visit friends, play golf and make personal appearance at various functions." No, he said he doesn't diet and he doesn't engage in any physical exercise.

As he was exiting the St. Anthony's Club en route to his room at the Hotel Du Pont "to get some rest" before the evening's banquet, he was mobbed by admirers. Some were seeking an autograph, some were snapping his picture with instamatic cameras, and others were just wishing to touch him.

At this point, it was evident that he was beginning to show some signs of fatigue. But he didn't brush aside a single request, always obliging with a big smile.

Art Daloise, a smallish, gray-haired, bespectacled man, pushed two old Yankee photos in front of DiMaggio and asked if DiMag would autograph them. They were 8-by-10 glossies taken in 1937. One showed DiMag together with Tony Lazzeri, Frankie Crosetti and then Yankee owner Col. Jake Ruppert. The other was a team shot of the 1937 championship Yankee team.

DiMag flashed a big smile as he studied the two photos, then signed them.

"I worked for a beer distributor in 1937 who handled Ruppert's beer and he got these photos for me," said Daloise, who lives across from the St. Anthony's Club.

Proudly admiring the two photos signed by DiMag, Daloise clutched them to his chest. "Nobody can buy these pictures from me for any amount of money," he said.

Reprinted with the permission of The News Journal

According to Matt, the interview was a satisfying experience, in Fournier Hall with only a few cronies seated alone in the large dining room.

Matt said after two hours, when he was running out of tape for his recorder, he tried to end the interview.

"The only guys left at the table were Joe, Ed Liberatore and me," said Matt. "DiMag was going on, and we were talking about a lot of things. Liberatore, who was seated next to me, poked me in the ribs, and said, 'Joe has been speaking for a long time.' So I'm taking my tape recorder and unhooking it, and Joe tapped me on the leg and said, 'Don't go yet. Let's keep talking baseball, Matt.'

"The climax of this whole thing was, about a week later, Ed Liberatore calls me, and says, 'I've got a message for you from Joe. He enjoyed the interview, and he appreciated the fact that you did not ask anything about Marilyn Monroe.'

"So I got the message from Joe DiMaggio to me that he enjoyed the interview. He wanted to thank me for using tact and not asking anything about Marilyn Monroe. He had a reputation when he played with the Yankees as being aloof—a lot of his teammates looked at him in awe— he was big, he was really famous. And he was courteous, polite and extremely friendly."

Matt interviewing Joe DiMaggio at St. Anthony's Catholic Club dining room. (Photo provided by Nick Grossi)

Jack Ireland

Sports Reporter
The News Journal

As a Delaware native from Wilmington, Jack Ireland said he always used to read Matt's columns and stories.

"I met Matt in the early 1970s," he recalled. "I was working at the *Seaford Leader.* I may have talked to him before that. I tried to get a job at *The News Journal.* I had been working six years downstate, and we stayed in touch. I didn't get hired, but Matt would put in a good word every now and then. We would run into each other. He was my mentor. He told me never to give up and to keep trying to put my foot in the door, and he always gave me encouragement and said something that would help me out. When I had a good chance to get on as part-time news assistant, he helped me get the job."

One thing Matt told Ireland was to grab any opportunity to land a job at Delaware's largest newspaper.

"Matt said to me, 'If the opportunity comes up to do something, don't dismiss it.' He told me to tell the editor that I'd be willing to do anything."

Ireland followed the advice and got a job in the Dover bureau when Monty Martin resigned to take a similar position in the Midwest.

The News Journal finally offered him a job in Dover since Ireland knew the area. They told him it would be for a year, but he still wanted to get back to Wilmington. When Izzy Katzman retired 10 years later, the horse racing beat opened up.

"They said I had a chance to cover horse racing," Ireland said. "Matt said to me, 'You can do that.' He encouraged me to take a shot at it. I started covering horse racing in 1986. There were a lot of little things he did. He gave me advice. He said, 'You'll pick things up. You'll meet a lot of different characters.' I have had a lot of fun doing my horse racing column and stories over the years."

Ireland recalled that Matt was always busy, writing columns for both the *Morning News* and *Evening Journal* while also doing a fair amount of layout work.

"He always encouraged me," Ireland said. "Some others were not as understanding, but Matt was. Whenever he was in the slot, if he saw you did something wrong, he would tell you and you learned from that. He was very encouraging to younger guys. He would try to show you stuff. I struggled when I first went to the paper. Without saying anything, Matt would look at you, and you would just feel better.

"I might have made a different decision if it had not been for Matt. He always told me, 'You can handle it.' He's always been positive."

And, like others who worked near Matt's sports desk, Ireland referred to the stories Matt told and the way he told them.

"He had a great personality and was just fun to get along with," Ireland said of Zee. "Matt just seems to know the right time to come up with a funny or interesting story. It gives you a few minutes to relax, in what can be a stressful job, meeting deadlines and coming up with good stories for the paper.

"I think Matt just got better with age. I love the guy. He's great. He's good for the paper and good for the community. He has more energy than a lot of younger people. I am truly indebted to him. He's a wonderful human being."

Gary Smith   **Writer**
Sports Illustrated

From 1969-1973, between the ages of 16 and 20, Gary Smith worked with Matt Zabitka at Wilmington's *News Journal*. That introduction into the world of sports reporting was followed by seven years at the *Philadelphia Daily News*. Smith's freelance articles have appeared in *Life, Esquire, Rolling Stone* and the *Washington Post Sunday Magazine*. He has been writing for *Sports Illustrated* since 1982 and has won the National Magazine Award for Feature Writing three times.

As was the case with most sports pages readers, Smith said he was aware of Matt's work when the teenager arrived for his first night on the job as a part-time clerk at *The News Journal's* downtown Wilmington offices at Ninth and Orange streets.

"Matt was super," Smith recalled. "There were a few guys who worked in *The News Journal* sports department who had a tendency to spit sparks under deadline pressure, and a few guys who burrowed into their work and remained aloof, but Matt, from day one, made young guys such as me feel welcome.

"I was just a lowly clerk, handling racetrack agate, high school box scores and two-paragraph shorts, but he was never, never a big shot. You could slip over to him and quietly ask him anything you didn't understand, questions you would be afraid to ask other guys who were more volatile under pressure.

Paula Illingworth

He'd patiently explain to you. He kept his sense of humor under duress. He always seemed to have a smile and a wise crack—a genuinely warm person."

Smith said he vaguely recalled Matt losing his temper once or twice. While Smith couldn't remember the exact circumstances, he said it was never at the expense of someone in a lower position in relationship to Matt.

"He made everyone who called the sports department or who walked through its doors feel welcome, no matter how obscure or small-time the sport," Smith said. "He'd flip those earphones over his head and begin hunting-and-pecking on that typewriter, banging out his notes and asking questions with a genuine passion and curiosity. He just gave a damn about people, plain and simple. Every second or third question, he'd say something or hear something through those earphones that got him to cackling, sometimes even laughing so hard he'd nearly double over in his seat. Or he'd lean back from that typewriter and bellow, 'You're kiddin' me!' His interviews were loud. Every staffer in the room was well aware of every question he asked in that raspy voice.

"Now and then, he'd pull out his comb and slick back that hair—had to be the same style for 60 years. Those dang earphones never seemed to muss up that hair a lick, but he'd still pull out the comb and give it a quick once-over now and then, just in case, take another swallow of black coffee and go right back to the phones. If that headset of his isn't in the Delaware Sports Hall of Fame, it ought to be."

With Smith working in the same profession as Matt, one wonders if the older writer may have influenced the star sportswriter in any way.

"I don't think that Matt's work influenced mine," Smith said, "but his ability to retain his zest for covering local high school athletics over so many years astonishes me. I have great admiration for that. I also greatly appreciate and respect Zee for how much at home he made me and a great many other young guys at *The News Journal* feel. He made it fun to be in that room at 10:49 p.m., when the gun was at your head and a stack of high school box scores and shorts were piled up on your desk. He made the business one that I could love and see myself doing the rest of my life.

"The older I get, the more I appreciate people who find a way to keep alive their zest for life, for work, for people, their capacity to be like a child—hell, to be silly. Matt could be gloriously silly."

As one might imagine, Matt had several memories of Gary Smith. After the former news clerk's bylines began to appear in national publications, Matt wrote a column that offered Wilmington readers insight into the background of the up-and-coming, prize-winning writer.

The News Journal

April 8, 1989   Wilmington, Del.

Gary Smith has come a long way
as a sportswriter

BY MATT ZABITKA

In a recent edition of *Sports Illustrated*, Donald J. Barry, in his "From the Publisher" commentary, wrote:

"Boxing has long attracted exemplary American writers, including Ernest Hemingway, Jack London, Norman Mailer and Joyce Carol Oates. Before he's through, special contributor Gary Smith may rank with the best of them as a chronicler of the sweet science.

"Indeed Oates herself says, 'That Muhammad Ali piece (SI, April 25, 1988) was brilliant. Oh, and that extraordinary one in which he led Mike Tyson into saying those amazing things was even more striking (SI, March 21, 1988). I can't praise this man highly enough. He represents boxing writing at its very best.'"

Are they really talking about the same Gary Smith I knew? A shy, soft-spoken, well-mannered young man I first got to know when he worked as a night clerk, at $2.50 an hour, in The News Journal sports department while attending Dickinson High?

Yep. The same guy.

Looking back, it's almost unbelievable that Smith today is being tossed in the same writing arena with such heavyweights as Ernest Hemingway, Jack London and Norman Mailer.

I vividly recall the first story Smith turned in. It was two paragraphs on a CYO kid basketball game. It contained a myriad of errors in grammar and punctuation. I know. I was on the desk as make-up editor that night.

In those days, as a clerk, Smith's job didn't include writing. His job was to handle race results off the wire machines and take results of games over the phone and turn over the notes to a full-time staffer.

One particular night, after taking some game notes over the phone, he turned the notes over to experienced writer Bill Schellhammer. Schellhammer, occupied with another story, blew a gasket.

"Damn it, you're a junior in high school and should be able to compose a two-graph story. Write it yourself," Schellhammer snapped.

Smith, taken aback at the outburst, did just that. It was bad. I should've saved it for posterity and gotten him to autograph it now.

177

Today, the 36-year-old son of former Dickinson High Vice Principal Harry Smith, ranks with the best sports writers in the U.S., maybe in the world.

He has honed his skills sharper than a Gillette blade. He strings words tighter like a jeweler strings together a necklace of pure pearls. His descriptions are explicit, extraordinary.

His brilliance started to surface at The News Journal as he was given more opportunities to write. Probably his first gem was an assignment to test security at Delaware's racetracks, to see if he could gain entrance to stable areas without being detected. He succeeded at every track and wrote about it.

I remember when, as a clerk handling race-wire results, he got interested in horse racing. Together, we went to Harrington Raceway one evening.

The track refused Smith permission to the clubhouse because he wasn't wearing a dress jacket. So that we could be seated together in the clubhouse, the track loaned Smith a green jacket bearing the Harrington track logo over a breast pocket.

Seated at a table in the front row of the clubhouse, he and I would handicap the standardbreds. Smith would get up to go to the mutual windows before each race and always asked if I wanted him to also place my bets.

From the glass partition that separated the grandstand from the clubhouse where we were seated, it might have appeared to fans that Smith, because he was wearing an official track jacket, was my runner. We joked about that on the ride back to Wilmington.

Today, Gary Smith might be able to buy Harrington Raceway and not be concerned about wearing a dress jacket to gain admission to the clubhouse.

I'm very happy for the success he has achieved. I can always boast of having known him way back when . . . when he wasn't touted as another Ernest Hemingway.

Reprinted with the permission of The News Journal

Recalling Gary Smith, Matt said, "He [Gary] said he didn't make that many errors. It was exaggeration. You exaggerate for the purpose of getting something across. Look where the hell I am. I'm nowhere. Gary made it big. Gary Smith said he saved the article. He even brought it up when he was in Australia for the Olympics. There's Gary sitting on top of the world. He wrote for the *New York Daily News.* He's made a really big reputation, but he's still the same shy guy. But he listens. He doesn't bluff.

Some people don't know anything abut a certain subject, but they bluff their way through it. He doesn't do that.

"You can tell when someone's bluffing right away. Gary was on a television talk show one night, and he said, 'I don't know much about that. Why don't you ask somebody else?' How many guys with his reputation would do that? They would just say something, bluff their way."

Chuck Lewis   Executive Director
The Center for Public Integrity

Chuck Lewis was back home in Newark to visit his mother and to be honored by his alma mater, the University of Delaware, for his outstanding professional achievement in the fields of communication and public policy. The Newark High School graduate had just completed a signing of his latest book—*The Cheating of America*—at Rainbow Books and Music.

Taking a seat on a couch in the back of the store, the former *60 Minutes* producer was genuinely excited to sit back and talk about Matt Zabitka "Zee"—the first of three mentors in his life. The other two, Lewis said, are University of Delaware political science professor James R. Soles and well-known television newsman and interviewer Mike Wallace.

Lewis described Matt as "one of my favorite people in the world." In the summer of 1971, when Lewis arrived at *The News Journal* sports department, the first person he met was "Zee."

"Matt was the first famous person I ever met," Lewis said. "Matt took an interest in me. He was a mentor. I'm grateful today."

Lewis spoke about the time he asked Matt's advice about writing a column. The young aspiring writer had become bored with short fillers and box scores. He was interested in getting noticed and wanted to produce a column that would be the talk of the town.

"Matt looked at me and said, 'You really want to do this? Shake things up? You want controversy?' and I said, 'Yeah.' And Matt said, 'All right. You've got to write things that have the ability to piss people off. Find out what people care about.' "

Lewis said he took Matt's advice and interviewed semi-pro baseball coach and

Center for Public Integrity

area sports icon John Hickman. In the column, Hickman made several disparaging remarks about the athletic ability of softball players, inferring that those who played the big-balled sport were inferior to hardball athletes.

"I wrote it and, oh my God, the letters came in. I went on WDEL and WILM," Lewis said, recalling the controversy surrounding his attention-grabbing column.

Soon after the story hit the papers and the buzz was in the area, Lewis said, Matt stopped the younger writer and said, "I think you found the right formula, there, Chuck."

As a result of that piece, Lewis was given his own column. He recalled typing his stories at a desk beside Matt. Apparently his affection for the older writer was obvious, and eventually, other staffers began referring to the two of them as Big Zee and Little Zee.

Lewis has a picture of Matt on the wall of his office in Washington, D.C., a short walk from the Capitol Building.

Visitors sometime ask him about the characters featured within the frame. He said the picture reminds him of those years from 1971 to 1975, when he worked in the sports department of a city newsroom, one of the last all-male bastions before women had entered the field.

"It was a lot like a fraternity," Lewis said. "We'd play baseball in the office, pitching paper wads glued or taped up tightly, swinging yardsticks and other metal implements we could find from composing, pull pranks and practical jokes. Sometimes Matt was the brunt of the jokes, and sometimes he'd participate in the pranks. But Matt never bitched and moaned. He was a steady performer, like clockwork. He was like an iron man, like baseball's Lou Gherig. He never complained."

After Lewis left the newspaper and worked in television reporting, he kept in touch with Matt through letters and Christmas cards. Their association continues. Whenever Lewis releases a new book, a personalized copy arrives in Matt's mailbox.

One Saturday morning, Matt proudly showed off Lewis' latest book to visitors in his home, then spoke fondly of his young friend with whom he had worked nearly three decades ago.

When Lewis quit *60 Minutes,* he wrote an eight-page, single-space letter to Matt, explaining his frustration and detailing why he had decided to move on. Lewis said he did so because he wanted to share his reasoning with someone he trusted. He respected Matt's judgment, and he wanted Matt to know that he wasn't a quitter. To Lewis it was important that his mentor understand the reasons for his life-changing decision. Lewis and others have described Matt as an "institution," but not simply because of the length of time he has worked. More importantly, Matt is known and respected because of the way that he worked.

"Matt was the Rock of Gibraltar," Lewis said. "Everyone loved Matt. No one ever had a bad word to say about him, because he was genuine and dependable. He didn't play politics, and he would always be encouraging."

From 'Delaware People'

In the Oct. 15, 2001, "Delaware People" *News Journal* column, Zee referred to the period during the mid-70s and early '80s "when a lot of fine, young talent was spawned in *The News Journal* sports department. He mentioned Gary Smith, who went to *Sports Illustrated*, Mike Sisak and Marty Gradel who went to *The News York Times,* Gene Quinn, who became executive sports editor of the *Chicago Tribune* and Caesar Alsop and Bill Fleischman, both at the *Philadelphia Daily News.*

But Matt singled out Chuck Lewis, presenting his readers with an overview of how Lewis ascended journalism's ladder of success.

"Today, Lewis is the founder and executive director of the Center for Public Integrity, a non-profit, non-partisan research organization that concentrates on ethics and public service issues. Lewis is also a hard-hitting author. He has authored four investigative books, the first two entitled *The Buying of the Congress* and *The Buying of the President* [1996 and 2000], in which he pulls no punches. . . .

"Chuck Lewis was a softball columnist and general sports news reporter during his teens and early 20s at *The News Journal*. Now he has become a "knockout puncher" in Washington, D.C., the political ring version of Madison Square Garden."

During the Newark interview, Lewis said, "I had a feeling Matt wasn't respected as much as some of the other reporters. He had never gone to college. But he was the top performer and important to the community. His columns always had people's names in them. You'd see 20 names in a single column. He cared about getting names in the paper. No one anywhere in America cared this much about people as Matt."

Vince Hyland Sr.   University of Delaware 1979 Division II National Championship Football Team

"Matt made me famous, and he did the same for my son, Vincent Jr." Hyland Sr. said. "Over the years, Matt has been great for people. One thing about Matt, whether you stayed at home or went away, Matt would find you. He goes out of his way. He digs up guys and lets you know what is going on in their life."

Vince Sr. played cornerback at Delaware, and, he said, Matt never seems to forget who people are or what position they played.

"He recently wrote a column about me and my son," Vince Sr. said. "He compared us. They sent a photographer out and took some pictures of Vince Jr. and me. For the next two weeks, after the column ran, everybody who saw the article told me about it. This was great, because a lot of people had lost track of me. It was nice also, because it let a lot of people know about my son, who played guard and forward for Concord High School. He graduated in May 2001."

Vince Sr. now works at Chrysler/Damlier, making Durangos, but his memories of Saturday afternoon on the field at Delaware Stadium are as close as the sports complex is to his worksite.

"Playing on that UD team was an incredible experience, it was like family," Vince Sr. said. "Some people say that you get your 15 minutes of fame, well, I think we all got something from that experience that lasts a whole lot longer. It was an incredible run (1979) with an incredible record. Tubby Raymond and his staff are great. You could take them and put them in any college and they would be winners. He's a genius.

"If we were in trouble at half, you know that Coach Raymond and his staff would make the necessary adjustments. Playing for that team did a lot for me.

"I have heard it said that being a part of greatness, no matter how briefly, always remains with you. No matter where you go or what goes on in your life, you can look back and draw on those situations."

Vince Sr. recalled playing Youngstown State in 1978, which came to be known as the "Shootout at Youngstown." The Hens were down at the half by 37-7, but won the game by a score of 51-45.

"That is a lesson that I cherish," he said. "That lesson, that I also tell my son, is that no matter how far down you are, if you keep on trying and have a positive attitude, things will work out."

To Vince Sr., getting that message across to others is important, and reporters like Matt serve that purpose well. Sports reporting is more than passing along statistics and scores.

"Matt is a great guy," Vince Sr. said. "He is a straight shooter. He asks the nice questions and the tough ones also. He is very candid and honest, and you really feel like he is a friend. You know he is going to write it just as you say it. Sometimes, when people have a certain success, they get a little above themselves. Not Matt.

"Matt Z is a Delaware icon. No matter where you go, or who you talk to, if you mention Matt, they know who you are talking about. Everybody knows Matt," Vince Sr. said.

Every fan and player in Delaware Stadium knew Matt Z was present in the spring of 1978, as the Hens were preparing for the coming fall season.

Along the sidelines, directing the Delaware White/defense through the annual spring Blue-White Game, was acting head coach Matt Zabitka. It's an experience that Matt, the coaches and the team members would remember for years to come. As an added bonus, Matt said, his appearance on the sidelines also gave many of his readers a chance to direct boos at one of their local sports columnists.

The News Journal

May 8, 1978   Wilmington, Del.

Blue Hen coach-for-a-day
grilled by angry fans
By Matt Zabitka

Less than three minutes remained before the half in Saturday's game that climaxed University of Delaware's 20-day spring football program. My White team was leading 17-6 over the Blue, coached by colleague Tom Tomashek.

My team had a fourth-and-three situation on the Blues' 12, or thereabouts.

Ed Maley, the Blue Hens' veteran linebacker coach, who was also on the White coaching staff, asked what I wanted to call.

"We've got the foot (George Pachucy), let's go for the automatic three points," I told Mal.

When the field goal "team" went out, the boos from the fans in the stands started slowly and lightly. As the jeers cascaded from the area of the press box, some 52 rows up and rolled down, they increased in tempo and volume. The crescendo grew into a giant stereophonic snowball and rolled right out of the stands and hit me like a tidal wave.

The fans were vocally expressing themselves as to what they thought of my coaching decision. Evidently, they felt being so close to the end zone, I should have tried for a first down or gone for a TD.

Maley, my chief adviser during the two days I was in the Blue Hen country, broke into a chuckle when he heard my name being used in

183

vain amidst the boos. "Look, when you're a coach you've go to expect that," winked Maley, referring to the jeering.

After Pachucy, a 6-foot-1, 190-pounder from Olyphant, Pa., easily executed a 23-yard field goal, his second of the half, the jeering subsided. My team took a 20-6 lead. I looked like a genius, and right then and there I was thinking about applying for Tubby Raymond's job as head coach.

But my ego was soon to be deflated when one of my White players questioned the decision for a field goal try, even after it was made. "Coach, you're a newspaperman and I thought all newspapermen were gamblers. So why didn't you gamble for a first-down or a touchdown?" 6-2, 241-pound offensive tackle Dan Riordan of Drexel Hill, Pa., asked. Dandy Dan wasn't sarcastic. He was just being inquisitive. And the polite way he addressed me as "Coach," I was ready to nominate him for Little All-American honors, even before the 1978 season starts.

I explained to Dan that we had a lead, that time was running out and we had a superfoot in Pachucy, who was an automatic three from that distance.

But the some 1,300 fans at Delaware Stadium had the last laugh before the initial half ended, when a play spilled over the sidelines into the area where I was standing and upended me . . . clipboard, sunglasses and all. I still feel Raymond called that play from the press box, steering it directly at me on the sidelines in retaliation for some of the nasty things I had said about him in the past. Fortunately, the only thing that was bruised in the spill was my ego.

My "Advisor," Maley, who was an outstanding tackle on Delaware's 1954-55-56 teams also pinched my ego. Mal asked if I wanted to address the White squad in the locker room before the game. When I said I did, Mal's face turned white as the jerseys my players were wearing. Evidently, he had been forewarned about my loquacity. "Okay," he said hesitantly, "but keep it short. You don't have to give them a Knute Rockne or Vince Lombardi type of talk." Mal requested I keep it to one minute; I gave them 2 1/2, maybe three. "Very well said," offensive backs coach John D'Ottavio, also on the White staff, said, shaking my hand after the brief talk. And that to me was like winning a Pulitzer Prize for the best pre-game talk in college spring football within a radius of five miles of Newark.

For me, it was a most interesting and illuminating two-day experience, looking inside the guts of the Wing T with the help of a bunch of real pros.

From my ringside observations, I want to forecast at this early date that the 1978 Fightin' Blue Hens are going to be extremely exciting to watch.

In the 5-11, 185 Ivory Sully and Gary Gumbs, the Hens have their human versions of Alydar and Affirmed. They don't really travel faster than sound, but they sure look like they do.

And Jeff Komlo at quarterback looks like a real winner in this his senior year. The Maryland whippet definitely figures to be a contender for Little All-American laurels.

One athlete who gets this "coach's" seal of approval as "the player to watch" is speedy Lou Mariani, a 6-0, 164-pound junior-to-be from Jessup, Pa. Larrupin' Lou, with his speed, move and guts, has the makings of a super back.

And the Hens this fall will be studded with state scholastic products. There's a ton of 'em, a lot of goodies like Tom Liszkiewicz, Joe and Jim Booth, Craig Swank, Vance Belcher, Bob Reed, Steve Baston, Gary Sterndale, Mike Young, Jim Baker, Mike Wisniewski, Vince Hyland, Jay Hooks, etc., etc., etc.

Reprinted with the permission of The News Journal

During an interview in the spring of 2001, Delaware Head Coach Tubby Raymond didn't mention anything about directing his player toward Matt's location during the 1978 spring Blue-White game and upending Matt on the sidelines. The legendary college coach did say he had great respect for Matt's fairness and described him as, "a real workman, a guy who did his job everyday right on the button.

"Matt stayed with it through all the good and bad times," Raymond said. "I have a great deal of respect for that. His love and commitment to athletics and the people that play sports have been remarkable."

Kevin Tresolini

Sports Reporter
The News Journal

Kevin Tresolini joined *The News Journal* sports department in the summer of 1981. Having grown up in Bethlehem, Pa., and graduated from the University of Delaware, Tresolini said he had a passing knowledge of the local sports scene. He knew of Matt Zabitka and the paper's other writers through their bylines. But it wasn't long before Matt made his presence known.

"One of the things that struck me immediately when I started at *The News Journal* in my early 20s," Tresolini said, "was I knew I had to soak up this guy, who was in his early 60s at the time—because I thought he probably wouldn't be doing this much longer. And he's still here. I was impressed with Matt's knowledge then, and he continues to impress me with his professionalism and energy. He just doesn't seem to tire.

"I admire his knowledge of the area. That is extremely important for a local paper, which must have a thorough knowledge of its audience and readers. If your sports section shows an unfamiliarly with its people and sports, your credibility is gone."

Tresolini said he and other younger writers continue to find Matt's contacts and memory invaluable.

Offering a recent example of Matt's assistance, Tresolini said he was assigned a feature on local football players who had a connection with the Army-Navy Game during times of war.

"The first thing I did was yell, 'Zee!' " Tresolini said, smiling at the memory. He said Matt paused a few seconds and said, "There was a kid from Mt. Pleasant. He was a center. He played for Navy. It was in the last 25 years."

Based on Matt's clues, Tresolini found a lead and conducted a phone interview with a Delawarean living in California who had been Roger Staubach's center.

"Zee was right on the money," Tresolini said, adding that Matt may have not had the player's precise name and game date, but the older writer's information saved hours of research.

"I can name anybody from 1980-81 on," Tresolini said, "but with Zee we can go back further. He's an historian sitting at a desk right in our newsroom. You throw out a name and he'll have a story, about local athletes and the nationally known players who came through town."

Matt proudly acknowledges his recognition as News Journal *Employee of the Month.*

186

When asked to use a word or two to describe Matt, Tresolini said, "He's a classic, a throwback in his diligence and his interest in people, not so much issues, but people—what they've done and who they are and what their histories are. We won't see many like him again. That he's done this for so long, and so well, is just amazing."

Tresolini particularly enjoyed talking about Matt's telephone interviewing techniques. Explaining that since Matt conducts all his work over the telephone, and his voice has a gruff, booming quality, other newsroom staff members get to hear Matt's side of the conversations.

When leaving a message, Tresolini said, Matt uses words to spell out his name. This is done so often that the office is familiar with the routine.

Tresolini said, "Matt will say, 'M like Mother, A like Animal, T like Tom, Z like Zebra, A like Anna, B like Boy, I like Indian, T like Tom, K like Killer and A like Albert.'

"The other day he was on the phone," Tresolini recalled, laughing, "and said, 'M like MURDER.' Five of us burst out laughing we were so surprised. He had never used MURDER before."

Tresolini mentioned fond memories playing on *The News Journal* softball team—called the ZeeStars—that was named after Matt. It started in 1983, first as a pickup team and then as a Sunday Only League entry and also played games against newspaper and radio station teams. "I idolize the man," Tresolini said. "He's such a wonderful example to sportswriters young and old, just with his enthusiastic and thorough approach to his work.

"When I first met him, he immediately struck me as the classic sportswriter. If they were going to do a movie about Matt's life, it's a shame that Walter Matthau died, because he could play Matt—with a cigar hanging halfway out of his mouth, banging on a typewriter, talking on the phone and working late into the night."

CHAPTER 10

On Writing and the Business of Sports

'The biggest changes are all related to money, the financial end of the business. Years ago, a top player would make thousands, today they're millionaires. Money is so damn big. . . . But what's still the same with baseball is, as always, there are three outs every inning, three strikes and you're out, and four balls and you walk.'

—*Matt Zabitka*

T
hroughout his career, people have asked Matt about writing and interviewing, plus his perspective on changes that have taken place in the big business of sports. Here are his answers to some of these questions.

Why did you decide to write about sports?

Because I was weaned on sports. That's what we did in those days to keep busy, for recreation. There was no television. My first football game we couldn't afford shoulder pads, so we wore three sweaters for padding. I was on a neighborhood club team as a teenager, playing at 15th and Highland Avenue, an open field. We would play anytime we had the chance, even in the rain. There were no fans and only three or four on a side at times.

There was no game clock. But St. Hedwig's Polish church, at 4th and Hayes Street in Chester, was about a quarter-mile away.

So we agreed beforehand to play until the church bells rang. They always rang at 6 o'clock. That would signal the end of the game.

We'd play baseball all day. We'd walk everywhere with bats and balls to play a game. Sometimes, when we would lose, we'd sit in our bedrooms and cry. We took it really seriously.

When I was growing up, I never saw a golf club. That was for the rich. I never played golf until I came to *The News Journal.*

When I was 16, I organized the Chester Morning Basketball League. In the wintertime we needed a place to play indoors. I suggested Douglass Junior High School. They asked who would be responsible in case of vandalism or if something got damaged. I said, "I would," and I signed the papers. I had no job. I was a freshman in high school. I had no money.

After I got out of the service, I organized the Delaware County Pinochle League. I put a notice in the paper, attended meetings of the policemen, firemen, Lions Club, got them all to sponsor teams, and I had never played pinochle.

Different clubs would host the matches, and set up food and sandwiches and beer for them and the visiting teams. Then there was a big banquet at the end, all the teams playing the same night at the Congoleum Nairn Cafeteria in Linwood. More than 100 men were involved in the league, participating on teams.

It was a good way to meet people. The banquet at the end was hilarious as hell. I was the toastmaster, and we'd have contests. People would sing, tell jokes, whatever came up at the spur of the moment.

[In addition to the pinochle group and morning basketball league, Matt also founded and organized Suburban Major Basketball Association, Suburban Major Football League, South Chester Twilight Baseball League, Leatherbelt Boxing Tourney, Soap Box Derby, Delaware County Girls Softball League, Chester Morning Baseball League and Delco Valley Jr. Baseball League.]

How did you learn to write?

I always had an interest in reading and writing, but I didn't go to any special school for writing. When you write a lot it comes naturally. You read a lot.

When I was doing make-up and writing at the paper, I had to visit a person, sit with the guy, finish the interview and then write the story rapidly. There was a lot of pressure on you, but that taught you how to get things done.

Can you share some of your techniques?

When I call somebody, I'll ask "What's your height and weight?" and they'll say, "What's that got to do with it?" But if they're 5 foot 2, or 7 foot 8, that may be a story. I'm looking for an angle. I'll ask 200 questions and only use some of the answers. I'll only use the answers that will go into a readable, interesting story.

Preparation is important in writing. Research. Before you do any interview, you should do your homework; find out about the person. Know all you can before you meet with him or her and start asking questions. That saves a lot of time. It reveals you have taken an interest in your subject.

You should be prepared for any assignment. Al Cartwright would always say, "Wear a necktie and a jacket when you come in, because you don't know where you are going to be sent or what you are going to cover."

How do you know what to look for or what to write about?

I look around the house, at the furniture, at the pictures. Is the place neat, does anything stand out? How does it look to me? I concentrate on the person's appearance. Is the hair white as snow? Does he wear glasses? How is his speech? I try to get a good description of the person. I look at him or her intently and do a study.

You try to put the person at ease so he or she will pour out their heart to you.

Talking about memorabilia is helpful. With Whitey Witt, who played outfield with Babe Ruth in the '20s, I met him in his old farmhouse in New Jersey. He lived by himself. I asked him if he had a scrapbook or any items from the old days.

He asked me if I wanted a beer. I said, "No. I'm working." He reached under the sink that was covered with a curtain, and pulled out a fifth of liquor. He said, "This is my good stuff. When Goose Goslin [a neighbor and former major leaguer] comes over, he's my friend, he mooches like hell. I hide the booze down there and offer him beer."

Whitey told me about the Blue Laws, when there were no Sunday games. No night games. After Saturday afternoon games in Philly, he would put up a tent in his yard. A lot of the ballplayers from the Yankees and the A's would come down to the tent and shoot craps until Monday morning. They had a spit with a pig roast outside. They were big social affairs. They'd gamble and eat, sometimes all weekend, into Monday morning.

He also talked about Babe Ruth. He played with Babe and he liked him a lot. Whitey said Babe used to have a good time, drinking and partying out on the town on some nights before a game. He would show up and not be able to run too fast in the outfield. Whitey used to cover for the Babe and catch fly balls in Babe's area, which the Babe was too slow to bag.

After the article came out, Whitey sent me a note on a ragged sheet of paper saying, "I enjoyed that column. If you want to write any more about me, let me know."

What do you like about writing?

It's an ego trip in a way, knowing that people are reading what you wrote and responding to it through letters and calls. It's like being an actor on a stage. When the audience applauds a line, it encourages him to continue. I'm not performing on a stage, but the things I write go out before the public.

You're hanging your wash on a clothesline where everyone can see it. In all professions everyone doesn't see and evaluate what you do. Usually, only a person's boss sees what he does and comments on a person's performance. In this job, everything can be judged by anyone reading the newspaper.

Did you ever get any comments from readers?

For most of my career my accent was on local people. When famous people came to Delaware or Delaware County, Pa., I'd interview them.

Sometimes I got telephone calls from people thanking me, and others complaining about something I wrote that they didn't like. They'd complain about things like, "You always favor public schools, not parochial." Then the next day I'd get calls saying just the opposite, that I wrote more about parochial schools.

They also tell me to put this in and that in, and I'd say, "Hey! I'm doing a story and not a paid advertisement!"

If you want to attract attention, just write something like, "I think it's time for Tubby [Raymond, University of Delaware head football coach] to retire," or something like that. You are going to get all kinds of comments, agreeing and heatedly disagreeing with you.

There was a guy, Bernie McCormick, who graduated from LaSalle. He worked for a weekly paper somewhere before he came to the *Delaware County Daily Times*. After a while, he got the opportunity to write a column every week. After the column appeared, he would run down to the first floor and check with the mailman before they distributed the daily mail.

He was looking for letters to him. Then, he would come upstairs with all the letters for the sports department. He would put a pile of mail on my desk. It was for me. None for him.

He said, "How do you get all this mail? I'm writing good columns and I'm not getting anything."

I said, "Do you want mail?"

He said, "Yeah, that's why I write columns. I want to get mail! I want to hear from readers!"

"Well," I said, "write something controversial. Write a column about Little Leaguers, for example, about how coaches are using them. That they are ruining the pitchers' arms, the arms are going bad before they even get to high school."

He wrote a column about that. Boy, did he get letters. People not only wrote letters, managers of Little League teams came in person to the office to berate him. That's when he turned to me and pleaded, "How do you stop this?"

You know how you can tell people read you? Make mistakes, errors, give the wrong dates. Say a guy hit a single, instead of a home run. Make a big error. Or just miss something important. Even make a slight mistake in punctuation or spelling and they will call you right away. That is, if they're reading you.

Most times, if it's fluff and nice stuff, they won't call. But people will call right away if they disagree with you. They will find the time to berate you, tell you what teed them off.

Why is it important to spotlight athletes from previous years?

As the years pass, people forget about the achievements made years ago. To an older person, who had an outstanding career, being remembered is important. As athletes, they loved the limelight and they miss it. To them the publicity means more than for a kid who's playing sports today, because they're young, active and still making news.

Look at Michael Jordan. He misses the adulation. That's why he wants to make a comeback. It's not for the money, he doesn't need the money. He wants the attention of the fans and the crowds.

A lot of the boxers miss the attention, because now someone else is the champion in their place. When you can put them back in the spotlight, even for a few days, a few minutes, they enjoy that and relive their memories all over again. With the aging population in Delaware, I suggested a column that would spotlight former athletes. I think it would attract a wide readership.

What was it like before computers?

You wrote the story on a typewriter, put it in a plastic tube and sent it to the linotype department on the second floor. That's where they set the type. That was back in the '50s and early '60s, not today.

Right now, I'm on my third computer in 15 years.

Before, you could feel the pulse of the newsroom, with the typewriters banging away. Now, with computers, the news room is like an insurance company office, where you are filing claims. The only thing is that now, you can write more, because it's so easy to make changes to the story without difficulty. It's much easier with a computer than using a typewriter.

There's no paper. Before, you would find paper flying all over the place, but now, you don't see that. You write more—faster. You make corrections right there on your computer. You are now your own proofreader.

I remember Bill Frank, a *News Journal* veteran of some 40 years. He was still there when they went with the first computer. He wrote an entire column blasting computers. He hated them.

When we got the first computers, they gave us lessons. It was easy for the guy giving the lessons. He knew everything. He was a pro. He was going so fast, you couldn't keep up with him.

I told my wife, "I'll never learn this damn thing." She said, "Stick with it." I kept saying, "I'll never learn. There are so many new things to learn." Once I became acclimated with the computer, I loved it. I said, "This is great! I'd never want to go back to a typewriter."

After I learned to use the first computer, here comes a new one, more sophisticated. I said, "I'll never learn how to use this one."

Well, we got a third set of computers. These are the most sophisticated of all. They have so many buttons and combinations. You might be typing a story, and if you press the wrong button, you could wipe out the entire story you are writing.

I said, "All I want to know was how you sign on, send the story and sign off." I've since learned much more.

How has sports changed over the years?

The biggest changes are all related to money, the financial end of the business. Years ago, a top player would make thousands, today they're millionaires. Money is so damn big. A number one player used to make big money, today a player gets $1 million right off the bat when he signs, and sometimes much more.

Baseball franchises that used to cost a million dollars 30 years ago, today they go for $200 million and more. As the price of teams and salaries go up, ticket prices go up, too.

I saw my first major league game when my older brother, Steve, took me to Philadelphia, to Shibe Park. It was played in the afternoon. There were no night games then, that's another big change—night games. We sat in the left field peanut gallery, and we could see a game for 50 cents. Ice cream used to be 5 cents, now it's $1.50. You could get a good box seat for a Phillies game for $5, now it's an astronomical price.

Years ago, they went to artificial surfaces, something new, AstroTurf. Now some new ballparks are reverting to grass. New ballparks today are like shrines. They have private boxes with refrigerators, private catering. It has changed completely.

But what's still the same with baseball is, as always, there are three outs every inning, three strikes and you're out, and four balls and you walk. The least changes in the game have been in baseball. More changes have been made in football and basketball.

Why have you continued working full time?

People ask me, "Why do you keep working?"

I talked to a lot of people who've retired, and they say, "Don't stop until you're forced to stop or are forced to retire because of a physical disability, or your company has a rule that you must retire at a certain age."

I enjoy work. I have enthusiasm for it.

I like to work and I get paid a decent salary. I think of ideas while I'm driving in the car, thinking of people to call. A lot of my peers I see now look like they're lost or don't have anything to do. Writing is what I like to do. At my age, if I wasn't doing this I'd probably be scrubbing my kitchen floor, which I still do, occasionally.

When I was a kid, I would make up the box score sheet, write a game summary and walk to the *Chester Times* six miles away to deliver the story and scores. That was long before I decided I would be working there one day.

Matt shared a few interesting interviews

Middletown football

When I came here [*News Journal*] during the football season of 1962, Bill Billings [Middletown High School football coach] had just started coaching in Delaware. Then they started winning, putting together one of the longest high school winning streaks in the country.

I had a story in *Crossroads*, not too long ago, about one Newark-Middletown game. How, about 1 o'clock in the afternoon, people were looking forward to the game and looking for seats—and the game was to be played that night. People were sitting in trees for a good vantage point. Interest in Middletown football was like an out-of-control August brushfire.

Where is he now?

One year, I covered the major league All-Star Game in Connie Mack Stadium. I sat behind the dugout. That's where many of the sportswriters sat, with a plank of wood placed across the front of the seats on which to write. A little guy was pitching for the American league—Bobby Shantz, 5' 5 or 5' 6. Tremendous fastball, a really good fielder. He struck out the National League's top three hitters in a row. In later years, just on the spur of the moment, I decided to track down Bobby Shantz, find out what he was doing today.

He had been in a partnership in a bowling alley on the outskirts of Philadelphia. I said, "What are you doing now?" He said, "I got this hot dog and ice cream stand."

I said, "What are you doing this very moment?" He said, "I'm frying hamburgers."

Bucket of Blood

I was the beat writer for the Blue Bombers. I traveled with the team. They played home games Sunday nights at Salesianum. They used to call the gym the "Bucket of Blood" because of the many fights that erupted there from close contact.

The Bombers were in the Eastern Professional Basketball League, which introduced the three-point field goal. The NBA always frowned on it, but the Eastern Basketball League came in and did it first. They had a guy from Allentown, George Lehman. He was fantastic with three pointers. He was the best in the league.

When the Bombers played, you could almost predict before the game there were going to be fights. It was a good league, but very rough.

There was a game when one player plowed into a fan. They started fighting. The player said the fan was picking on the player's wife and making derogatory comments.

That resulted in a big free-for-all, blood flying. They had to stop the game and get the janitor with the bucket and a mop to sop up the blood. So that's where the term came from.

Another time, there was such a big melee they had all 10 players on the floor in a pyramid of bodies. They had to call in extra police.

One final question

Talk about a rough interview. It was at the Salesianum Sports Banquet, which is held every year. That's where they honor senior athletes. They walk in, it's really picturesque, all these young kids all wearing tuxedoes, sitting in the front of the dais.

One of the featured speakers was Greg Luzinski. The banquet started, and they are starting to serve food, and no Greg Luzinski showed up yet. Finally, he appeared wearing a red jacket. He had a lot of weight on him.

After the banquet, I walked up and asked, "Greg, do you have a few minutes for an interview?"

The interview is going good. He is answering everything, but one question, the last one, was: "What do you weigh, Greg?"

He said, "What the hell does that have to do with it?" I just folded my writing pad, thanked him and walked away. He was really pissed. The interview was going good, but once I asked him what he weighed, that was it.

That was probably the most talked about part of the interview. The weight.

After the story was published, readers called, thanking me for a good story, bringing up the weight part, which I used in the article.

What was your most embarrassing experience?

At a high school football banquet at a downstate school one year, I was the toastmaster. I was introducing all the guests at the head table, which included one female.

I asked the audience to give a great welcome to Mrs. Dave Nelson (the wife of the University of Delaware football coach at the time). No one applauded. The silence in the auditorium was broken up only by bits of stifled laughter. The man seated next to me at the head table whispered to me that the lady I was introducing was actually the wife of the school's head football coach.

After 10 or 15 seconds that seemed like 10 to 15 hours, I corrected myself and the audience erupted with applause. Mr. and Mrs. Dave Nelson were seated in the audience.

When did you know you wanted to be a sportswriter?

I always loved sports, loved to play them, loved to write about it. Years ago, when I had the flood in my basement, I had so many items that were destroyed. There was four-and-a-half feet of water down there. I had a big oak desk, filled with pictures and autographs, newspaper clippings. The water swelled the wooden drawers and I had to get an axe to chop them open. I pulled out clumps of paper, all stuck together and ruined.

One of the things I lost was my Chester High School *Annual*, a yearbook. Years later, I received a package in the mail from Norma Handloff, my former French teacher, who many years later became mayor of Newark. Inside was a copy of that annual. In a note she wrote me, she said, "Matt. You were the only one who knew what he wanted to be."

That's because underneath my picture in the book, where they write something about you, it reads, "Matt Zabitka. Future work: sports writer."

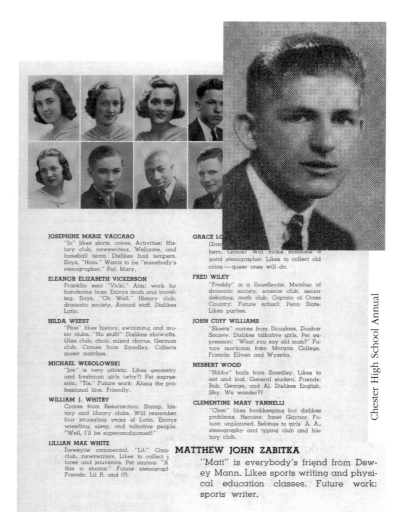

JOSEPHINE MARIE VACCARO
"Jo" likes skirts, cakes. Activities: History club, newswriters, Welcome, and baseball team. Dislikes bad tempers. Says, "Ham." Wants to be "somebody's stenographer." Pal: Mary.

ELEANOR ELIZABETH VICKERSON
Franklin sent "Vicki." Aim: work for handsome boss. Enjoys math and traveling. Says, "Oh. Well." History club, dramatic society, Annual staff. Dislikes Latin.

HILDA WEEST
"Pete" likes history, swimming and music clubs. "No stuff!" Dislikes show-offs. Glee club, choir, mixed chorus, German club. Comes from Smedley. Collects queer matches.

MICHAEL WESOLOWSKI
"Joe" is very athletic. Likes geometry and freshman girls (why?) Pet expression, "Tis." Future work: Along the professional line. Friendly.

WILLIAM J. WHITBY
Comes from Resurrection. Stamp, history and library clubs. Will remember four struggling years of Latin. Enjoys wrestling, sleep, and talkative people. "Well, I'll be superamalgamed!"

LILLIAN MAE WHITE
Deweyite commercial. "Lil." Cam-club, newswriters. Likes to collect 1 tures and souvenirs. Pet saying: "A this a shame." Future stenograph Friends: Lil R. and (?).

GRACE L[...]
Gra[...]
hero, Grace? Will make someone a good stenographer. Likes to collect old coins — queer ones will do.

FRED WILEY
"Freddy" is a Smedleyite. Member of dramatic society, science club, senior debating, math club. Captain of Cross Country. Future school: Penn State. Likes parties.

JOHN CUFF WILLIAMS
"Skeets" comes from Douglass. Dunbar Society. Dislikes talkative girls. Pet expression: "What you say old man?" Future mortician from Morgan College. Friends: Ellven and Wyzetta.

NESBERT WOOD
"Nibby" hails from Smedley. Likes to eat and loaf. General student. Friends: Bob, George, and Al. Dislikes English. Shy. We wonder??

CLEMENTINE MARY YANNELLI
"Clem" likes bookkeeping but dislikes problems. Heroine: Janet Gaynor. Future: unplanned. Belongs to girls' A. A., stenography and typing club and history club.

MATTHEW JOHN ZABITKA
"Matt" is everybody's friend from Dewey Mann. Likes sports writing and physical education classes. Future work: sports writer.

Chester High School Annual

The Last Word

Ed Okonowicz

When authors Ed Okonowicz and Jerry Rhodes first approached me relative to writing a book about me, I was flabbergasted, I mean really speechless with amazement.

While being flattered, I wanted to know why me? I really hadn't done anything to merit being the subject of a book.

And what prompted them to single me out?

Then the truth came out.

One of my dear grandsons, Bobby McCreary, whose exploits I followed from the day he broke in as a catcher with a baseball team in the Brandywine Youth Organization, in which he also played football, and my loving daughter, Shirley Ann McCreary, pushed the button that whetted the writing appetites of authors Okonowicz and Rhodes to write a book.

For weeks, as the authors invaded my home to garner information for a book, I kept rebuffing them. I kept insisting there would be no interest in a book about me.

About the fifth week of interviewing at my home in Afton, as Okonowicz was leaving my home, he had a big smile on his face. "This was the first time since we've been interviewing you that you didn't give us an argument about writing a book," he said.

And he was right!

My ego had supplanted my reasoning.

Matt Zabitka: Sports

As the authors dug deeper into my past as a sportswriter, radio sportscaster, athlete, coach, manager, promoter and survivor of a Japanese Kamikaze attack on the aircraft carrier *U.S.S. Randolph* (CV 15) on which I served during World War II, I got enthused about my past. Hey, I thought to myself, this might make an interesting book.

I started searching through the countless volumes of scrapbooks, letters and other memorabilia I kept, mostly from my 38 years as a sportswriter at *The News Journal*, and came across stories I had written that lit up my memory bank. I figured, for example, that young sports fans of today would be interested in reading some facts about the days of the old Negro National Baseball League, in the days when blacks were banned from the all-white major baseball leagues. I researched all the living black athletes in Delaware who played in the all black leagues—athletes like Judy Johnson, Bubby Sadler, Toots Ferrell, Rats Henderson. They poured their hearts out to me, recalling their good and bad times, their ups and down while playing in the Negro National Baseball League. This is historical stuff, about another time, another era.

And through my career as a sportswriter, I met, dined with and interviewed world boxing champions like Rocky Graziano, Jersey Joe Walcott, Mike Tyson, Billy Soose, Tony Zale, documenting their experiences.

On the local boxing scene, I churned out stories on boxers Al Tribuani, Art Redden, Lou Brooks, Willie Roache, Jimmy Lancaster, Tony Aiello, Lou Renai, Jimmy Willis, Freddy Sammons, Ron Branch, Joe Barbizzi, Maynard Jones, Johnny Aiello, Stevie Martin, the Tiberi brothers (Joe and Dave), Henry Milligan, Mike Stewart and dozens of others. They all had interesting stories to tell.

Interesting personal feelings were extracted through interviews with Cal Ripken Jr., Ted Williams, Joe DiMaggio and Stan Musial, all members of baseball's "All Century Dream Team."

Interviews with baseball hall-of-famers Goose Goslin, Judy Johnson, Ralph Kiner, Duke Snider and Bill Veeck revealed a lot about themselves and their thoughts, as did talks with NBA stars Wilt Chamberlain, Bob Cousy, Neil Johnston, Paul Arizin and Tommy Heinsohn.

Danny Murtaugh, three-time National League manager of the year with the Pittsburgh Pirates, and Mickey Vernon, two-time American League batting champ, both of whom should be in Baseball's Hall of Fame, were always available for interviews, despite their tight schedules.

I'll always remember candid interviews with so many athletes who surfaced among the most interesting sports personalities of the 20th century, in addition to those already mentioned. People like Jim Bunning, Andre the Giant, A.J. Foyt, Tommy Bolt, Arnold Palmer, Gary Player, Gorilla Monsoon, Hank Stram, Ray Malavasi, Jessie Owens, Joe Montana,

Al McGuire, Yogi Berra, Dick Vermeil, Rocky Bleir, Larry Csonka, Delino DeShields, Dave May, Bobby Shantz,, Jimmy Caras, "Boom Boom" Mancini, Billy "White Shoes" Johnson, Whitey Witt, plus Gene Autry (ex-movie star who owned a major league baseball team), Eddie Gottlieb (who owned the Philadelphia 76ers and made up the NBA schedule every year) and "Sleepy Jim" Crowley and Elmer F. Layden (both of whom played football under legendary Notre Dame coach Knute Rockne in 1922-24 and gained fame as members of the Four Horsemen backfield).

Among the most poignant interviews, actually visits, were with ex-Phillies pitcher Chris Short and third baseman Judy Johnson of the Negro National Baseball League. They were both near death at the time, unable to speak, unable to take care of themselves; Short at Christiana Care Hospital, Johnson at a retirement facility in Wilmington. They were sad visits that evoked tears.

My memories of a sports writing career that was ignited at 13, making $5 a week writing a sports column for a weekly paper in Chester, Pa., still bless and burn.

I've been fortunate.

I was rarely out of work in the sports field.

I was recruited by Joe Grieco to write a sports column for the *Progressive Weekly* in Chester; recruited to write a sports column by Joe Trout, for the *Weekly Chester News*; was recruited by Bill Burk (my childhood idol as a sportswriter) to write and be a partner and owner in *Sportweek*, a weekly all-sports paper in Delaware County, Pa.; was recruited by Ralph Mitosky to write and edit the *Kensington and Juniata Guide*; was recruited to write and edit the *Marcus Hook Herald*; was recruited by Bob Finucane to join him on the sports staff of the *Chester, Pa., Times*; was recruited by radio station WDRF manager Cy Swingle to do a daily 90-minute sports show; and was recruited by Al Cartwright to join his sports staff at *The News Journal* in late 1962.

About nine years ago, I was touched by a letter I received at *The News Journal* from Dan Parker of New York, who was recognized as being one of the top national sportswriters in America during the 1930s, '40s and '50s.

Parker read a piece about me in *Editor & Publisher*, a nationally circulated magazine for people in the newspaper business. In the article, I offered some tips to young people who aspired to be sportswriters, like Red Smith and Dan Parker.

Parker, whom I never met but knew by reputation, wrote me a beautiful letter, thanking me for mentioning him in my story.

It meant a lot to me, a nobody, to be recognized and thanked by Parker just for mentioning his name in one of my stories.

In the west end of Chester, Pa., where I was born and raised, I was a baseball-crazy kid.

My older brother, Steve, was a baseball player, who owned a glove and baseball spikes.

When my brother was at work, I'd sneak his glove, go outside and look for someone with whom to have a catch.

Across the street where I lived, resided a scraggly old man, who got free lodging in the cellar of a private home in return for putting out the trash and sweeping the sidewalk. I'd rarely seen him with his face shaven. He walked slowly, always chewed tobacco and always appeared to be under the influence of John Barleycorn. But I admired and respected the man because I was told he was in the major league around the turn of the century. I had never spoken to him.

One day, while outside with my brother's baseball glove, he sauntered up to me and asked what position I played. I told him I was a pitcher. He, shockingly, asked for my glove and requested I pitch to him, to see what I had on the ball.

I lobbed the ball to him a few times, slowly, realizing he couldn't see too well, was up in age, and his reflexes just weren't there.

After a few lobs, he yelled, "Don't throw too fast!" A few more lobs and he returned my glove.

He snarled, "You'll never make the majors, but you might make a few big bucks as a pitcher." And he walked away, slowly and weaving.

The name of the man was Ernie Augustus Vinson. He's in the all time major league record book. Look it up. He was born March 20, 1879, in Dover, Del., and died on Oct. 12, 1951, in Chester, Pa. He played for Cleveland in 1904-05, and with the Chicago White Sox in 1906.

He was right.

I never made the major leagues.

I never made "a few big bucks" as a pitcher.

But I did gain satisfaction, and in some ways, gratification, pursuing sports in another field—as a writer.

Through my career that spans more than six decades, which includes my start as a 13-year-old, I've had the good fortune to work under such talented sports editors as Bill Burk (*Sportweek*), Bob Finucane (*Chester Times*) and Al Cartwright, Jack Chevalier and Ron Fritz (*The News Journal*). And I experienced the pleasure of being surrounded (at various papers I worked for) by such top-notch writers as Hal Bodley, Mike Sisak, Bill Fleischman, Kevin Tresolini, Chuck Lewis, Gary Smith, Bill

Schellhammer, Martin Frank, Doug Lesmerises, Jim "Prince" Albert, Ed Gebhart, Ray Finnochiaro, Karl "Turf King" Feldner, Jack Ireland, Tom Tomashek, Kevin Noonan, Jim Swann, Gene Quinn, Aaron Rivers, Matt Galella, Caesar Alsop and dozens and dozens of others.

In addition to interviewing and writing about major sports personalities, I never forgot the "small" guys—from the sandlots, in high school and in college. They were my main source through most of my career, the major subjects of my stories.

It has been one helluva ride, doing something I've always liked, and the time passed by all too rapidly.

Matt Zabitka

Matt Zabitka
Dec. 20, 2001

Matt Zabitka columns
reprinted in this book

Matt Zabitka
Foundation for Children

The friends and family of longtime Delaware sportswriter Matt Zabitka, a member of the Delaware Sports Hall of Fame and the Delaware County Chapter of the Pennsylvania Sports Hall of Fame, have launched a campaign to help children with life-threatening illnesses and their parents enjoy some much-needed quality time together.

Founded by Matt's grandson, Bob McCreary of Wilmington, the Matt Zabitka Foundation for Children's goal is to raise $5 million to build a ranch where youngsters can enjoy time in a country setting—riding horses, playing games with their parents and other children, swimming and enjoying recreation in a natural setting.

Because many children patients come to the Wilmington-Philadelphia area for treatment from the around the country, McCreary said, the ranch will serve children, and their family members, while the youngsters are being treated at local hospitals. These include the DuPont Hospital for Children, Children's Hospital of Philadelphia, Seashore House, area Ronald McDonald's houses and other organizations and facilities that serve children's needs. He said the ranch also will function as as summer camp site.

McCreary said the idea for creating a foundation honoring his grandfather seemed to make sense, especially since throughout his long and successful sportswriting career Matt "Zee" Zabitka has directed a spotlight on young athletes, often at the beginning of promising scholastic and professional careers.

"Because of all the work my grandfather has done in writing about young people in his columns," McCreary said, "we wanted to do something that would honor his name. We also want the ranch to be a place where young people can come with their parents when a break in their treatment allows them to do so."

Currently, McCreary said, the foundation is looking for a natural outdoor site in the Chadds Ford, Pa., area that is close enough to metropolitan area treatment centers to be easily accessible.

The foundation also would like to see the ranch used to host support groups for parents of seriously ill children. Instruction in coping skills will help parents deal with their child's illness and prognosis and also build friendships with those in similar situations.

206

McCreary said he hopes members of the sports community, who have been served so well by Matt Zabitka for the last half century, will support the foundation through contributions and volunteer work at the ranch.

"We would like to get figures from the sporting world involved in this," McCreary said, "and we would like to have athletes and team mascots visit the ranch and spend some time with the kids. Above all else, we just want young people to come out here, take advantage of the site, have fun and just be kids."

For more information about the Matt Zabitka Foundation, details on how to contribute or how to become a volunteer, call (302) 777-KIDS (5431), or visit the web site at [http://www.fightforchildren.com/dev/matt.html].

A portion of the proceeds of this book is being donated to the Matt Zabitka Foundation.

Index

209

213

Myst and Lace Publishers, Inc.

Myst and Lace Publishers Inc. was established in 1994 and specializes in regional books featuring a variety of topics, including biographies, folklore, murder mysteries, history, ghost stories, Mid-Atlantic culture and traditions and oral history.

Matt Zabitka is featured in our national award-winning coffee table-style book *Disappearing Delmarva: Portraits of the Peninsula People*, which won two first place awards in 1998 from the National Association of Press Women— for best general book and best photojournalism.

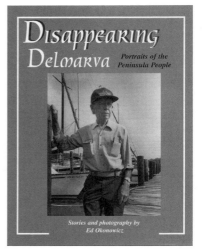

Since 1994, we have published 18 books. Thirteen of them are collections of ghostly short stories that are based on true experiences relayed to Ed by local residents. They include nine volumes in our Spirits Between the Bays series, two books about haunted antiques and collectibles, one book about terrifying tales at the beach, and our recent title *Ghosts*.

All of our titles are available at major chain bookstores, local independent book dealers and Internet web sites, including [amazon.com] and [barnesandnoble.com].

Ed also has written two murder mysteries, *FIRED!* and *Halloween House*. In this DelMarVa Murder Mystery series, readers follow the same group of protagonists as they solve murders in the fictional state of DelMarVa.

Kathleen Okonowicz, a watercolor artist and graphic designer, who is a member of the Baltimore Watercolor Society, creates the layout and design for each of our books. Ed Okonowicz conducts the interviews and takes most of the photographs.

Jerry Rhodes is the first new author to have his work published by Myst and Lace. However, Cecil County, Maryland, historian Mike Dixon is working on a regional historical book that is scheduled to be published by Myst and Lace in 2003.

For information about our company, our books, Kathleen's paintings, prints and exhibitions, as well as Ed's public performance storytelling schedule and special events, including ghost/history tours and cemetery tours that are offered as fundraisers for nonprofit agencies, visit our web site at

[www.mystandlace.com]

Myst and Lace Publishers, Inc.
1386 Fair Hill Lane
Elkton, Maryland 21921
(410) 398-5013

Myst and Lace Publishers, Inc.
Order Form

Name _____

Address_____

City_____State_____Zip Code_____

Phone Numbers _(____)_____(____)_____
                         Day   Evening

For information on future books, visit our web site [www.mystandlace.com] or fill out the above form and mail it to us.

I would like to order the following books:

Quantity	Title	Price	Total
_____	Matt Zabitka: Sports	$24.95	_____
_____	Ghosts	$ 9.95	_____
_____	Terrifying Tales of the Beaches and Bays	$ 9.95	_____
_____	Pulling Back the Curtain, Vol I	$ 8.95	_____
_____	Opening the Door, Vol II (temporarily out of print)		_____
_____	Welcome Inn, Vol III	$ 8.95	_____
_____	In the Vestibule, Vol IV	$ 9.95	_____
_____	Presence in the Parlor, Vol V	$ 9.95	_____
_____	Crying in the Kitchen, Vol VI	$ 9.95	_____
_____	Up the Back Stairway, Vol VII	$ 9.95	_____
_____	Horror in the Hallway, Vol VIII	$ 9.95	_____
_____	Phantom in the Bedchamber, Vol IX	$ 9.95	_____
_____	Possessed Possessions	$ 9.95	_____
_____	Possessed Possessions 2	$ 9.95	_____
_____	Fired! A DelMarVa Murder Mystery(DMM)	$ 9.95	_____
_____	Halloween House DMM#2	$ 9.95	_____
_____	Disappearing Delmarva	$38.00	_____
_____	Stairway over the Brandywine, A Love Story	$ 5.00	_____

*Md residents add 5% sales tax.

Please include $2.00 postage for the first book, and 50 cents for each additional book.
Make checks payable to:
    Myst and Lace Publishers

Subtotal _____
Tax*_____
Shipping_____
Total_____

All books are signed by the author. If you would like the book(s) personalized, please specify to whom.

Mail to: Ed Okonowicz
1386 Fair Hill Lane
Elkton, Maryland 21921

Visit our web site at: www.mystandlace.com

216